NEW BEGINNINGS

CONSTITUTIONALISM AND DEMOCRACY
IN MODERN IRELAND

D1476257

BILL KISSANE

UNIVERSITY COLLEGE DUBLIN PRESS

PREAS CHOLÁISTE OLLSCOILE BHAILE ÁTHA CLIATH

First published 2011
by University College Dublin Press
Newman House
86 St Stephen's Green
Dublin 2
Ireland
www.ucdpress.ie

ISBN 978-1-906359-51-5 pb

CIP data available from the British Library

*The right of Bill Kissane to be identified as the
author of this work has been asserted by him*

Typeset in Scotland in Adobe Caslon and
Bodoni Oldstyle by Ryan Shiels
Text Design by Lyn Davies
Printed in England on acid-free paper by
CPI Antony Rowe, Chippenham, Wilts.

Contents

—

Acknowledgements

I began this book while a Visiting Professor at the Keough-Naughton Institute of Irish Studies at the University of Notre Dame in 2005–6. I would like to thank Chris Fox and his faculty for making it such a pleasant environment to be working on Irish politics. In 2007 I attended a week-long seminar on constitutionalism, organised by Maeva Marcus, at the Institute for Constitutional Studies, George Washington University. I learnt a great deal from the participants, and especially from Professors Mary Bilder and Avi Soifer, who proved to be excellent teachers.

The following year, with Nick Sitter, I co-hosted an ECPR (European Consortium of Political Research) workshop on Constitutionalism and National Identity in Modern Europe, and I would like to thank the participants for their contributions. Much of the material that went into this book has been presented to different audiences: Irish Studies Seminars, at the University of Notre Dame, and the University of London; the Irish Politics Colloquium at the London School of Economics; and seminars on Irish History at Hertford College Oxford, University College Cork, and Trinity College Dublin. My thanks go to the organisers and their audiences. I taught a Master's class in Irish Politics at the LSE for over ten years. Inevitably, getting the students to dwell on the 'manifesto' aspects of Bunreacht na hÉireann was an interesting exercise, and I learnt much from their responses. The link between constitutional history and national history in general is strong in Ireland, and the sources are many. On the 1980s I am grateful to Peter Sutherland for sharing his memories of that traumatic decade with me, and providing me with some useful documents. On the 1990s Professor Michael Laver shared his recollections of the Constitutional Review Group. The current crisis has again raised questions of constitutional reform, but in terms that are seldom new. Indeed my contention is that constitutional reform was an integral goal of the Irish independence movement, and I have been able to reclaim much that is new about the period between 1905 and 1922. Most of the archival research for this book has been done in Dublin, and I thank the staffs of the National Archives in Dublin, the Archives Department at UCD, the library of Trinity College Dublin, and the National Library of Ireland. Finally, my thanks go to Barbara Mennell for the efficient way she has produced this book and to the two anonymous reviewers who helped give it shape. The usual disclaimer applies.

BILL KISSANE

London School of Economics and Political Science

March 2011

Abbreviations

—

D/T	Department of the Taoiseach
DUP	Democratic Unionist Party
ECHR	European Convention on Human Rights
EEC	European Economic Community
EU	European Union
IRB	Irish Republican Brotherhood
LSE	London School of Economics and Political Science
NAI	National Archives of Ireland
NLI	National Library of Ireland
OECD	Organisation for Economic Co-operation and Development
PR	Proportional Representation
RUC	Royal Ulster Constabulary
SDLP	Social Democratic and Labour Party
STV	Single Transferable Vote
TD	Teachta Dála
UCDA	University College Dublin Archives
UUP	Ulster Unionist Party

Introduction

—

At crucial turning points in the twentieth century Irish people have had to make fundamental decisions concerning the basic rules which govern their collective life. The acid test of such 'new beginnings' is whether they have transformed the nature of Irish democracy. Constitutionalism does not always enhance democracy: many see a logical contradiction between the principle of majority rule and a strong system of checks and balances. At the precise moment of drafting a constitution politicians have to choose whether the new documents are intended to further democracy, or to make democracy more manageable. In Ireland the choice has often been between the claims of idealism or experience. Since experience has tended to prevail, prudence has generally pre-empted genuine democratic transformation, and strong elements of continuity mark the constitutional record. This continuity should not be condemned. Any enduring reconciliation of constitutionalism to democracy is worthy of respect. Each chapter of this book examines a distinct episode in Irish constitutional history when the connection between constitutionalism and democracy was at issue. Combining history and political science, these chapters show how culture, ideas, and institutions have combined to produce the distinct constitutional order which exists today.

NEW BEGINNINGS

Much of the impetus behind Irish constitutional development stems from the existence of a revolutionary past. All revolutions are linked to the existence of fundamental norms and values which are then expressed in constitutions. The short 1919 constitution followed the Proclamation of a Republic in 1916, and its (re)declaration in January 1919. It began with a statement of Irish sovereignty, as did the 1922 and 1937 constitutions. All three symbolised the appearance of new entities on the world stage. The Dáil's 1919 constitution was for an Irish Republic, and the 1922 and 1937 constitutions marked the appearance of 'the Irish Free State' and 'Éire/Ireland' respectively. The latter had a section on Nation and State, making the connection explicit. When the 1937 constitution was challenged in the 1970s, the question of what could appropriately be put in a constitution became a touchstone of political differences. The debate subsided in the 1990s, but the Belfast Agreement of 1998 also begins with a statement about Irish values: for an island of diverse traditions.

For any constitution to have normative force, it needs to be changed – at critical turning points – so that it reflects the community's experiences and changes in its culture.[1] This is especially the case in Ireland, where the national revolution (1916–23) has a strong hold on public consciousness. Indeed, all five episodes documented in this book reflect the failure of previous attempts at settlement of the national question. These 'new beginnings' for the Irish people reflect the 'incompleteness' of the nationalist project, and the absence, thus far, of a successful constitutional formula for reconciling Irish divisions. The 1916 republic found its nemesis in partition in 1920, and the civil war which followed the signing of the Anglo-Irish Treaty on 6 December 1921. This Treaty allowed for the adoption of a constitution for an 'Irish Free State'. Though its preamble expressed confidence that the unity of the island would be restored, the day after its ratification at Westminster the six counties of Northern Ireland 'opted out' of the Free State. The 1922 constitution remained in force until the adoption of Bunreacht na hÉireann in 1937. Approved in a plebiscite, 'de Valera's constitution' symbolised the rejection of the 1920–1 settlement, and the establishment of Éire or Ireland, claiming authority over the whole island. The Northern Irish conflict (1969–98) has forced reconsideration of the claim to the North. With the 1998 peace agreement, the Republic of Ireland recognised the permanence of partition, unless overturned by a majority of Northern Ireland's electorate. 'Unfinished business', a metaphor for much of contemporary Irish history, also applies to the constitutional record.

Key in the general relationship between constitutionalism and democracy, one issue provides a good test of Irish nationalism's claims as a legal ideology. Why should a nationalist movement, in the process of asserting its sovereign claims as an indigenous majority, make concessions to a minority opposed to that project? A variety of approaches mark the episodes in this book. The Home Rule bills guaranteed religious freedom and equality before the law. The 1922 constitution provided for minority representation through the Senate and PR. The 1937 constitution stuck with PR/STV and, as in 1922, allowed for federal tiers of government. After 1968 critics wanted to redefine constitutional identity by changing the bias towards the values of the majority (Catholic and nationalist) community in the constitution. The 1998 Belfast Agreement breaks new ground with its minority rights provisions. From Home Rule onwards, minority rights have generally been seen as a necessary part of the case for independence and unity. Two facts have had to be reconciled. The incomplete nature of independence results in a stress on sovereignty. The fact that a minority opposes full independence raises the question of how this value can be reconciled to minority rights.

A second reason why any society would limit its own sovereign power through the adoption of a written constitution is bound up with the ambition to establish a state based on the rule of the people.[2] When Darrell Figgis, chairman of the 1922 constitutional committee, advertised the constitution of the Irish Free State to the wider world, his analogies were with the revolutionary precedents of France and the United States. Popular sovereignty was invoked as its guiding constitutional principle.[3] The 1916 Proclamation symbolised a determination to establish a state based on this principle. The 1919, 1922, and 1937 constitutions followed this (specifically republican) tradition. In 1919, the first Dáil's unicameral character was seen as a symbol of national sovereignty. In 1922, a constituent assembly was responsible for ratifying the constitution. In 1937, the people approved the constitution in a plebiscite. Adopting a constitution, as an assertion of separate identity, confers a sense of popular ownership of the state. The constituent assembly in 1922 and the referendum in 1937 were seen as ways in which the people 'gave themselves' their constitution. The prescription of fundamental rights promoted the idea that there are popularly accepted limits to the state's power. After 1922 the people were to be involved in subsequent decision making through the referendum.

Popular sovereignty is central to the nationalist constitutional tradition. Yet in 1922 Figgis also defended those provisions which provided for a British-style cabinet government. Was he simply paying lip service to the principle of popular sovereignty, while employing a range of constitutional devices to keep the popular impulse at bay?[4] Implicit in the idea of a new beginning is the ambition to establish a new kind of state.[5] In 1918 democracy had been achieved in the United Kingdom, so the question was what type of democracy the Irish constitutions would provide. The truth is that as a working democracy emerged after 1921, the range of options quickly narrowed. Sinn Féin drew its initial inspiration from the wider crisis of liberalism before 1914, when radical constitutional reform was on the agenda. The approach in 1922 was also experimental, but the outcome unreflective of this approach. In 1937 the approach was more conservative, and the task that of legitimating existing institutions on the basis of first principles valued by Sinn Féin before 1921. After 1969 the goal of those wanting change was to redefine constitutional identity to make it more inclusive. Major institutional change was not a serious option. The task of the Belfast Agreement was to provide a new institutional basis for co-existence in a divided society. Yet the Agreement was more 'a gradual instalment' than a new beginning. In short, the tension between evolution and transformation has tended to be resolved in favour of the former.

Should we then read these new beginnings only symbolically, as 'milestones' in the history of Irish nationalism, rather than as genuine 'constitutional moments' which transformed prevalent conceptions of democracy? Ackerman sees in the history of American constitutionalism three 'moments' of inspired change, when popular involvement in constitutional debate changed the basic contours of political life. The 1786 constitution, the Reconstruction Amendments, and the New Deal, demonstrated that the exercise of popular sovereignty, even outside normal amendment processes, could lead to progressive constitutional change.[6] The 'constitutional moment' is marked by *discontinuity* (a moment of radical sudden change), and *transformation* (ordinary politics is rendered very different).[7] The model cannot easily be applied to Ireland. The 1919 Dáil constitution was short and provisional. The 1922 constitution lasted fifteen years, below the standard lifespan for modern constitutions. The campaign for a new beginning after 1969 failed, and the Belfast Agreement is ultimately transitional.

The rhetoric of new beginnings is ever present, but only 1937 produced a lasting constitution. 1937 was a *radical* moment in the sense that the 1921 Treaty settlement did not allow for the replacement (as opposed to amendment) of the 1922 constitution. The 1937 constitution also transformed constitutional life in several ways. After 1937 the Irish constitution was more respected as a higher law. A distinction between ordinary and constitutional politics was reasserted, whereas the 1922 constitution had been repeatedly amended by ordinary legislation. Strong judicial review and a rights jurisprudence eventually developed, and new institutions like the presidency have grown in importance. These are attributes of a constitutional moment. Yet popular involvement in 1937 was confined to the process of ratification. A crucial attribute of a constitutional moment is that the decisions made during it are binding on later generations because of the quality of the popular involvement, marked by principled deliberation of constitutional issues. In Ireland, the deliberation took place only at the elite level. The main opposition party opposed the constitution in the plebiscite, when only a small majority of the voters actually backed the new document. The 'constitutional moment' was unaccompanied by much enthusiasm, and the plebiscite was held on the same day as a general election.

For Ireland we need a different model of constitutional development. Each chapter in this book addresses a distinct mode of constitution making. Before 1922 the advanced nationalist press and an emerging civil society pushed for radical reform. In 1922 responsibility fell on an expert constitutional committee. In 1937 a small group of civil servants drafted the constitution in tandem with de Valera. After 1968 the pressure for change came from opposition parties and civil society. The engine behind the Belfast Agreement was inter-governmental. Comparisons of the outcomes suggest two things. When the impetus for change came from only civil society, change did not follow. Party politics mattered. Secondly, some elitism has been compatible with constitutional innovation. Those civil servants chosen by de Valera to draft his new constitution were not radicals, but their constitution has lasted more than seventy years.

IRISH CONSTITUTIONALISM

Yet if 1937 was 'a constitutional moment' in terms of consequences, but not in terms of popular involvement in higher-lawmaking, what general model of constitution making fits Ireland? An answer requires consideration of three factors bound up with Ireland's relationship with Britain. Almost every text-book on the Irish political system begins with a discussion of the Westminster model. Since 1922, it has provided the backbone of the political system and has limited the extent to which Irish constitution-makers have really intended radical change. Unlike in 1922, in 1937 the drafters assumed strong government on the British model, but also wanted a fresh system of checks and balances. If there was a constitutional moment it was one where the existing Westminster machinery of government was reconciled to the concept of the constitution as a fundamental law. Figgis had described the 1922 constitution as *Reacht* (legis-lation) or *Bunreacht* (fixed or foundation legislation). The name for the 1937 constitution, *Bunreacht na hÉireann*, returns us to the former approach. Hence 1937 was crucial in providing for Westminster-style government within the framework of a fundamental law.

Culture also made the constitutional moment different. The American people were (in some ways) constituted by their constitution, but the Irish had a long history prior to their state. Their constitutional documents were intended to symbolise the recovery, not the establishment, of sovereign status. Hence they partook of a tradition which valued not social transformation but loyalty to the past. Before 1921 Sinn Féin had seen the creation of a new state as a return to origins, and its constitution would not so much found a polity, but attempt to discover and express the characteristics of a polity that already existed. These characteristics were those that distinguished Ireland from Britain. The constitution thus had an expressive aspect. In 1937 the Taoiseach, Éamon de Valera, declared:

> There is a stage in the life of every community in which its customs as well as its philosophy of life naturally pass into laws. A system of law which is divorced from the convictions, the beliefs and the spiritual character of a people is in no sense a national code [8]

The expressive approach had two consequences. It allowed the 1937 constitution to first develop in 'harmonious conjunction with the socio-cultural environment within which it came into being'. Its values naturally appealed to a highly conservative not to say static society.[9] However, when (in the 1970s) the constitution became 'disharmonic', those who wanted change staked their claim in the sphere of values not institutions. They wanted to make the identity of the constitution more reflective of contemporary values, not to transform democracy. There was no new beginning in institutional terms after 1969.

A third factor making for a constitutional moment was the rejection of Treaty-based law. Since the late nineteenth century two paradigms of constitutionalism have competed in Ireland.[10] The first existed (in embryonic form), during the Home Rule era (1885–1914). Under it, constitutions would gradually emerge from a formal process of decentralisation – from centre (London) to periphery (Dublin) – and as the periphery gradually gains new powers a shift from 'Treaty' to 'constitution' takes place. This was the hope of those 'Home Rulers' who hoped for the establishment of an Irish parliament in Dublin, with powers that would gradually grow. Under Home Rule, co-ordination between different power centres and monitoring respective spheres of competence would have been the stuff of constitutionalism. This tradition survives in Northern Ireland under devolution. Yet with the 1916 rising the Home Rule tradition became anathema. In the second, alternative paradigm, constitutions are 'milestones' in a nation's history, symbolising 'new beginnings' for the nation, and the repudiation of an oppressive past. Co-ordinating powers and functional issues are less important, and constitutions have a strong symbolic role in legitimising fundamental transitions in the life of nations. The 1916 Proclamation and the 1919, 1922, and 1937 constitutions belong to this tradition.

Yet if 1916 symbolised the ambition to form a new kind of state, the Government of Ireland Act of 1920 and the Anglo-Irish Treaty of 1921 established limits to that freedom. The 1922 constitution was subordinate to the Treaty for most of the next fifteen years, and opinion differed as to whether a constitution could grow out of the Treaty. In 1933, section 2 of the 1922 Constituent Act was repealed by de Valera's government, depriving the Treaty of force of law, and by implication denying the 1922 constituent assembly its sovereign status. De Valera complained that the 1922 constitution 'was made subject to a Treaty admittedly imposed by the threat of force'.[11] What followed in 1937 was 'a constitutional revolution', brought to completion when the Republic of Ireland, declared in 1948, left the Commonwealth. Thus only in 1937 was the dependence on Treaty-based law broken, and the commitment to national sovereignty completed the national revolution south of the border.

This had an important consequence. The 1937 constitution was drafted before the war, during an international crisis, and international agreements, as in later European constitutions, did not *ipso facto* prevail over its provisions. This eventually slowed down European integration (itself requiring 'a constitution to Treaty' process), and was a measure of the constitution's stature as a new beginning.

HEGEMONY AND DESIGN

Bunreacht na hÉireann was the product of a specifically Irish constitutional moment because of the way these three factors came together. By 1937 it was clear that the Westminster model provided the backbone of the political system. The ability of the 1922 constitution to express a nationalist vision of society was limited by a British veto, and by the need to secure unionist assent to an end to partition. The year 1937 produced a more appropriate moment for the expression of more autochthonous values. Changes in Commonwealth relations also meant that the 1921 Treaty settlement was unravelling, and the constitution largely completed a process of revision which began in the 1920s. It could claim to be the constitution of a free people in the way that of 1922 could not. Yet if only 1937 was a genuine constitutional moment we still have to ask why the constitution has lasted so long. Its longevity reflects a mixture of hegemony and design.

Ackerman's is a dualist theory of democratic politics. 'Constitutional politics' are different from 'ordinary politics' in that responses to crisis lead people to transcend calculations of self-interest, and make constitutional choices which serve the common good. What is missing is a consideration of party politics, which was key in Ireland. 'Partisan entrenchment', when a party with a guiding ideology gradually gains control of state institutions, can also produce a new constitutional order. Fianna Fáil's hegemony was completed by the constitution and reflected the three factors discussed above. The 1937 constitution provided for a Westminster-style executive, but since 1932 only Fianna Fáil have been able to form single-party governments. Until the 1960s the constitution's religious values (backed by a powerful Catholic Church), were unchallenged. Fianna Fáil's emphasis on national sovereignty did not become a legal problem until Ireland wanted to join the EEC. In other words, the 1937 constitution reflected and perpetuated the party's hegemony.

A sense of universal ownership, stemming from public involvement in the constitutional debate, or from a consensual drafting process, are not needed for a constitution to endure. A constitution can also endure when the consti-tutional moment delivers clear signals that the new charter articulates a *fait accompli.* If the referendum generated a high degree of legitimacy for the new document, as it did in 1937, it also fostered co-ordination around this new set of rules.[12] Fine Gael and Labour simply acquiesced in the new constitutional order, because (*a*) they recognised that a more powerful mass of other actors (including the Catholic Church) recognised the rules of the constitution, and (*b*) there were insufficient resources to communicate an alternative set of rules around which mutual expectations could build.[13] When the possibility of change came with the Troubles in 1969, both pushed for a new document.

The concept of hegemony helps explain why the 1937 constitution endured. Its value commitments first allowed Irish society to develop consensually, free of major ideological conflicts. Yet they raised a common problem in the relationship between constitutionalism and democracy. If these values were those of 1937, why should later generations accept the constitution's authority, allowing 'a dictatorship of the past over the present'? Up to the 1960s the values *were* hegemonic, but they have been declining ever since. No democratic constitution can be explained entirely in terms of hegemony. Much has depended on Fianna Fáil itself upholding its principles when exercising power, thus removing a reason for their opponents to want a different constitutional order. There must have been a clear sign of what constitutes a transgression of the limitations the constitution placed on government power, and here judicial review and the constitutional referendum have been crucial. Transgression is most likely to emerge during crises (like the Northern Irish conflict), and a constitution must prove adaptable.[14] The rigidity provided by the referendum requirement for constitutional change, combined with successive symbolic amendments, has allowed expectations to be co-ordinated in a non-hegemonic way. Just as judicial review has allowed lawyers to 'discover' a more progressive document, the balance between rigidity and adaptability has reinforced the authority of the constitution by allowing changes reflecting shifts in popular values.

In explaining this outcome, design factors, reflecting the drafters' intentions and values, were crucial. Daly sees the 1937 constitution as an exception to two general models: a diffusionist model where democratic constitutions are produced in 'waves', and a strategic 'rational actor' model which predicts that constitutional choices will reflect personal and factional interests.[15] The prescription of the STV electoral system was an example of how de Valera actually broke with an authoritarian wave of constitution making in the 1930s, but did not behave in a self-aggrandising way either.[16] The puzzle of a constitution producing the positive consequences of a constitutional moment, but lacking much public deliberation, points to two factors (beyond hegemony) key its design: leadership and the nature of Irish nationalism as a legal ideology. Scholars generally stress the incompatibility of constitutionalism and nationalism. To Kedourie 'constitutional politics' is associated with the protection of life, the mediation of conflict, and the rule of law. The 'ideological politics' of nationalism leads to a perpetual and destructive tension between ends and means.[17] Garvin also draws a strong 'either or' contrast between constitutional and Irish republican traditions, suggesting that the latter contributed little to the 1922 and 1937 constitutions. Kelly contrasts 'the bare law' of the 1937 constitution with those 'manifesto' articles that expressed a vision of Irish society. Chubb contrasts the liberal legacy of British rule, with the authoritarian aspects of Irish political culture.[18] Yet my approach is to see Irish nationalism not as a value system which pervades all of Irish constitutionalism, but to see Irish constitutionalism as an autonomous part of the political culture, where a *blend* of constitutional and nationalist values has produced a distinct constitutionalism.

This book follows a historical approach to constitution making. Each chapter provides a historical reconstruction of an actual or potential constitutional moment. This approach may bring objectivity, adding substance to the normative debates the constitution gives rise to. Only a historical approach can establish what politicians were actually trying to do when making or amending constitutions. It can answer the question of whether the 1937 constitution was a hegemonic project, or the 'power grab' feared by Fine Gael. In so far as constitution making is a human-interest story, it brings out the drama of the moment when elites try to covert the ideals of their youth into legal and institutional reality. The balance between change and continuity is a constant theme and is an issue which faces constitutional reformers today. The current constitution can be viewed retrospectively, in terms of the values of Irish nationalism before 1921, or by way of comparison with 1922. Chapters two and three provide such vantage points. Alternatively, the constitution can be viewed in terms of the critique of the 1970s and 1980s, or in contrast to the very different Belfast Agreement. Chapters five and six provide such perspectives. Since my ambition is to place Ireland's current constitutional order and debate in historical and comparative perspective, it follows that chapter three, on the making of the 1937 constitution, should be the longest of the book.

ONE

IDEALS

FROM HOME RULE TO SINN FÉIN

—

In 1800 Ireland became an integral part of the United Kingdom. Its constituencies were represented at Westminster, the British legal and bureaucratic system extended to every part of the island, and this system underwent a succession of reforms before independence in 1921. After the Great Famine of 1845–52, with its massive loss of life and subsequent emigration, the linguistic assimilation of Ireland into the UK gathered apace. This was the period when mass democracy pressed its claims, and as extensions of the British suffrage were followed by similar reforms in Ireland, Chubb argues that 'Irish people acquired democratic values and habits'.[1] Certainly, during the Home Rule period (1885–1914) there was substantial overlap between Britain and Ireland on constitutional issues. Yet the Home Rule cause found its demise as part of a wider 'crisis of liberalism' in Britain, which led many to look beyond 'the Westminster model'. When the Home Rule party was defeated by Sinn Féin in the 1918 general election, more subterranean currents came to the fore. Sinn Féin's founder Arthur Griffith looked to the Hungarian Dual Monarchy, established in 1867, for a solution to Irish divisions. Yet Sinn Féin's was 'a constitutional revolution that never was'. The British system had been brought to the point of civil war, a native civil society and intelligentsia were being formed, but the idealism of early Sinn Féin ran aground on the rocks of partition and civil war.

THE HOME RULE BACKGROUND

Irish independence was a long time coming. The product of a revolt against British rule between 1916 and 1921, the preference for complete independence emerged late in the history of Irish nationalism. Before then, for at least four decades, nationalist politicians pursued 'Home Rule'. Home Rule was a form of what we now call 'devolution', under which Westminster would devolve legislative power over areas of Irish concern to a Dublin parliament. It was compatible with Westminster sovereignty over Ireland, and with membership of the British Empire. Since the Home Rule movement's immediate objective was the establishment of a native parliament, the movement clearly failed. Yet while the failure of three Home Rule bills (1886, 1893, 1912) led to the displacement of the Home Rulers by Sinn Féin in 1918, the era proved a fertile breeding-ground for constitutional ideas. Home Rule was debated in a context where Britain, not only Ireland, was preparing for democracy, and the tension between democratic ideals and the grip of social hierarchies on politics produced fresh thinking. Leading British thinkers applied their minds to Irish problems, and Irish nationalists shaped a British debate in which Home Rule became an issue of democracy and justice.

Home Rule took centre-stage because of the strength of Irish nationalism. An Irish parliament had existed in the late eighteenth century, and it was widely believed that the calamities which befell the island after 1800 would not have occurred had a native parliament existed. Nationalists pointed to demographic decline, mass emigration, and the Great Famine, as evidence of the Union's destructive impact. Unionists argued that a general 'Anglicisation' benefited Ireland. With the Union came the promise of democracy, but regular elections, equal citizenship, and mass involvement in politics also sharpened differences between Catholics and Protestants. As the local majority, Irish Catholics hoped that legislative reform could improve their status on the island, and identified with causes generally associated with democracy and equality. Yet as their ambitions amounted to more than the amelioration of socio-economic conditions, but also concerned the island's constitutional status, Protestants came to identify with the Union as the guarantor of their socio-economic position.

'Home Rulers' knew that Britain would never accept complete independence, and sought to reassure the British elite that legislative autonomy was compatible with maintenance of the Union. They argued that Home Rule would assuage nationalist grievances, allow the Irish to make policies better suited to that island, and relieve Westminster of an enormous burden of legislation. Home Rule might also allow Catholics and Protestants find common ground in Ireland. Falling short of federalism, it was compatible with the British constitution.[2] These arguments were reinforced by the fact that the Irish Parliamentary Party – 'the Home Rule party' – gained huge Irish majorities at parliamentary elections between 1885 and 1914, practically monopolising representation in the south and west of Ireland. The British government could not govern Ireland without the goodwill of a party which repeatedly gained over 70 of the 105 Irish seats in the House of Commons. When the party held 'the balance of power' at Westminster, the case for Home Rule became overwhelming. Thus liberal British governments tried to pass Home

Rule Bills in 1886, 1893 and 1912. The first was defeated in the Commons, the second vetoed by the Lords, while the third was put on the statute book in 1912, to come into operation when the Great War ended. Home Rule's legislative career reflects the wider story of British democracy in this era. Only the removal of the veto power of the House of Lords in 1911 allowed the passage of the third Home Rule Bill through the parliament the following year.

From the 1880s on the question in the UK was how to make democracy work, which concentrated minds on institutional issues.[3] In the background was Chartism, with its strong Irish contribution. The Chartists had maintained that constitutional change was a necessary prelude to social reform, and formulated a specific set of constitutional objectives reflecting this belief. The Home Rulers' demands for franchise reform, the substitution of elective county boards for grand juries, and the payment of Irish members of parliament, found strong support in radical British liberal circles. Home Rule led to a fundamental re-evaluation of British democracy.[4] Resistance to monopoly – 'landlordism' in Ireland, 'financial power' in Britain – meant that both liberals and nationalists saw the desirability of land reform. The Irish could argue for the recovery of their 'constitutional rights' in the face of 'alien' institutions, but their conception of reform was rooted in the British radical tradition. Their claim that the state was denying Irish 'constitutional' rights, by relying on institutions such as the Royal Irish Constabulary, found a sympathetic audience in British radical circles.[5]

The 1893 and 1912 bills were firm on the types of undertakings an Irish parliament would involve. The parliament would not be permitted to establish or endow religion, restrict the free exercise of religion, set religious tests for office, or require a child to attend religious instruction in a public school.[6] Equality before the law was guaranteed. Yet there was ambiguity. The English anti-imperialist L. T. Hobhouse noted that in no other constitution in the Empire were such extensive clauses thought necessary. The Home Rule leader John Redmond argued that express limitations on the power of an Irish parliament, in order to protect the Protestant minority, were a positive aspect of Home Rule.[7] The Cork Home Rule MP J. J. Horgan thought they were necessary only because of the 'raving' of 'Orange bigots'.[8]

None of the Home Rule bills was 'federal', since the powers devolved to an Irish parliament could have been revoked by ordinary legislation at Westminster. These powers would not touch on defence and foreign policy. Specifically colonial institutions, such as that of Lord Lieutenant, figured prominently. He would perform the Crown's functions in Ireland: with the power to appoint ministers; summon, prorogue, and dissolve the legislature; and give or withhold the royal assent to bills. The 1893 and 1912 bills abandoned the two 'orders' of parliament elected on different franchises outlined in 1886, and proposed conventional bicameral parliaments. Major differences between the houses would be resolved by the two chambers sitting and voting together. The 1912 bill also stipulated that money bills originating in the lower house could not be blocked by 'the Senate'. All three bills retained a right of appeal to the British judicial authorities. Ward rightly stresses the essential continuity between these bills and later documents.[9] The 1922 constitution also created a bicameral parliament, with the lower house having primacy over the 'Senate', which had no power to block money bills either. A right of legal appeal to the Privy Council of the House of Lords was retained, the Lord Lieutenant was replaced by the Governor General, and the provisions on religious discrimination were kept, almost word for word.

Between 1800 and 1918, the United Kingdom went from being a competitive oligarchy to a full democracy, with (almost) full adult suffrage, a democratic parliament, and a vibrant civil society. Property ownership was ceasing to be a qualification for voting. These changes gave Home Rule a democratic imprint, enabling these bills to serve as blueprints for later constitutions.[10] For nationalists, democracy required an Irish executive with autonomous power. In 1885 the Home Rule leader Charles Stewart Parnell proposed that the Lord Lieutenant should act only on the advice of Irish ministers on Irish issues, but this did not become constitutional law until 1922, when the Governor General of the Irish Free State was expressly instructed to act on the advice of the Irish Executive Council. As Ackerman notes, one form of constitutionalism begins with the devolution of power from a centre to a periphery, and after a treaty is signed, and power becomes more decentralised, a move 'from treaty to constitution' takes place.[11] Here monitoring respective spheres of competence, and enabling co-ordination between different power centres, becomes the stuff of constitutionalism. It was in the first sense of constitutionalism that British supporters had welcomed *The New Irish Constitution* in 1912, when their debate about Home Rule in this book focused on the respective spheres of competence between London and Dublin.[12] Debates about the role of the Lord Lieutenant, the powers of the Irish parliament, and judicial review, encapsulated this 'Treaty constitutionalism'. It remained the dominant Irish constitutional paradigm until 1918, but also influenced the 1922 constitution.

Home Rule was the *casus belli* of 'constitutional nationalism', which favoured the express provision of rights. Britain was the most liberal of the European Empires, but its political values were usually left implicit. Irish nationalists – from O'Connell to Sinn Féin – favoured the express provision of rights. Parnell outlined his first scheme for Home Rule in October 1885, under the title of 'A Proposed Constitution for Ireland'.[13] 'Constitution' would recover a status for an island which had ceased to a separate kingdom in 1800. Status mattered to all sides. Unionists like Alfred Milner used colonial analogies to specify what status would be consistent with a viable settlement. The relationship of the federal units to the Canadian federation would work, but that of Canada with the United Kingdom could evolve in the direction of complete independence. Such an outcome would please nationalists but not unionists. 'A Treaty to constitution' scenario thus divided Irish opinion. The debate took place in a late Victorian and Edwardian context obsessed by issues of imperialism, liberty, and democracy.[14] With the 1921 Anglo-Irish Treaty, the obsession with status, the colonial analogies, and the connection between empire and democracy, would return with tragic force.

Home Rule's claims have been subject to rival interpretations. If there was substantial 'overlap' between Britain and Ireland, the case for a liberal Home Rule project seems compelling. Biagini argues that the Home Rule cause was deeply suffused with liberal ideas of freedom and citizenship.[15] Yet its fate was bound up with divisions within Ireland. The Home Rulers shared the liberal commitment to an expanded suffrage, but while its general logic was to increase the number of social groups whose rights could be respected, in Ireland the logic was to increase the electoral power of the majority at the expense of a dominant minority. Home Rule could point in the direction of a Catholic nation, entitled, by virtue of its numbers, to govern the whole island. In 1902, one nationalist declared that 'we must fight with all our might until we have raised our hands on as much of the power, place, and position of this country as our numbers and our unabated historical claims entitle us to demand'.[16] There was clearly a tension between advocating Home Rule as a solution to Irish divisions, and the fact that its electoral mandate increasingly reflected 'a religious headcount'.[17] The movement was always divided between those who *were* idealists in this sense – who made a moral case for Home Rule – and those for whom self-government became 'an instrument' of the Catholic rural middle classes: 'the materialists'.[18]

The Home Rulers had focused on issues – the franchise, the paramilitary nature of the Royal Irish Constabulary, and the unrepresentative nature of local 'Grand Juries' – which challenged Protestant dominance in Ireland. Many Irish Protestants saw here the claims of Catholic power. Critics quoted John Redmond saying on 9 October 1906:

> I have always held the view that it was a strength to the National Movement, and not a weakness, that England should realise that there was behind the men who were conducting the constitutional movement on the floor of the House of Commons a Great Unknown Power, waiting for an opportunity which might arise, to have recourse, if necessary, to other methods to advance the cause of Ireland.[5]

The founding rules of this 'Unknown Power', the Ancient Order of Hibernians, in 1836, were that all members should be Roman Catholic, and Irish or of Irish descent, and of good moral character. None could join in any secret societies contrary to the laws of the Catholic Church.

While the British radicals' emphasis was on denuding elites, cliques, and monopolies of power, Irish nationalists attributed their religious divide to the influence of an oligarchy. For them the issue was between 'popular rights' and 'democracy' against aristocratic privilege.[20] In 1911 one complained:

> We hear a lot about 'law and order' from the Irish Unionists. When they talk about maintaining law and order they mean the maintenance of ascendancy and partisanship on the judicial bench, on the county court bench, in the magistracy, and in the police administration. So long as the administration of the law is biased and this influenced, so long as the overwhelming majority of appointments are Protestant and Freemason, the Irish people can have neither confidence in nor respect for the system.[21]

Conversely, William Joseph O'Neill, John Patrick Prendergast, and William Lecky – three important Irish intellectuals – withdrew their support from Home Rule, because of its populist impulse and allegedly radical aims. They stressed the need for a moderate middle ground, the importance of respect for property and for human life, and the dangers of land reform.[22]

Many nonetheless hoped for reconciliation under Home Rule. In 1872 George John McCarthy had made *A Plea for the Home Government of Ireland*, on the grounds that there were no people on earth less disposed to 'ultra democracy' than the Irish, with their respect for tradition, family, and religion. Sir John MacDonnell, Professor of Comparative Law at the University of London, believed that the forces for toleration in Ireland – intermarriage, the press, and American secularism – could prove stronger than any constitutional safeguards.[23] In *The Framework of Home Rule*, the Home Rule MP and author Erskine Childers compared the minority safeguards of the 1893 Home Rule bill to some of the slavery amendments to the US constitution. He also supported PR if valued by the unionists. In 1912 Griffith proposed that no parliamentary legislation on the linen trade passed by a Home Rule parliament could become operative without the agreement of the majority of Ulster representatives. The religiously monthly, the *Catholic Bulletin*, later favoured the idea that an Ulster Committee would have the power to modify legislation applying to Ulster, and proposed that the Home Rule parliament would meet in alternate sessions in Dublin and Belfast [24]

This idealism was reflected in the conception of a second Irish House as more than 'a correctional chamber'. The provisions for a nominated Senate under the third (1912) bill testify to the vitality of a concept largely rejected by British radicals after the Lords' crisis in 1911. These proposals were welcomed in Ireland, although nominated chambers had already fallen from favour in New Zealand and New South Wales.[25] The bill proposed that the Senate would be elected after a five-year interim period from four Irish provincial constituencies. Nationalists proposed specific arrangements to guarantee unionist influence. J. J. Horgan advocated election by PR and a minimum age of 40 for senators. The *Irish Citizen*, a radical periodical edited by Francis Sheehy Skeffington and his wife Hanna, argued for a nominated senate for a five-year transitional period. William O'Brien, leader of the 'All for Ireland League', proposed that any law passed by an Irish parliament, which was opposed by a majority of the representatives from Ulster, should be suspended for five years, until approved by Westminster. In 1914 Griffith's daily *Sinn Féin* proposed a house evenly divided between nationalists and conservatives nominated by the Imperial Executive. To the Irish Convention in 1912 Griffith proposed Senate elections from one national constituency to guarantee Unionists enough representation in Munster and Connaught.[26] In 1917 Darrell Figgis, deputy chair of the 1922 constitutional committee, proposed that one third of the senators be elected by PR from large constituencies, with two thirds from the various county councils acting as electoral colleges. The 1922 constitution established a Senate, first consisting of government appointees and elected Senators, and after an interim period of four years, elected under universal suffrage from one national constituency.

In 1913 D. P. Moran's 'Irish Ireland' newspaper, *The Leader*, observed that political debate had ceased to be about the nature of the Home Rule parliament, but focused on Ulster, civil war, and the coming electoral contests.[27] Home Rule would find its demise as part of the crisis of a wider liberal value system. Its liberalism was appropriate to the task of reconciling a dominant minority to the power of the majority, on the assumption that legislative autonomy be given to the majority. It had no answer to the question of what to do when the British system failed to introduce Home Rule, just as it was intent on introducing adult suffrage. Conceptions of national identity also changed. Some argued that Home Rule was a model only for those of the same race as the colonising nation, such as the USA, whereas the Irish were 'foreigners'. Acceptance of it would be tantamount to acquiescence in British imperialism, a sentiment later expressed by Sinn Féin.[28] Moreover, constitutional innovations in the colonies might require more fundamental changes to the British constitution than represented by such bills. Indeed, as the crisis of liberalism deepened, more radical reform schemes were mooted in Britain itself. The debate ceased to be about reconciling Irish self-government to the British constitution, but about reconstituting democracy itself.

THE CRISIS OF LIBERALISM

The death-knell for Home Rule, supported by the majority of Irish MPs for four decades, was sounded by the paramilitary mobilisation of Ireland on the eve of the Great War. The mass signing of the Ulster Solemn League and Covenant in 1912 had demonstrated to Herbert Asquith's Liberal government that Home Rule would have to be forcibly imposed on Northern Unionists. Asquith decided that Home Rule would be implemented after the war, with the special position of Ulster taken into consideration. The execution of the leaders of the 1916 Rising further discredited the constitutional nationalist tradition.

Yet the collapse of constitutionalism had begun long before 1916. In 1901 it had been suggested that the nineteenth-century belief in parliamentarianism, linked to British prestige internationally, was being reversed all over Europe. William O'Brien saw *The Downfall of Parliamentarianism* in terms of a *long-term* degradation of Irish party politics. His complaint that 'a cheque from the British Treasury' enabled an Irish MP to make light of the Irish question for a whole parliamentary term, while 'an expert electioneering machine' guaranteed him re-election, restated radical liberal themes. 'Party government' became a term of abuse. Griffith complained that there was nothing in the third Home Rule Bill preventing its parliament from becoming 'a creature of party'. J. J. Horgan hoped that Home Rule would eliminate a party of 'selfish place hunters' whose aim was the maintenance of 'a corrupt sectarian ascendancy'. *Sinn Féin* asked what the Home Rule Party had actually achieved – beyond Irish taxpayers' subsidising government departments, more jobs for the boys, and Home Rule MPs whose prominence was due only to their membership of the Ancient Order of Hibernians.[29]

Nationalist dissatisfaction focused on Asquith's (1908–16) governments, which had proposed only 'a few glorified County Councils without an Irish parliament'.[30] *The United Irishman* thought the central plank of Irish parliamentarianism, 'the balance of power', discredited. The republican propagandist Aodh de Blácam wrote of 'The Passing of Liberalism'. Asquith's wartime cabinet was described as 'a close oligarchical corporation' by the *Catholic Bulletin*.[31] Yet the wider crisis was not about particular governments, but over how to 'adapt' the whole Westminster system to the complex social order that was emerging. The strength of industry, the density of urban living, and the rise of collectivism, all meant that institutional change was needed to provide a more responsive form of representation. From the 1880s on the question had been how to make democracy work, which concentrated minds on institutional issues.[32] These concerns found their climax in the Lords' veto crisis in 1911, when even unionists such as Albert Dicey took a strong interest in reform. Gradual extensions of the suffrage also meant that the liberal–conservative party divide could cease to be pivotal, and equal suffrage meant that gender equality would be inserted into the British constitutional tradition. The interest in reform was strongest on the left, and the new labour movement worked out policies on the referendum, functional representation, proportional representation, equal suffrage, and the second chamber.[33]

The UK was of course still 'a composite Monarchy' and developments in the Commonwealth affected thinking on issues such as federalism, the referendum, and responsible government.[34] Liberals could embrace those parts of the Empire where democratisation was proceeding most rapidly, and supporters of Irish Home Rule raided it for models of reform. By September 1913 the possibility of a federal UK had become the subject of discussion among a British elite forced to think through the ramifications of Irish partition. Indeed, the Irish crisis concentrated minds on how to defuse its potential for conflict. Griffith looked to the Austro-Hungarian Dual Kingdom founded in 1876, a monarchical form of federalism, for a solution to Irish divisions. It was widely believed on both sides of the Irish sea that the resolution of the constitutional issues in Britain would provide a solution to the Irish divisions. For Ramsay MacDonald in 1905, the need was for structures which would link society 'organically' to the state, a theme which exercised Irish minds up to 1922.[35] The inability of the existing system to accommodate change, and the presence of different democratic forms elsewhere, gave the Irish debate a strong comparative dimension. The Belgian electoral system, the Swiss referendum, US municipal government, the Austro-Hungarian monarchy, and dominion federalism, became common reference points.

The central question was whether the Westminster model still provided for adequate democratic representation. The control of parliamentary business by the cabinet, the use of party discipline to stifle independent thinking among MPs, and the ability of special interest groups to influence legislation, meant that 'party government' had supplanted 'parliamentary government'. The traditional representative model no longer worked. For radical liberals such as J. A. Hobson, author of *The Crisis of Liberalism* in 1909, 'popular self-government' could not be achieved without institutional reform, and in classic Chartist fashion those that wanted social and economic progress would have to struggle against a range of electoral, legislative, administrative, and judicial processes, through which elites protected their interests.[36] Hence his interest in the Single Transferable Vote (STV) system, the referendum, and a unicameral parliament. Such authors abandoned liberalism's concern with the limited state, and rather sought ways of restructuring it to expand the opportunities for individual development and social service provided by the industrial age.

In Ireland the crisis proved of some consequence. Only there did the idea of an elected second chamber representing a national elite survive the Lords crisis. In 1907 the *Fortnightly Review* published an article by Alfred Wallace, proposing a second chamber drawn from the professions, with county council-lors acting as the electoral college. This was partially provided for by the 1937 constitution.[37] The idea that a dispute between the two chambers could be resolved by a referendum originated in the Lords veto crisis, and found its way into both the 1922 and 1937 constitutions. The Boer war had galvanised interest in PR, which became linked to the idea of 'minority rights'. Sinn Féin became committed to equal suffrage early on, and to the 'electoral justice' provided by PR. Thus rather than there being a Westminster 'model' between 1905 and 1914, both British and Irish radicals claimed that the people were being deprived of their rights under this system.[38]

There were concrete reasons why an Irish interest in constitutional reform should have continued. The prospect of Home Rule still raised the possibility that one of these bills would become 'a constitution for Ireland', distinct from that of the UK. It was hoped that Home Rule would transform the Irish political landscape: *The Leader* predicted that a very 'mixed up' country would divide into many combinations after Home Rule.[39] Secondly, the inability of the Liberals to deliver Home Rule, and the Irish Parliamentary Party's dependence on 'the balance of power' at Westminster, heightened nationalist dissatisfaction with 'party government'. In June 1912 the *Irish Citizen* ran an article stating that the suffrage and the PR questions were interlinked, with the party system the main obstacle to reform.[40] Crucially, these debates took place against a backdrop of increasing electoral polarisation between nationalism and unionism, and PR was seen as a device to assuage the widening divide. In 1913 the *United Irishman* published 'Civil war and local government', suggesting that the small number of Unionist members who were elected outside Ulster encouraged perceptions of discrimination against Protestants and thus opposition to Home Rule.[41]

Concrete criticisms of the Westminster model were also made. James Connolly, the socialist leader who signed the 1916 Proclamation, thought that its chief weakness was that the majority in the Commons did not represent a majority of the people. The British constitution was so full of 'illogical and apparently impossible provisions', that were someone to propose it for a new country, it would be too ridiculous to consider. The Liberal success in the 1906 general election led Griffith to propose a *de facto* assembly for Ireland – 'a council of three hundred'– which would govern through a strong committee system. This proposal appeared in the last issue of the *United Irishman*. In 1914 the journalist Arthur Clery had remarked that justice for Ireland now required a change to the whole British system of government. In 1916 the writer AE (George Russell) wrote that a government based on the general will would 'require something better than the English invention of representative government'. Darrell Figgis wanted to dispense with territorial constituencies altogether. For de Blácam, the Irish experience of the Westminster parliament had doubled Sinn Féin's commitment 'to have no institution modelled upon it'.[42] The attack on the liberals was also an attack on the system which produced them.

Interest in the referendum predated the war. One unionist critic of the first Home Rule bill, Baden Powell, had believed that the referendum could better represent public opinion than 'party caucuses' or 'professional politicians'. Another, Albert Dicey, saw it as a way of providing a check on an elected first chamber after the Lord's veto crisis. James Connolly lamented the fact that the electorate had little control over how their representatives made laws, except through elections, 'to return other gentlemen under similar conditions and with similar opportunities for evil-doing'. Since the assumption of elections was that the public should influence legislation, the Rev. John Kelleher, a professor of theology at St John's College Waterford, maintained that they should be consulted on 'every vital measure' rather than being forced to vote on the totally unconnected items of party manifestoes. The Swiss model was often alluded to, which *Sinn Féin* claimed was of Celtic origin, sharing the Irish ideal of arbitration in politics. Indeed *Sinn Féin* maintained that the people should have both the right to make policy and choose their governing institutions. Later Alfred O'Rahilly, author of draft C of the 1922 constitution, thought this meant that they should have *ultimate* control, exercised through the referendum and the initiative.[43] The 1922 constitution would give the people a veto on unjust legislation, and allow the public initiate a referendum on issues being ignored by the parliamentary elite.[44]

The crisis of the British system gave the nationalist intelligentsia an opportunity to propose a more indigenous form of representation. This again raised the question of how democratic institutions could be 'organically' rooted in society, without reproducing its inequalities. Hopes for a new Irish polity were subsequently expressed in George Russell's *The National Being: Some Thoughts on an Irish Polity* (1916), Darrell Figgis's *The Gaelic State in the Past and Future* (1917), Aodh de Blácam's *Towards the Republic: A Study of New Ireland's Social and Political Aims* (1919). These reflected the corporatist, 'new pluralist', and socialist models of democracy, which became popular after 1914. Russell believed that the liberal state had been justified when it was defending general rights, such as religious freedom, but became anachronistic when parliament began legislating on relations between labour and capital. 'Democratisation' should lead to arrangements whereby capitalism would be subject to democratic control, and the Irish co-op movement was the model for 'cooperative democracy'. For Figgis, parliaments had proven, like local government, 'corrupt servers of special interests', and responsible government based on parties needed to be supplemented by bottom-up structures that would represent social and economic sectors of society. He proposed a Senate, with one-third of the Senators elected by PR from large constituencies, and two-thirds from various councils acting as electoral colleges. De Blácam dedicated his book to Connolly. Parliament had taken power over so many spheres of life, that it had become 'a jack of all trades and master of none', falling victim to the party system and corruption. In 1921 he proposed a governance structure whereby the Dáil would entrust administrative responsibilities to organisations like the Gaelic League, the Irish Agricultural Wholesale Society, and local councils.[45] All three authors believed that the traditional parliamentary model was outmoded. They were not just Irish fantasies. In 1909, in *What is the Use of Parliament?*, the British radical, F.W. Jowett, had also recommended substituting the traditional cabinet system, based on ministerial responsibility, with a system of committee government similar to that operating in county and local government.[46]

Since 1908 the Irish Women's Franchise League and the Irish Women's Suffrage Federation had been campaigning for equal suffrage. The Home Rule leadership was unwilling to demand this under the third Home Rule bill. The party had actually helped defeat a women's suffrage bill at Westminster in November 1912. To Hannah Sheehy Skeffington, the chapter of constitutionalism was now closed:

> It was a pretty tale, full of friendship and election pledges and platform appeals from those who 'have always been our best friends', but who were always fatally debarred from action at 'critical junctures', and who in the sacred cause of party were regretfully obliged to shelve our cause when there was a likelihood of it winning'.[47]

Her journal the *Irish Citizen* abandoned the Home Rule Party after 1916. It had concluded that women were the true constitutionalists, since they were outside the scope of constitutional rights. Prominent Irish feminists became more militant. Margaret Cousins spent a month in Mountjoy jail. Hannah Sheehy Skeffington went on hunger strike with three others. Dr Kathleen Lynn attended the strikers as a medical officer.[48]

In 1914 *The Leader* had noted that the third Home Rule Bill allowed the Home Rule parliament to decide on the suffrage question after five years. The examples of the Gaelic League and the Irish National Teachers Organisation suggested that it would be extended to all those active in the economy, male and female.[49] Sinn Féin became committed to equal suffrage early on. In 1911 it had joined a Dublin protest against their exclusion from the franchise under the Home Rule bill. Griffith, unlike John Redmond, supported them. There was thus first common ground between republicanism and feminism. The constitution of Cumann na dTeactaire (League of Women Delegates), formed by female members of Sinn Féin, pledged itself to co-operation with suffragette organisations and the appointment of women to all public bodies.[50] During the 1918 election campaign another republican women's organisation, Cumann na mBan, would use speeches from Hannah Sheehy Skeffington for electioneering.[51] After almost full suffrage was granted in 1918, Cumann na mBan issued a circular to its branches outlining the qualifications needed for voting, and directing local secretaries to secure women's right to vote in the different counties. Countess Markievicz, chosen as Minister of Labour by Sinn Féin in 1918, thought the national, women's, and labour causes, one. Yet Cumann na mBan would eventually wrest the initiative away from the purely feminist organisations. In 1914 the *Irish Citizen* had had to rebut republicans like Mary MacSwiney, who were opposed to the policy of putting the suffrage question ahead of independence. Sinn Féin's Jennie Wyse Power thought women should get the vote from an Irish parliament and not go seeking it from a British one.[52]

The British interest in reform bridged the Home Rule and Sinn Féin periods, when ideas of cultural revivalism and republicanism came to dominate. Biagini suggests that the Irish commitment to constitutionalism had been 'renewed and intensified' between 1900 and 1906, but rules out that this could also have occurred in the violent era on its way.[53] Yet Sinn Féin first drew on the same strand of constitutional idealism we now associate now only with Home Rule. The commitment to PR/STV was its most tangible legacy. Before 1912 support for PR had been confined to a small circle of thinkers. George Gavan Duffy's *A Fair Constitution for Ireland* (1892), had proposed that constituencies should be part of the fundamental law by which an Irish constitution would be established. In 1911 Erskine Childers argued that if PR were perceived by the unionist minority to be safeguarding their interests, then it should be welcomed. In response to a Royal Commission on Electoral Methods published in May 1910, the *Belfast Newsletter* and the *Northern Whig* expressed unionist support for PR for elections to the Irish House of Commons, and for county and borough councils. In January 1911 the pro-Home Rule *Freeman's Journal* ran a series of articles on electoral reform, and John Redmond supported change in principle. The third Home Rule Bill of 1912 adopted P.R. for the election of senators, and also, from constituencies returning three or more representatives, for the new Commons. The proposals were welcomed by the electoral expert, James Meredith, who argued that Unionist opposition to Home Rule could not be unrelated to the fact that they were exclusively represented in Westminster by members returned from Ulster constituencies. PR would end their underrepresentation outside Ulster, and strengthen that of nationalists in the North. It would also enable that change of government on which the English system depended. Because of the fixity of preferences on Home Rule in Ireland, this was impossible under 'first past the post'.[54]

The most influential supporter was the PR Society of Ireland, a deputation of which had been received by Asquith, Bonar Law, and the Ulster Unionist leader, Edward Carson, in 1912. While the Fabians were interested in whether PR would produce a more efficient administration, for the British and Irish PR Societies the accurate representation of public opinion was more important. With Sir Horace Plunkett as President, Lord Dunraven as Vice-President, and a council representative of all Irish parties and interests, the Irish PR Society was formed in 1911 to campaign for 'electoral justice'; PR, greater electoral choice, freeing candidates from dependence on financial interests, and minority representation. Griffith was a founding member. Irish supporters of PR feared that the 'list' system would perpetuate the current party system, and advocated the STV system instead.[55] Griffith's *Sinn Féin* pointed to Finland to argue that electoral reform could do away with the 'absurd' and 'corrupt' ward system. The British system it described as 'the most anomalous system of representation in the civilized world'. A combination of PR, the referendum, and elections from a single constituency, would combine democracy with minority representation.[56] Sinn Féin wanted to stand for ideals over and above those of the contending parties. It had won no majority in any constituency in the 1910 general election, and made common cause with moderate Unionists in arguing that the whole Home Rule parliament should be elected by PR. Sinn Féin followed the lead earlier given by the liberal Unionist, Lord Courtney, in asking for countywide and three-seater constituencies, so that anyone with at least fifteen per cent of the vote could secure a seat. In 1912 it ran a series of articles in *Sinn Féin* showing how minorities would be under-represented under the Home Rule bill. In South Dublin, where Unionists and Nationalists had 5,000 votes each, the Home Rulers would have three seats to none under the existing system.[57] Griffith proposed to the Irish Convention in 1915 that an Irish parliament be elected by STV, with large multi-member constituencies to give Unionists more representation.

To Garvin the prospect of Home Rule, not of separation, exercised the nationalist constitutional imagination.[58] The provisions for religious freedom, PR, and the Senate, all means of reconciling Unionists to some form of Irish self-government, reflected the ideals of an era committed to democracy as 'minority rights'. Griffith broke with the classic republican tradition (expressed in the IRB 1858 constitution) in prioritising safeguards for the minority, and seeing them as compatible with national unity.[59] Yet the crisis of liberalism was also a crucial influence. A persistent theme of British radicalism, shared by Irish nationalists, had been that popular self-government was distorted by elites and special interests, and that institutional reform was needed for popular democracy. In 1911 *Irish Freedom*, controlled by the Irish Republican Brotherhood (IRB), pointed to a constitution which would provide for religious toleration, free education, the prevention of poverty, democratic control of the legislature (through referendums or triennial elections), and universal adult suffrage.[60] This article was actually written by P. S. O'Hegarty, later an important figure in Sinn Féin. Sinn Féin's commitment to equal suffrage, functional representation, and the referendum (as well as to STV), also shows how the crisis of liberalism updated the nationalist tradition in institutional terms. It remained to be seen whether it would take the Irish beyond the traditional Westminster model.

SINN FÉIN'S NEW BEGINNING?

Some scholars have suggested that Sinn Féin paid little attention to the question of what the constitution of an Irish-Ireland would be like. Laffan remarks that Sinn Féin simply did not concern itself with citizenship, and sees revival of the Irish language as their key policy aim.[61] Others argue that '"a familiar and acceptable model" – Westminster – was available and simply taken over'[62] Yet Sinn Féin had developed a critique of that model, which rested on the conviction that the reform of institutions was necessary for national revival. Whether expressed in Padraig Pearse's views of the educational 'murder machine', in dissatisfaction with local government, or in disenchantment with electoral polarisation, nationalist thinkers believed that British institutions had brought the country to a demoralised *impasse*. Revival needed new institutions, as well as new values. At the first annual convention of the National Council of Sinn Féin in January 1905, Griffith proposed a policy of national self-development through the recognition of the 'duties and rights of citizenship' on the part of the individual. This remained Sinn Féin's policy up to 1921.[63]

The most important constitutional change was the introduction of near universal suffrage in 1918. Victory in the Great War legitimised the Westminster model in Britain, and the Conservatives dominated the first democratically elected Commons. In Ireland British rule was discredited by the executions of the 1916 leaders, and Sinn Féin's 1918 electoral victory raised the question of what constitution could be consistent with 'Ourselves Alone'. Sinn Féin followed Griffith's 'Hungarian policy' by abstaining from Westminster, and founding Dáil Éireann in January 1919. This parliament's unicameral character was a symbol of national sovereignty. The principles of 'liberty' and 'self-determination' were invoked in the Dáil's 'message to the Free Nations of the World'. The Dáil 'ratified' the declaration of the Republic in 1916, and 'Republic' and 'Commonwealth 'were used in a *Democratic Programme* promising liberty, equality and justice for all.[64] This programme was influenced by Irish Labour, and the Dáil elected a woman, Countess Markievicz, as Minister for Labour. The Dáil also committed itself to the use of 'every available means' to end British rule in Ireland. It remained an illegal parliament up to 1922. The day it met, the IRA had already begun a military campaign intended to remove British forces from Ireland. This campaign would last until July 1921.

A vote for Sinn Féin was a vote against the parliamentary tradition: only two of Sinn Féin's 45 TDs in 1919 had been MPs. The Home Rulers had pressed for rights under the British constitution. Sinn Féin's source of legitimacy was the Irish nation which had 'reasserted' its sovereignty by voting for the complete independence of the island in 1918. The results of the (local) 1920 and (general) 1921 elections strengthened this claim. To Griffith 'a native Irish constitution' had always existed: under the Union the Irish people had been prevented from exercising their constitutional rights by force, and the constitution of Grattan's parliament (1782–1800) would continue to exist, until the Irish people voluntarily agreed to its abrogation. After 1800 Irish constitutionalism had meant either support for the Union, or the use of purely moral force against it. Now conventional constitutionalism was deemed 'criminal' by radical nationalists, and the real constitutionalists were the anti-constitutionalists.[65] As in later anti-colonial movements, a 'hidden constitution' had superior claims to allegiance to the existing constitution.

Irish feminism became more radicalised. In 1921 Cumann na mBan reported the existence of almost 800 branches in Ireland, England and Scotland. Formed in Dublin in November 1913, it first considered itself 'The Women's Section of the Volunteer Movement'. The organisation had adopted a uniform in October 1915.[66] After the 1916 Rising it initiated the 'Defence of Ireland Fund' for the arming and equipment of the Volunteers. In 1918 the government declared it a dangerous organisation. Cumann na mBan was pledged to follow the 1916 Proclamation by training women to take up their proper position in the life of the Irish nation, as 'perfect citizens of a perfect state'. During the War of Independence (1919–21), it assisted the IRA in many ways. When one republican Eithne Coyle was later interviewed for a proposed history of the organisation, she mentioned the provision of safe houses, work on the republican courts, and the support of prisoners' dependants.[67] Feminist ideology became influenced by the Gaelic Revival. Cumann na mBan endorsed the Sinn Féin view that in the old Gaelic civilisation there was no bias in citizenship rights. Its 1914 manifesto had stated that its aims were 'solely national'.[68]

Culture had become important to constitutionalism. In 1905 D. P. Moran had declared that 'politics is not nationality', and lamented that various political movements had made no effort to enable men and women grow up Irish.[69] With its policies of abstentionism, economic protectionism, and language revival, Sinn Féin was best placed to advance his 'Irish Ireland' ideals. Many of its members had a common background in the Gaelic Athletic Association, or the Gaelic League. Sinn Féin proclaimed that 'democracy could only be realised through Irish nationality', which suggested that its constitutional ideals reflected those of the Revival.[70] By 1918 the Revival was decades old, and had sought to relocate the moral centre of the nation away from the legal bureaucratic state on to the historic Irish community.[71] Revivalists conceived of a Gaelic world prior to hierarchy, class, and private property. This world was seen as one where Irish society had fulfilled its potential for creative self-expression. Hence the Revival's interest in literature and folklore, the Gaelic land system, and the Brehon laws (the Gaelic legal system). It became commonplace to contrast its creativity and harmony with the values of class, sectarianism, and materialism, that had supplanted it under British rule.

Sinn Féin's new beginning was thus conceived of as a return to origins. Bulmer Hobson's *The Republic* suggested that Irish Republicans wanted to obtain, not the constitution Wolfe Tone, had died to abolish, but the one he died to obtain. Sinn Féin thought the new constitution could only be constitutional if according to some fundamental laws, it located the sovereign power in individuals or bodies, designated or chosen in a prescribed manner, and defined the limit of that power so that rights could be protected from the assumption of arbitrary authority. Since the authority of a constitution derived from its fidelity to a set of prior values and rights, this constitution would be a fundamental law. Griffith (sometimes accused of anti-clericalism) thought the Irish people a free people by 'natural rights' and 'constitutional law'.[72] His *United Irishman* thought that these rights, usurped with the original British conquest, were historically prior to any political order, and extended to ownership of all the material wealth and resources of the island, as argued by the Fenian leader, John Mitchel. The approach was romantic and subversive rather than revolutionary, since the constitution would express the characteristics of a polity that once existed. Hence it would take on an expressive aspect, to express a set of values, rights, and norms – to de Blácam 'the dictates of nature and tradition' – long suppressed. To Figgis, there was something arresting about a nation whose 'distinct laws and procedures' had been trampled underfoot, but which had maintained them through centuries of oppression in its 'instincts and intuitions'. For *Irish Freedom*, anything standing in the way of the creation of the state working to give expression 'to the soul of the nation' must now be overcome.[73] Just as language revival would return Ireland to the Gaelic World, the constitution would symbolise the recovery of Ireland's ancient rights.

The idea that the modern democratic Irish nation had its roots in the pre-conquest era, and could recover its Gaelic features after centuries of British rule, was appealing to many. In Britain, two traditions of thinking about the state had solidified on the left by 1914. One was idealist, almost utopian, and became committed to such a strong notion of democracy that it wanted to transform the state utterly. The other accepted the democratic possibilities of the British constitution with some reservations.[74] In Britain, the cautious view prevailed because certain reforms, such as PR, did not resonate with British political culture as well as equal suffrage.[75] In Ireland the first tradition appealed to a society with a long tradition of alienation from the state. Popular sovereignty was invoked both to reject British rule, and to establish a new political system grounded in the rule of the people. Sinn Féin's 1918 election manifesto promised a constituent assembly to speak in the name of the Irish people, and to develop Ireland for the welfare of the people as a whole.[76]

As in classic republican theory, the virtue of a republican state was contrasted to the corruption of the existing system. The Home Rulers had seen legislative autonomy as the means of reversing Irish decline, but Sinn Féin saw that tradition as a source of corruption itself. *The Republic* argued that the examples of Belgium, France, and Switzerland, showed that democratic states prospered, and associated monarchy with heavy taxation and military spending. To the *United Irishman* monarchy embodied the despotic principle, and the English King, soon to visit Ireland in the person of King Edward, encouraged feudalism. The Sinn Féin priest, Father Michael O'Flanagan, also criticised the social hierarchies promoted in monarchical systems, and linked them to the favouritism through which 'men of influence' now corrupted the electoral process:

> In a kingdom, therefore, or even in a country in which the mind of the people is in a muddle between monarchism and republicanism, favour is all important. Even at elections candidates go round from man to man and ask for votes as a personal favour – it produces the most pernicious form of individual, the 'man of influence'. The man of influence is able to get votes for a friend, and then he will be able to go to his friend and get jobs for his supporters. Woe betide the people who are governed by such a system.

O'Flanagan advocated a presidential republic, and thought that republics would not go to war because they were more democratic and meritocratic.[77]

There were two responses to this corruption. By 1921 the Dáil had succeeded in wresting control of local government from the British Local Government Board, and was running elected local courts to dispense justice and resolve land disputes. Dublin Castle, the seat of British rule, was specifically blamed for Irish corruption. The underground Dáil government set up a Department of Local Government, with William Cosgrave as minister, and Kevin O'Higgins as his deputy. Well before the Anglo-Irish Treaty was signed in 1921, all county and most boroughs in the future area of the Irish Free State had recognised the authority of this Ministry.[78] Cosgrave and O'Higgins fought against vested local interests and corrupt officials in their drive to reform, standardise, and centralise the system. In its 1919 constitution Sinn Féin committed itself to the creation of a National Civil Service, embracing all local government employees with appointment only by merit. In its manifesto for the 1920 local elections, Sinn Féin stated that all its candidates stood for appointment by merit, open competitive examinations, and an end to 'the insidious system of jobbery and corruption'.[79]

In contrast, the 'intellectual Sinn Féiners' looked to new models of representation. For de Blácam, the role of parliaments had been reduced to those of a second chamber, and the 'multitude of interests' in society could not be represented under party government. A more sensitive instrument than the electoral constituency was needed for popular control of the legislature. He pointed to vocational representation. Figgis also thought the local government system had reduced political life to 'a tangle of conflicting and corrupt interests', and that 'functional representation' would remove dependence on traditional bureaucracies. Russell thought the larger the state the more the dominance of economic interests. The purpose of reform should be to 'let the general will have free play', in contrast to the tendency for parliament to act as 'a device' enabling 'all kinds of compromises to be made'. He also supported 'functional representation'.[80] These intellectuals returned to Hobson's question of how democratic institutions could be 'organically' rooted in society without reproducing its inequalities. De Blácam brought Hobson to his logical conclusion:

> The state in the past has been a parasite of the community: an external authority, created and maintained by the antagonism of classes. When class conflict passes, the state passes with it, according to Marxian belief. In Ireland we expect to see the external or central state dissolved, absorbed and assimilated, as the powers engrossed by the parliamentary form of government are assumed by the natural institutions of society. Administration of the new order will be the natural, reflex action of the heading organism, not the artificial act of an ascendancy riding that organism.[81]

Various new representative models, influenced by European trends, had been proposed. Griffith's *de facto* 'council of three hundred' from 1906 would have combined members of local government councils, poor law boards, and harbour boards, with parliamentary members elected from territorial constituencies. This was proposed as a sturdier model than Grattan's (1782–1800) Parliament. Figgis also suggested a dual system, in which government ministers would be presidents of functional councils, and make legislation in consultation with specific social and economic groups. AE saw in the co-op movement a form of co-operative democracy which would end the influence of 'the gombeen man'. De Blácam proposed governing through self-governing colleges, which would rely on groups such as the Gaelic League, the Irish Agricultural Wholesale Society, and the county councils, to administer laws. Sinn Féin's 1917 constitution actually proposed a protectionist system for Irish industry and commerce, by combined action of local councils, poor law boards, and 'other bodies directly responsible to the Irish people'. It hardly mentioned the word parliament. Instead it made its *Árd Fheis* the 'supreme governing and legislative body'.[82]

A tension thus existed between Sinn Féin's centralist and bottom-up tendencies. With the goal of establishing an independent state accepted by the international community, 'political nationalists' typically organise along legal-rationalist lines, forming centralised organisations which mobilise groups for this end. Lacking central or official means of advancing their ideals, cultural nationalists typically first organise in non-official and decentralised societies embodying values such as civic co-operation and self-reliance. Sinn Féin combined both tendencies. To Davis Sinn Féin had a strong centralising tendency, and its 1917 constitution, which allowed the 'bosses' to co-opt 20 members, made it more so.[83] Others thought the constitution 'almost Soviet in its decentralisation', and anticipated the democracy 'of the future', purged of Bolshevism and state socialism.[84] With no ambition to fight the Home Rulers in parliamentary constituencies, Sinn Féin was first based on local government bodies. Its constitutional ideals were thus connected to its size. The 1917 constitution, suspicious of parliamentary leaders, had located voting power at its annual convention, Árd Fheis, in local branches, or *cumann*. Parliamentary representatives were deprived of a vote unless they were delegates from Sinn Féin clubs or *Comháirle Ceanntair*. Not more than one third of its standing committee could be members of its parliament.

Did this approach survive the increase in size which followed Sinn Féin's electoral success? The first Dáil passed a short provisional constitution in January 1919, resting on the British concept of responsible government, which vested all legislative power in Dáil Éireann.[85] Yet de Blácam wrote of a 'Sinn Féin constitution' to emerge from the workings of the suppressed Dáil (1919–21), and the writings of Irish Ireland propagandists.[86] There was ambiguity. One clerical 'Sinn Féiner' thought that by integrating organisations like the Gaelic

League, the Industrial Association, and the Farmers' Organisation into government departments, the Irish executive could be destroyed only by the destruction of the Irish people.[87] His assumption was that the leaders of such organisations would become 'Directors' of government departments. The Officers and Directors report from the first 1919 Árd Fheis commented that the work originally undertaken by Sinn Féin had now become the province of Dáil Éireann. Among its tangible results were the projected Arbour day, the development of the Irish fisheries, and the commission of inquiry into industrial opportunities, all signs of an evolving self-reliant Irish state.[88] In truth, of the eleven government departments arranged for by the Dáil, the four most important (Finance, Home Affairs, Foreign Affairs and Defence) were placed under ministerial responsibility in the 1919 constitution. It remained to be seen how Sinn Féin would cater for areas closer to its heart, such as the Irish language. One report of its April 1919 extraordinary Árd Fheis noted the need for a new constitution to reconcile Sinn Féin to Dáil Éireann.[89]

The 1916 Proclamation had promised a Republic which 'cherished the children of the nation equally'. This committed the Republic to an egalitarian and non-sectarian future. Pearse shared the social radicalism of the land agitator, James Fintan Lalor, who believed that popular sovereignty required both the nation's right to ownership of the soil, and the right to make laws for itself. A nation's sovereignty thus extended to all its material possessions, and no right of private property was good against this. The radical liberal argument that laws made by elites not fully representative of the people were 'a usurpa-tion', was also found in Pearse's 1916 'Sovereign People', which argued that the widest possible franchise was necessary to achieve full representation. Pearse quoted Wolfe Tone and Thomas Davis's views that the gentry and merchant classes had corrupted the Irish cause in a way that 'the people' would not. The Irish nation was under 'a moral obligation' to secure 'strictly equal rights and liberties' to every man and woman. Other arguments Pearse found in Tone, that the Irish claim to freedom was based on fundamental human rights, that English-held property in Ireland could be confiscated, and that the country would never be free or happy without independence, were consistent with this radical legacy.[90]

Yet a strong juridical or secular conception of the republic had not deve-loped before independence. In 1907 *The Republic* claimed that the concept was not really understood outside Presbyterian Ulster. The *United Irishman* pointed out that when General Humbert declared a Republic of Connaught in August 1798, it operated according to 'a war constitution'. Pearse's the *Sovereign People* implied that the Republic symbolised the rejection of the British value system, more than a commitment to a new type of state. James Connolly had wanted a 'socialist republic' with nationalisation of all land, and all national property controlled by public associations accountable to a democratic congress. *Irish Freedom* was controlled by Tom Clarke and Sean MacDermott of the IRB. Its editor, P. S. O'Hegarty, placed independence above any specific framework of government. He accepted the Treaty in 1922. In 1918, the nationalist priest, Walter O'Brien, argued that only the 'militant' Sinn Féiners' wanted the establishment of a Republic, while the 'constitution-alist' Sinn Féiners' followed Sinn Féin out of alienation with the 'parliamentary misrepresentation and ministerial trickery' of the pre-war era. The latter supported an appeal to the Peace Conference, but would have been satisfied with a form of Home Rule as existed in the White Dominions.[91] Sinn Féin's 1917 policy was to declare a Republic, and once independence was achieved, to allow the people, in a referendum, to freely chose their own form of govern-ment. In 1919, however, both 'Militant' and 'Constitutionalist' Sinn Féiners agreed on the necessity of physical force.

Sinn Féin espoused a 'national internationalism'.[92] Its 1918 policy was to appeal to the Versailles Peace conference to recognise its claim to self-determination, and should that approach fail, Sinn Féin would pursue its objectives by force. Key to the Wilsonian vision was the idea that small nations' rights were equal to those of larger states, and de Valera campaigned for this principle in the United States in 1920–1. He wanted a new 'Covenant' or Treaty for the League of Nations to establish equality of rights between large and small states, not another 'Holy Alliance', dependent on the goodwill of the Great Powers.[93] His campaign was unsuccessful. After major conflicts caused by Great Power rivalry, intellectuals often put their hopes for peace in the creation of smaller political units and decentralised power structures. In Ireland, the standard liberal justification for Home Rule had been that the Irish were a permanent minority within the UK, their rights were infringed, and legislative autonomy would allow them to contribute more fully to the culture of humanity.[94] After a war which shattered European empires, these arguments were displaced by more organic ones. Hobson argued that inter-national morality now required the self-determination of nations, and invoked 'a sound organic principle' of moral conduct – from each according to its power, to each according to its needs – in defence of this principle. *Sinn Féin* suggested that there were two conceptions of the state: the Roman one, where the state was held together by a central authority, and a Gaelic one, where the state was held together, not by military cohesion, but by a spiritual com-munity of self-governing communities. For Pearse, the nation, like the family, was a natural unit held together by spiritual ties, unlike 'unholy' empires, whose ties were of mutual self-interest and brute force. In 1913 *Sinn Féin* had published an article arguing that the pre-feudal Celtic system in Ireland and Scotland, free of any central authority, favoured 'divided' rather than centralised power arrangements. The balance of power these provided expressed the Irish constitutional ideal. De Blacam thought the era of self-determination heralded a return to the pre-Reformation era. He saw in the dissolution of the European Empires into smaller units, which could then devolve sovereignty to their constituent communes, the only guarantee of international peace. For William O'Brien, the concept of self-determination was also as old as Europe itself, and transferred the power to determine Ireland's future from 'sham English party managers' to the Irish themselves.[95] The crisis of the Westminster system was thus linked to the weakening of Empire in the international sphere.

The Gaelic Revival provided grounds for thinking that the native Irish tradition was somehow 'agin the state'. Since the flowering of Gaelic civilisation had preceded the development of European feudalism, the native tradition was to resist the power of the state and the material culture associated with it. W. B. Yeats saw in the Gaelic past a harmonious and creative social order, which combined love of locality with cultural unity. Its small-scale individualised communities had been destroyed by the mass British culture of materialism, class divisions, and imperialism. Yeats saw the centralised clergy and the men of science as agents of this change, but his equation of a centralised source of morality with authoritarianism was also a critique of the modern state. Pearse's *Murder Machine* was another. De Blácam also thought nation states intolerant of diversity, and associated them with militaristic and capitalist institutions. *The Republic*, with Ulster in mind, supported a Federal Republic which combined multi-nationality with popular sovereignty, as in Switzerland. For language scholar Eoin Mac Neill, the first Minister of Education in the Free State, the essence of the 'Irish-Ireland' movement was a rejection of state worship, and the basis of the political fabric should be strong local government, with little delegation of power to the centre. The Gaelic *tuatha* were a historical model. He attacked the idea that the Anglo-Norman invasions had brought Ireland out of backwardness, by imposing a unified legal and political system. Rather the Celts had had a democratic system resembling the Greek city states, in which the decentralisation of power allowed for cultural creativity and technological progress. Representative government produced atrophy of citizenship, and 'hypertrophy' of the state, because it delegated too much responsibility away from the citizen. O'Neill also rejected the inequalities and excessive specialism of modern education, and thought the medieval values of local initiative and autonomy could achieve a meritocratic system without a strong central authority.[96]

Yet this anti-state tradition could easily be reconciled to the Catholic preference for 'subsidiarity', especially in education. The Catholic Church's belief in subsidiarity was developed in Pope Leo XIII's 1891 encyclical *Rerum*

Novarum, which advocated a 'third way' between capitalism and communism. Since the principle was that matters ought to be decided by the smallest, lowest, or least centralised authority, it suited Sinn Féin's anti-centralist tendencies. With the crisis of liberalism Catholic nationalism had become stronger, and the materialist approach to self-government persisted. This was suggested by the formation of the Catholic Association in 1902, and the Catholic Defence League in 1905. In 1906 the *United Irishman* rejected the idea that the Irish House of Commons should be elected on the same basis as the English chamber, since this could exclude Catholic ecclesiastics. In 1913 *The Leader* suggested that both state and Church were 'divinely ordained', and would operate in their respective spheres for the common good. The *Catholic Bulletin* suggested that Christ was the founder of democracy, and that the world revolution towards freedom, equality and fraternity, had its roots in the Christian faith.[97] Clerical supporters of Sinn Féin, like the Rev. P. Gaynor, emphasised that its parliament would conform to 'God's law', as a 'natural' and 'lawful' authority.[98] Few saw in the Catholic Church a source of monopoly to rival that of landlordism and big finance.[99] There was little secularism in their Republic.

Subsequent history would show that Catholic nationalism could combine with Sinn Féin constitutionalism. The combination marks the work of Alfred O'Rahilly, Professor of Physics at University College Cork, who wanted to marry Swiss direct democracy to Irish Catholicism. In a series of articles in *Studies* from 1918 to 1921 he tried to intellectually repatriate the concept of democracy to the Gaelic/Catholic world by denying its British roots. To O'Rahilly, the seventeenth-century jurist, Francis Suarez, had found in Church democracy the 'balance of power' ideal. The English and American embrace of democratic ideas also came from their rejection of the 'machinery' of the state, and from the application of religious values to the secular life in the seventeenth century. He contrasted the liberal and socialist view of the state as an 'impersonal arrangement', with the idea that its authority was derived from the people as an 'organic' whole. The task of modern constitutionalism was not the separation of powers between different government functions, but the maintenance of a balance of power between authorities of a different nature. He envisaged an Irish constitution based on natural law, self-governing councils, and a balance between Church and State.[100] Naturally, he championed the 1937 constitution.

Yet O'Rahilly also believed in popular sovereignty. Recent history had shown how 'political machines' and 'financial interests' had undermined the value of elections as a means of providing democracy. These 'machines' had resulted in 'caucus control', 'secret funds', 'front bench collusion' and 'coalitions'. Indeed, parliamentary sovereignty itself was incompatible with popular sovereignty, since the last English attempt at true democracy was that of the

Levellers. Cromwell's subsequent dictatorship, with its acceptance of the property order and its imperial foreign policy, defeated the republican idealism that could have sustained an English democracy. Since then English popular sovereignty, like its Irish counterpart, had also been suppressed.[101] O'Rahilly was prescient enough to see the potential conflict between his *de jure* theory that only the constituent will of the community can form the moral personality of the state, and any theory that derived political obligation from the *de facto* existence of an external framework of order. The moral requirement to obey an inauthentic or illegitimate state, simply because it provided for public order and social continuity, could be sustained only in the short run, and the tension might produce civil war.[102] Indeed O'Rahilly's work was an unconscious premonition of the Irish civil war.

Did Sinn Féin experience a constitutional moment? The 1916 Proclamation established popular sovereignty as the basis of any future system. The first and second Dáils symbolised new beginnings, rejecting traditional constitutionalism and British law. Radical reform continued to be discussed in the advanced nationalist press. Yet the task of turning ideals into reality was deferred. Only one page long, the 1919 constitution was provisional, and liable to alteration upon seven days' written notice of motion for that purpose. The short period between January 1919 and the truce in July 1921 then gave little time for the creation of new constitutional structures. The Dáil met rarely, and when it did, reliance on British rules for the conduct of its business suggests a degree of 'parliamentary literacy' among its inexperienced TDs. Despite the efforts of educators like Thomas Davis, Griffith, and Pearse, mainstream constitutional thinking had long been focused on Westminster. Yet the radical literature of the era suggests a desire for something new, and independence would test its seriousness of intent. The 1922 constitutional committee consulted an eclectic set of sources, including on functional representation, with their roots in the crisis of liberalism. Yet when the committee sat, tensions between the Sinn Féin leadership and local power-holders one the one hand, and within the IRA on the other, were intensifying. Sinn Féin's split over the Treaty had led to a governmental vacuum, in which Cosgrave and O'Higgins emerged as important figures. There is always a risk with utopia that it might not quite believe in itself.[103] Indeed their resolution of this crisis suggested the existence of an Irish 'state tradition' obscured by the themes of the Gaelic Revival.

CONCLUSION

Since 1880, Britain, not just Ireland, had been preparing for democracy, and there was overlap between the two. In terms of the legal dimension to constitutionalism, Home Rule had focused minds on legal principles and judicial mechanisms for the protection of minority rights. In terms of institutional provisions for limiting power, the crisis of liberalism took nationalists beyond the Westminster model. Since Sinn Féin sought to repudiate, not regulate the connection with Westminster, its institutional legacy was less concrete. It was strong on mobilising people, and its intellectuals hoped to convert the emotion of 'Ourselves Alone' into novel institutional structures. Yet Sinn Féin would have needed 'a century of propaganda' to realise its vision of Ireland.[104] The link between new models of representation and socioeconomic progress would soon be forgotten. Sinn Féin's legacy was primarily normative. Its understanding of a constitution as 'a new beginning', with the doctrine of popular sovereignty supplying the principle of legitimacy, proved central to the 1922 and 1937 constitutions. Its expressive approach to constitutions was linked to the idea a fundamental law, and contrasted with the flexibility of the British system. The Republic, proclaimed in 1916, has remained key to social and political discourse, North and South.

Sinn Féin had begun as a fringe ideological movement. Constitutional reform proposals seldom originated within Ireland, but the 'intellectual Sinn Féiners' generally supported them. The idealist strain lasted until 1922, when Figgis, a poet and critic, was made deputy chair of the constitutional committee. *The Drama of Sinn Féin* had reflected the tension between its effectiveness as a political 'machine' and its hopes for 'a spiritual democracy'.[105] This tension lasted into 1922. Sinn Féin encountered the specific difficulty the Home Rulers faced – of advancing a majority case for self-government without alienating the Unionist minority – and its strongest liberal commitments stemmed from this conundrum. After 1922 both wings of Sinn Féin, Cumann na nGaedheal and Fianna Fáil took on the characteristics of parties of social integration, pursuing materialist not idealist ends.[106] The organic conception of the constitution, articulated by O'Rahilly, appealed to many in the 1930s. Indeed, to the republican left the Free State had become the 'instrument' of the Catholic middle class, and by 1937 Sinn Féin commitments, to functional representation for example, were being diverted to Catholic ends. Partition provided the perfect framework for an alliance between Church and State to re-emerge. Griffith's Dual Monarchy had been proposed for a bi-national island, not for a partitioned state. The prospect of independence had sustained a tradition of constitutional idealism among advanced nationalists. Once it came, consolidation became imperative, and constitutional life given a different stamp.

Was it force of circumstance or of character that had given Irish nationalism this idealist stamp? When nationalists saw some prospect of self-government in a 32-county context, an idealist approach prevailed. The writer Frank O'Connor thought Sinn Féin 'playacting' at revolution and were shocked by the reality they created with the civil war. Sinn Féin had wanted to reverse the course of 700 years of Irish history, but partition and civil war saw the emergence of a strong centralised state amidst a general disillusionment of ideals. Sinn Féin had come to prominence during one (international) war, and was destroyed by another (civil) war. The 1920s in Ireland, as in Europe, were then marked by retrenchment. Ambiguity about the ability of Irish ideals to survive independence had been long standing. In 1908 the Rev. John Kelleher remarked that the people were equipped for resistance against despotism, not for the exercise of power. He cited historical examples, like the English Commonwealth, to show the tendency for revolutions to produce a transition from despotism to democracy, and then to return to despotism again. P. S. O'Hegarty, after proposing a radical constitution in his 1911 *Irish Freedom* article, suggested that the best government for Ireland for twenty years or so, would be a military dictatorship under an Irish Cromwell. In 1919, de Blácam concluded that whatever the aims of Irish-Ireland idealists, in a revolutionary or transitional stage, paternalism or centralised control was necessary.[107] This was a persistent theme of the Irish constitutional mind before 1921, and an appropriate guide to the fate of many anti-colonial movements throughout the following century.

TWO

EXPERIMENT

THE 1922 CONSTITUTION

—

The Anglo-Irish Treaty of 1921 gave Sinn Féin the opportunity, for the first time, to express its values in a legal constitution. This opportunity arose in a European context that was fertile ground for constitutional experiments, and for the concept of a constitution as a new beginning. In the wake of the collapse of several European empires, over fifteen new republics emerged after the First World War. These typically marked the transition from Empire to Republic with democratic constitutions. Darrell Figgis called the 1922 constitution *Bunreacht* (foundation or fixed legislation), which suggests the passing of a fundamental law symbolising a new beginning.[1] Yet its provisions for religious freedom, the office of the Governor General, and the bicameral parliament, spoke to the older Home Rule tradition. Britain had been victorious in the Great War, and the first clause of the 1922 constitution stressed the constitution's subordination to the Treaty. The constitution suffered from the tension between its ambition to mark a new beginning, and its subordination to that agreement. Pro-treatyites saw no inconsistency, and thought the Irish could move 'from Treaty to constitution', achieving the objectives of Irish nationalism on the way. For the anti-treatyites, a new beginning was incompatible with continued membership of the Empire. Thus the two conceptions of constitutionalism were opposed, and the result was a contested constitution. In the background was the deepening crisis of inter-war Europe. This began early in Ireland, with partition and civil war, leading to a general disillusion of ideals. By 1936 the constitution was in tatters, and its ultra democratic components were first to go.

THE 1922 CONSTITUTIONAL COMMITTEE

The collapse of the European land empires during the First World War led to the creation of more than fifteen new states, all based on the nationality principle. Only Hungary did not adopt a new constitution. Most were 'new' states, with no previous experience of statehood, and their creation involved reordering the territorial map of Europe. This meant that their constitutions were 'foundational' documents on many levels. The preamble to 'The Constitution of the Irish Free State' proclaimed the establishment of a (26-county) state, 'in the confidence that the national life and unity of Ireland shall thus be restored'. Whereas in 1914 there were only a few European republics, after the war this number trebled. One aspect of the republican approach to constitution making was to convene a constituent assembly, with the authority to amend, ratify or reject, the new document. This was the French model, and as the 1922 constitution was only published on the morning of the 1922 election, 16 June, the Provisional Government hoped to legitimise it in this way. The Labour Party was strongly in favour, naively hoping that the document would reflect the Dáil's 1919 Democratic Programme. The third Dáil was elected as a constituent assembly on 16 June, and first considered the constitution on 18 September. After several amendments, it ratified it on 25 October. Following approval by Westminster the previous day, the constitution became law on 6 December 1922.

Figgis compared the new political system to a pyramid, with the people at the base, and the executive at the top.[2] The European transition from Empire to Republic saw popular sovereignty emerge as the central organising principle. In Ireland this concept had to be reconciled to the 1921 Treaty framework. This Treaty had created an Irish dominion with the same constitutional relationship to Westminster as that of Canada. This ruled out a formal Republic, although Irish Free State was a translation of *Saorstat Éireann*, the Irish name Sinn Féin had used for Republic since 1919. The Treaty also upheld partition, as long as the Northern majority wanted it. The Free State would assume a certain portion of the public debt of the UK, key ports would remain under British control, and members of parliament would be required to swear an oath to the Free State constitution and the British Crown. When the constitution was published, to some the explicit statement of popular sovereignty in Article 2, which had no dominion parallels, indicated Irish sovereignty.[3] Others argued that it created 'Hamlet without the Prince of Denmark', and the rival claims of Monarchy versus Republic would persist.[4] The tension between Treaty and Sinn Féin constitutionalism would remain.

The Treaty required the constitution to be adopted no later than 6 December 1922. Although the Treaty had been approved by a small majority of the second Dáil on 7 January, to the constitutional committee the constitution was a domestic matter. After its enactment, the six counties of Northern Ireland could opt out of the Free State, remaining within the UK, or become part of the Irish state. Thus the 1922 constitution was drafted with the possibility of unity in mind. When submitting two drafts to Michael Collins, the Chairman of the Provisional Government, Figgis remarked that

Northern Ireland could come in without amendment.[5] Should Northern Ireland opt out, the final border between Northern Ireland and the Free State would be decided by a Boundary Commission. It was widely believed that the commission would render Northern Ireland non-viable if reduced to four counties. When debating the Treaty in January 1921, the Dáil had been divided by the question of status, not partition.

The 'Wilsonian moment', which promised an international order based on the principle of self-determination after the Great War, allowed new states to envision their future in idealistic terms. Their constitution makers wanted to give constitutional form to the advanced principles of democracy, and to ground their newly acquired national existence in this form. When the Irish committee first met on 24 January 1922, Collins pointed to the first clause of the Treaty, which conferred on the Free State 'co-equal' status with Canada. The committee was to bear in mind not the legalities of the past, but the possibilities of the future.[6] The other imperative was to draft a democratic constitution. The Irish were not tied to the Canadian model of government. Lloyd George declared that the powers of the second house were not his concern.[7] It was only after the committee had completed its work, that negotiations took place between the British and Irish governments over the draft (B) they produced. Moreover, while the committee met, Sinn Féin had not formally split over the Treaty. Ultimately Collins produced his own short draft, intended to show that the constitution was compatible with republicanism. Winston Churchill had warned him that the British government would be as tenacious on questions of symbolism as the republicans.[8]

Drafted by an expert committee, the constitution was intended as a non-party document. Five members were legal experts, and four were civil servants. Three were former leaders of the Irish White Cross, and one, James Douglas, a Quaker businessman, would figure in peace initiatives during the civil war. Insulated from the bitterness of the Dáil, they continued on the idealism of early Sinn Féin. This was expressed by George Gavan Duffy, Minister of Justice in the Provisional Government, who told Collins on 15 March that Ireland would soon prove itself 'the First of the Small Nations':

> Ireland's day has come. The oldest nation in Europe, Ireland is the youngest in spirit. She has warm friends everywhere throughout the continent of Europe, and no enemies. She will buy into a tired world a freshness of vision, coupled with a directness and tenacity of purpose, that will gradually make her an active force in the redemption of Europe.[9]

The committee first met on 24 January and subsequently held 27 meetings. Collins attended only the first meeting. Figgis chaired in his absence. On 7

March 1922 a committee report was sent to Collins. Only drafts A and B were formally submitted by the committee, with C never seriously considered by the government. The committee heard from expert witnesses, notably on electoral practice and financial administration. Where possible its recommendations were kept simple and flexible, given uncertain conditions, north and south.[10] The committee contained a wide range of academic, administrative, business, legal and political expertise. Formally, it consisted of Collins, head of the Provisional Government, Figgis, Vice Chairman and secretary, James Douglas, Hugh Kennedy (law adviser to the Provisional Government), James Murnaghan, James McNeill, Alfred O'Rahilly, C. J. France, Kevin O'Shiel and John O'Byrne. Kennedy was a barrister, as were O'Byrne and O'Shiel. Murnaghan was a Law Professor. MacNeill, a brother of the Minister of Education, had been a high-ranking British civil servant in Calcutta. Figgis had been involved in Sinn Féin's Commission into Industrial Conditions between 1919 and 1921. O'Byrne had experience of the British Land Commission, while O'Shiel had been involved in Sinn Féin's Land Courts. O'Rahilly, Professor of Mathematical Physics in University College Cork, had published *A Case for the Treaty* in 1922. Kennedy had served as legal adviser to the Treaty negotiators in 1921.

Given their backgrounds in British administration and law, the broad frame of reference was noteworthy. Figgis's use of *Bunreacht* reflected linguistic practice on the continent, where the concept of a constitution as a basic or fundamental law prevailed in countries as linguistically diverse as Finland, Germany, Turkey, the Soviet Union, and Norway. In 1932 Kennedy recalled that the committee was 'happily free from any obligation to accept existing British or Dominion models', and looked for inspiration elsewhere.[11] Constitution makers of that era typically sought to adapt the most prestigious foreign models to local circumstances. The French Third Republic was widely admired. The 1922 committee consulted many constitutions, published in a 1922 volume presented to the Dáil by order of the Provisional Government called *Select Constitutions of the World*. It contained those of Yugoslavia, Poland, Austria, Estonia, Czechoslovakia, Germany, the Soviet Union, Mexico, Denmark, Australia, France, Switzerland, Canada, Belgium, Norway, Sweden, and the United States. The committee also had collections of specialist documents, on functional representation, the southern unionists, the executive, the referendum, the judiciary, and the referendum. On conflicts between the two parliamentary chambers, ten constitutions – eight European, and those of Australia and South Africa – were consulted. For the electoral arrangements, Figgis specifically thanked Professors Bastable and Oldham, Professors of Economics at Trinity College Dublin and University College Dublin respectively, Mr Waterfield of the British Treasury, Mr Humphries of the

British PR Society, and the committee of the PR Society of Ireland. On financial administration, after hearing witnesses, the committee opted for the British practice of an Auditor and Controller General, rather than the French system, leaving it open for the Dáil to prescribe a Court of Accounts, if desired, without the need for constitutional amendment.[12] The suffrage provisions were also influenced by British legislation.[13] The 1922 constitution enfranchised women under thirty, before Britain did so, but the legislation simply amended the British 1918 Representation of the People Act, simply changing the references to Westminster and the United Kingdom, with Dáil Eireann and Ireland.[14]

None of the drafts were long. A characteristic feature of contemporary European constitutions was the pre-eminence of personal rights, included early in the documents. In conception these were influenced by Hans Kelsen, an Austrian legal scholar who helped draft Austria's 1920 constitution. Kelsen believed that constitutions should prescribe only rights that actually existed, (which the state could protect), rather than general principles from which rights can be imputed. The 1922 constitution contained a list of civil and political rights (Articles 6 to 10). As an aid, the secretariat had provided the committee with an index to the constitutions presented to the Dáil. This provides a guide to thirteen European and five non-European constitutions. When discussing the rights provisions, the constitutions of Australia, Belgium, Czechoslovakia, Estonia, and Denmark were most referenced. On the right of free assembly and the right to form associations, the Belgian, Czech, Estonian, Mexican, Austrian and Danish constitutions were consulted. On equality of the sexes, reference was made to the Czech and Austrian precedents. On liberty of conscience and belief, the Australian, Czech, Estonian, Swiss and Danish constitutions, were referred to.[15]

It is possible to check these sources against the final provisions. Article 9 of the 1922 constitution was unusual in combining the right of free expression of opinion, the right to assemble peacefully, and the right to form associations and unions, in one article. The constitutions most consulted – the Belgian (1831), the Czech (1920), the Danish (1917), the Estonian (1920), and the Mexican (1917) constitutions – had separate articles for the rights of assembly and of freedom of expression. The Irish provision of a right to assemble peaceably 'without arms' was contained in most of them, but Article 9 of the 1922 constitution was longer and more complex. It specifically mentioned the right to form unions, crucial considering labour unrest during the civil war. The broad right to free expression of opinion had American precedents, and went beyond the right to express 'ideals' found in the Estonian and Mexican constitutions. It also went further by stating that laws regulating the exercise of these three rights shall contain no political, religious, or class distinction.

Thus, although comparative reference was made, creative drafting took place. Generic language was present in other provisions. The principles of proportional representation, rather than a specific electoral system, were prescribed. There was an affirmation of the civil and political equality of men and women. Functional representation was also allowed for in an abstract way, but specific social and economic groups were not mentioned. The rights of the unionist minority were provided for, although no specific minorities were named. These were standard European approaches at that time.

Draft A was signed by Figgis, MacNeill, and O'Byrne; draft B by Douglas, France, and Kennedy; and draft C by Murnaghan and O'Rahilly. None of the drafts mentioned the Treaty. As with some contemporary European constitutions, like the 1919 Weimar Constitution, the drafts had early clauses claiming the right to self-determination, and asserting Irish sovereign status. Irish terms were used: *Dáil Éireann* (lower house), *Seanad* (Senate), *Cathaoirleach* (Speaker), and *Uachtarán* (President). *Dáil Éireann* invoked continuity with the revolutionary first and second Dáils, which had been unicameral, whereas the *Oireachtas* (parliament) of the Free State would be bicameral. When an objection was raised to this ambiguity, the signatories to A and B were unanimous in insisting on continuity with the revolutionary Dáils.[16] In other new states, such as Finland and Turkey, sovereign unicameral parliaments also symbolised new beginnings for the nation. The European mood for 'popular self-government' was reflected in the drafts' provisions for parliamentary control of the executive, proportional representation, and the use of the referendum and popular initiative. The authors of C thought party government could be avoided by giving people the opportunity to 'legislate directly' through the referendum and initiative.[17] Drafts A and B had similar provisions for the referendum and the initiative. Figgis hoped that these would destroy the power of parties.[18]

Preambles express the purposes for which new states are founded. Those in the *Select Constitutions* usually declared fidelity to universal principles. Leo Kohn noted that the 1922 preamble also enunciated, in accordance with continental models, 'the spiritual source' and 'higher purpose' of the constitutional enactment. It stated that all authority came from God to the people, and invoked the 'exercise of undoubted right' in the enactment.[19] By referring to the Dáil as a constituent assembly, it emphasised its sovereignty and continuity, not its derivation from the Treaty.[20] To Sinn Féin, independence meant the recovery of sovereign status. The signatories to A believed that the constitution marked the renewal and re-establishment of the ancient Free State of Ireland.[21] The preamble to B included a reference to Robert Emmet's vision of Ireland taking its place 'among the Nations of the Earth'. To counter anti-treaty criticisms, the committee had been advised by Professor Edward

Culverwell, of Trinity College, to make the statement of sovereignty explicit. They first thought the constitution 'assumed sovereignty in a form stronger than any possible protection of it', but later agreed.[22] For O'Rahilly a combination of Christian and Swiss democracy would oust 'English political ideals and the party system', and the Swiss executive, PR, referendums, and the initiative, were recommended to this end.[23]

The committee agreed that the constitution should express fundamental principles: not on what they should be.[24] On 22 January 1922 O'Rahilly had told Figgis he disagreed with practically every section of the draft being produced by the committee, and announced his intention to draft his own. Although Murnaghan supported him, draft C was O'Rahilly's own work. Its 'Rights and Duties' section stressed the duty to uphold the basic Christian ideals of parental authority, family life, religious education, and private property. Murnaghan and O'Rahilly considered this section their draft's most characteristic feature, and argued that the majority of the people expected the incorporation of their ideals into the constitution.[25] Article 53 committed the state to the protection of marriage, and attacks on the position of the family would be forbidden. There would be no state monopoly of education, no infringement of the right of parents to secure religious instruction for their children, and no interference with the academic autonomy of learned bodies. O'Rahilly also proposed a distinct structure: section A on fundamental principles and rights, section B on the structure of the state and the machinery of government, section C on principles to which the machinery of the state must conform, and section D on amendment to the constitution.[26]

After James Douglas had published his views on the constitution in April, O'Rahilly asked Figgis whether he was also free to do so.[27] Figgis conveyed Collins's view that no member of the committee should publish their individual views before the constitution was published.[28] The religious issue was potentially explosive. O'Rahilly had corresponded with Edward O'Byrne, Archbishop of Dublin, and Archbishop Harty of Cashel. O'Byrne expressed confidence that Catholic interests would be protected, with 'earnest Catholics like yourself and others' on the committee.[29] Harty saw no difficulty establishing a committee of bishops to examine the constitution from a Catholic point of view, if the Provisional Government were willing to submit it for examination.[30] The committee possessed copies of the 1827 Greek preamble, which began 'In the Name of the Holy and Indivisible Trinity', and the Polish 1921 preamble, which recalled gratefully 'the heroic and persistent sacrifices of the struggles in which every generation spent itself in the cause of Independence'.[31] Divisions over religion were reflected in the draft preambles. The preamble to A began with 'We the People of Ireland', and referred to a state, founded upon principles of freedom and justice, but committed to preserving and developing 'the spiritual aspirations of our people'.[32] The preamble to B acknowledged 'that all authority comes from God', and C's stated that 'political authority comes from God'.[33] The signatories to A did not want to 'parade the deity' in the preamble, but conceded, in view of popular feeling, that 'Invoking the blessings of Almighty God' could be joined to 'We the People of Ireland'.[34] Drafts A and B were otherwise largely secular. Kennedy was determined to keep the clergy out of politics, and adamant that ecclesiastics should not sit in either house, as was later proposed by the future President of the Executive Council, William Cosgrave, who wanted a theological Senate. Kennedy persuaded MacNeill, O'Byrne, Douglas, France and Figgis to agree to a formulation under Article 16 whereby the bishops would agree to stay out of the political arena.[35] This was never adopted.

Although the dependence of the new European states on majority communities was obvious, their constitutions did not usually make this explicit. The post-war preambles usually avoided reference to a pre-existing national self, or nation, and committed the state to act in accordance with universal principles. The final 1922 preamble was also short, and did not use 'nation', as opposed to expressing confidence that 'the National life and unity of Ireland' shall be restored. Article 2 stated that all sovereignty emanated from 'the people' not the nation, a word used rarely in the constitution. The clauses on citizenship for example did not use 'nation', and made no distinction between citizenship and membership of the nation. Sex distinctions in citizenship laws were ruled out. The Catholic Church was not accorded a special position, and there was an express prohibition against establishing a Church. English was recognised equally as an official language, although Irish was named the national language of the Free State, as was proposed in B.

Yet the final draft obscured much. The signatories to A had wanted the preamble to say that the constitution was the renewal and re-establishment of 'the ancient Free State of Ireland'.[36] Yet the final preamble omitted this, despite the fact that the rest of the constitution was largely based on A. The British government were unhappy with A's preamble, which read:

> We the people of Ireland, in our resolve to renew and re-establish our State and found it upon principles of justice, take control of our destiny in order that Ireland may take her place among the Nations of the world as a free democratic state. In the exercise of our sovereign right as a free people and to provide the welfare and to preserve and develop the heritage and the spiritual aspirations of our people we hereby declare Saorstat Éireann established and give it this constitution.[37]

The preamble to B was equally nationalistic:

Whereas in the good providence of God an end has been made of foreign rule in
Ireland and the sufferings and sacrifices of its people have been rewarded with
freedom by divine mercy, we, the people of Ireland, acknowledging that all lawful
authority comes from God, and in the exercise of our national rights, do hereby
proclaim this to be the Constitution of Saorstat Éireann.[38]

Its religious conception of history, also expressed in the Polish 1921 constitution, would find full expression in 1937. 'Acknowledging that all lawful
authority comes from God' in the final preamble was clearly a compromise
made with O'Rahilly and Murnaghan, since the original preamble to B had
stated only that 'all authority comes from God'.[39] C's remarkable formulation
was that all 'political' authority came from God.

The Constitutional politics differs from ordinary politics in the greater number
of actors possessing veto power.[40] Sinn Féin had established a committee in
early May to consider a joint panel for the June election. The Collins–de
Valera electoral 'pact', signed on 20 May 1922, promised a coalition between
pro- and anti-treatyites, and was designed to avoid civil war. Draft B allowed
for eight out of twelve ministers to be 'external ministers' not bound by
collective cabinet responsibility.[41] Anti-treaty ministers could participate in a
coalition in this way without being responsible for foreign policy. Yet Article
17 of the Treaty required all members of the Provisional Government to sign
a declaration of adherence to the Treaty. There was no stipulation in the
electoral pact that the anti-treaty ministers would do so. If this clause was not
applied, the British warned that the transfer of powers from London would
not continue. Not wanting to be seen interfering in the internal affairs of a
dominion, their acceptance of the pact was subject to one condition: it did not
prejudice their right to raise any question of non-conformity between the
Treaty and the constitution.[42] This proved crucial.

The Provisional Government had wanted no reference to the Treaty in
the constitution. The committee had accepted that an implicit approach to
sovereignty was no longer sufficient, and draft B had an explicit statement of
Irish sovereignty.[43] This was consistent with Griffith's view that the Treaty
had been signed between two sovereign states.[44] The prospect of membership
of the League of Nations also made such a statement appropriate.[45] Collins
brought the Irish draft, based on B, to London on 27 May. On 2 June the Irish
side acquiesced in a redrafting carried out by Kennedy and Lord Hewart,
Attorney General during the Treaty negotiations. This took almost a week,
and negotiations over the rights of the southern unionists prolonged discussions
until 15 June. To Hugh Kennedy, British law and precedent was 'an alien
imposition', and the Treaty had recognised the Irish right to chose their own
form of government in accordance with its traditions.[46] He quickly backtracked.

The British vetoed those articles which asserted Irish sovereignty. Drafts A and B stated that popular sovereignty extended to the nation's material resources, in language taken from Pearse's 1916 'The Sovereign People'. The economist and lawyer George O'Brien had objected to draft B's declaration that 'all right to private property is subordinate to the public right and welfare of the nation'. He also urged the omission of a clause from draft B stating that, in return for willing service, each citizen had a right to receive an adequate share in the produce of the nation's labour.[47] The committee invoked Pearse, and argued that an express limitation on state expropriation of private property would be 'obstructive'.[48] However, anything of 'a communist tendency' was removed in the redrafting with Lord Hewart.[49] Article 2, with a broad commitment to gender equality in an Irish 'Commonwealth' (a concept from the 1919 Democratic Programme), was dropped altogether. Kennedy remained firm on retaining an article on the principle of popular sovereignty, but quickly gave way on what Austen Chamberlain (Lord Privy Seal), called 'The Soviet character' of these articles.[50] The issues would be returned to in the constituent assembly in the autumn, when amendments were proposed allowing for the state to expropriate private property 'for reasons of public utility', as well as for constitutional recognition of a right to a livelihood, or welfare provision in its absence.[51] They were rejected by the assembly.

The move from Treaty to constitution proved problematic and the two species of constitutionalism were not easily reconciled. The claims of an old nation were new to the Commonwealth and co-equality had not been expressly claimed by any other dominion.[52] The British did not want to give the other White dominions a pretext to enlarge upon their autonomy. On 1 June 1922 Lloyd George wrote to Griffith stating his view that Ireland was no less a member of the British Empire than she had been before the Treaty. The other members could not permit her to adopt a constitution not in harmony with an order under which they enjoyed 'freedom and security'.[53] On 2 June Collins told the Irish cabinet that Lloyd George wanted to know whether the Irish stood by the Canadian analogy. This analogy defined the limit of the Free State's autonomy, but pro-treatyites saw it as a basis for evolution. Collins proposed a skeleton constitution, leaving out the objectionable parts of the Treaty, but having the Treaty attached to it. The following day, Griffith reported to the cabinet that the British were willing to go back to war over the constitution.[54] The British thought the Irish draft a 'negation of the Treaty' and a Republican constitution 'almost without disguise'.[55] On 5 June it was decided to send Griffith and others back to London to negotiate further.[56]

The Provisional Government were forced to accept the British conception that the King was part of the individual constitution of each dominion.[57] On 11 June Kennedy reported to Collins his further discussions with Lord Hewart.

'Assuming the British interpretation of the Treaty', he advised that the Irish should introduce the King as part of the Oireachtas, as the formal expression of the Executive, and as the appointer of judges. The summoning and dissolution of parliament in the King's name, the assent to, and reservation of legislation in the King's name, and an appeal to the Privy Council, were also necessary.[58] The Treaty was annexed to the constitution, as Collins proposed, but draft B was rejected in favour of a revised draft based on A. Kennedy also told the British that if they were not satisfied that the oath was sufficiently incorporated into the constitution through the Treaty, it would be 'expressly set forth in the constitution as the oath required of the members of the Parliament'.[59] The extern ministers had been seen by the British as a subterfuge to evade Treaty commitments, and members of the Oireachtas would now be constitutionally obliged to take this oath.[60] The anti-treatyites, after their defeat in the civil war, would abstain from the Dáil until 1927.

The Provisional Government had tried to reconcile the two forms of constitutionalism by distinguishing between Treaty and constitution. Ties to the Empire were accepted in the Treaty, but the constitution should provide for a form of government in accordance with Irish traditions. In this way a 'treaty to constitution' process could develop. Yet matters of 'form' to the British, such as the Governor General, were 'substance' to the Irish, and the distinction collapsed.[61] Article I was redrafted to express the Free State's status under the Treaty, and 'co-equal' status with Canada preceded the claim to popular sovereignty. Article II was redrafted to exclude from its reach property owned by the War Department, the Local Government Board, and Crown Lands.[62] The term *Erse* for the Irish language was omitted altogether, 'Irish Free State, was substituted for *Saorstát Éireann*, and reference was to 'The Irish Free State (*Saorstát Éireann*)', throughout the constitution. *Uachtarán* was replaced by 'President of the Executive Council', and *Árd Chúirt* by High Court. Article 5 was amended to allow the Crown to confer titles of honour to Irish citizens for services to the Empire.[63] Articles 5 of A and 46 of C had actually provided for the phased abolition of all hereditary titles. Article 79 was amended to state 'the passing and adoption of this Constitution by the Constituent Assembly *and* the British Parliament'. Specific provision was made for the continuation of the British courts, a sign that the underground Dáil courts, functioning since 1919, would be dispensed with. After a meeting between the British side, mostly Treaty signatories, and Griffith and Kennedy on 15 June, it was finally agreed that the constitution was in conformity with the Treaty. It was published the next day, the morning of the election. The court provisions, and the right of Westminster to ratify the constitution, were withheld from publication by Kennedy.[64] There was now little prospect of a coalition. Any future constitutional amendment repugnant to the Treaty provisions would be void and inoperative.

Disappointment was expressed by some of the intellectual Sinn Féiners. O'Rahilly later complained that the process of founding the Free State had been assimilated to that of establishing a colony.[65] George Russell had supported a Swiss executive, and would initiate a peace initiative during the civil war.[66] Gavan Duffy had encouraged Collins to be 'unyielding' in the face of the British attempt to get the oath into the constitution.[67] He later resigned as Minister of Justice in protest at the suspension of *habeas corpus* during the civil war, complaining that 'the old corrupt gang' of judges were still in control of the King's Inns.[68] Republican objections were 'grounded in the fact that the King was to be part of the parliament, that he is to have a veto on legislation, and that executive authority is to be vested in him'.[69] In contrast, the British constitutional expert, Arthur Berriedale Keith, argued that the constitution recognises the sovereignty of the people of Ireland, 'leaving utterly vague' the relations of Britain and Ireland.[70] The *Irish Independent* contrasted the express claim to popular sovereignty with the Canadian model, where authority proceeded downwards from the monarch.[71] Kennedy noted that Free State was still a translation of *Saorstát*, the name used by each Dáil as a description of the Irish polity established in 1919.[72] Griffith had been unimpressed by the committee's drafts. Unenthusiastic about denying the cabinet power to dissolve the Dáil, he opposed the extern ministers idea, and wrote 'against all precedent' against both proposals, just as he opposed a Dáil committee system in 1919.[73]

When civil war began on 28 June 1922, hopes for a coalition government evaporated. The anti-treatyites would not attend the constituent assembly, which pro-Treaty Sinn Féin dominated in the autumn. Continuity was retained through the adoption of 'third Dáil' as the assembly's name, as proposed in draft A, but the Provisional Government told Labour in advance that it would not consider amendments inconsistent with the Treaty.[74] A plan to get members of the constitutional committee to address the assembly did not materialise, with Sinn Féin's William Magennis, remarking that 'we may do this, but [a] steamroller will crush us'.[75] The Provisional Government wanted the constitution to be ratified before Lloyd George left office, and rushed the constitution through the assembly. They kept secret the draft originally submitted to the British. Figgis, who backed draft A, was satisfied, claiming that the existence of a written constitution was 'practically identical' with a statement of national sovereignty.[76] The British had diminished its symbolic appeal, but a distinction between the external and internal dimensions to the constitution could still be made. A distinctive model of democracy was envisaged by a committee, which were largely faithful to its second instruction – to write a democratic constitution.

INSTITUTIONAL ANALYSIS

The *Morning Post* derided the 1922 constitution as 'a characteristically English liberal document of a pre-war type'.[77] Yet the prominence it gave to personal rights, its minority provisions, and the desire for popular control of the executive, were also consistent with a European attempt to achieve popular democracy. This followed the introduction of full adult suffrage, of PR electoral systems, and the formation of social democratic governments across Europe after 1918. 'Popular government' was associated with strong unicameralism, popular control of the executive, and individual and minority rights.[78] In 1932 the *Irish Free State Official Handbook* reflected that the committee's draft was designed 'to embody in definite terms democratic principle in its most developed form'.[79] Yet just as there was no new beginning in symbolic terms, such were the claims of the Westminster model that a new beginning also proved hard to accomplish in institutional terms.

Since 1848 much of European constitutional history had been shaped by the need to reconcile the functions of a representative assembly with hereditary monarchical rulers.[80] This issue had dominated the Home Rule debates. Four models mattered: the British system of responsible government, the US separation of powers, the Swiss collegial executive (without responsibility), and the German monarchical example.[81] The 1922 committee was divided by the claims of the British and Swiss systems. All three drafts had proposed 'extern ministers', elected by the Dáil, but not necessarily members of either house, to ensure less executive dominance of parliament. These would provide stable government from a parliament made up of a large number of groupings. In support of the pact, some committee members had been approached by outsiders, with a view to preserving unity. In both B and C, the extern ministers would not share responsibility for foreign policy.[82] The signatories to B suggested to Collins that the February Árd Fheis of Sinn Féin had shown the need for co-operation in internal affairs, while 'we' would be responsible for external affairs.[83] Murnaghan and O'Rahilly wanted to 'get people into government who did not agree with foreign policy'.[84] The signatories to B and C had met separately, and without having seen draft B, O Rahilly thought that they could have produced 'a composite report'.[85]

Their advocacy of Swiss-style executive arrangements led to other members preparing draft A.[86] They proposed ministerial responsibility to ensure popular control of the executive, citing French, German, Belgian, Italian, Czech, and Estonian, as well as British models.[87] Irish words (*Uachtarán* for President, *Áireacht* for Executive, *Áiridhe* for Ministers) were used for a cabinet responsible to and removable by Dáil Éireann. Ministers would be chosen by the President of the Executive Council, with the assent of the Dáil, and no confidence motions could apply to one or all ministers. They rejected draft B and C's proposals for ministers elected by committees of the Dáil by PR. The executive should not be fixed 'in a rigid and unalterable mould', as in Switzerland.[88] Yet Patrick Hogan, Minister for Agriculture, suggested that ministers should have a fixed tenure of three years, and not be removable by votes of confidence. O'Rahilly also wanted extern ministers, not members of the house, independent of party caucuses.[89] Figgis, who denounced the pact and campaigned as an independent in the June election, proposed that the executive would consist of no more than nine ministers, six of whom must be from the parliament, and all of whom would responsible to and removable by Dáil Eireann.[90] The British government backed Figgis's draft A, which prescribed collective cabinet responsibility. Lionel Curtis, a civil servant in the Colonial Office, thought the Irish 'saturated with American ideas'. Based on his experience with the drafting of the South African constitution of 1910, he predicted that prior experience of responsible government would persuade them of the folly of their experimental proposals, and was determined to ensure this outcome.[91]

The signatories to B and C thought that a combination of the referendum and the popular initiative would provide for *popular* control of the executive. All three drafts had contained provisions for their extensive use. A and B also required constitutional amendments to require approval by referendum. The 1922 constitution made referendums on constitutional amendments mandatory (after an eight-year transitory period had elapsed), gave the Oireachtas the right to initiate referendums on controversial bills, and also allowed a petition of 75,000 voters the right to initiate referendums on legislative proposals and constitutional amendments. In the Commonwealth, only the Australian 1901 constitution required referendums for constitutional amendments.[92] In Ireland, constitutional rigidity was provided for by the requirement that a majority of the voters on the register, or two thirds of votes cast, was necessary for a valid verdict on amendments, but a bare majority for referendums on ordinary legislation The provisions were drafted by Douglas, France and Kennedy, but were uninfluenced by the Swiss model. The voting arrangements closely resembled those of the 1920 Estonian constitution, a state which also experimented unsuccessfully with direct democracy in the 1920s.[93] The provisions could also have been taken from the 1909 constitution of the State of Washington, then in the possession of the committee. Its constitution gave the people the power to propose constitutional amendments, reject laws, and to initiate legislation independently of the assembly, through both the referendum and the initiative.[94]

The 1922 constitution gave the people a veto on unjust legislation, and allowed the public to initiate a referendum on issues being ignored by the parliamentary elite.[95] The people's veto idea went back to the Lords veto crisis in 1911. For Albert Dicey the referendum could replace the Lords as a check on the Commons, reduce excessive partisanship, and prevent unpopular laws (such as Home Rule) being passed.[96] The Irish veto was also linked to the interests of the Anglo-Irish minority, who would be overrepresented in the Senate. Creating a power of initiative independent of the government made the 1922 referendum non-majoritarian in conception. As across Europe, the provisions for a popular initiative also allowed well-organised minorities to initiate referendums. Dicey's belief that the referendum would be used rarely, without the popular initiative, was rejected by the committee, for whom a combination of PR and frequent referendums could kill off the party system. Kevin O'Higgins, Minister of Home Affairs, at first thought frequent referendums would bring people closer to their state.[97]

It was thought that proportional representation would produce so many groups in the Dáil that party government on the British model would be impossible. The British government had first experimented with STV in a special election to Sligo Corporation in January 1919, just a month after the 1918 general election. In Sligo, the mainly Protestant Ratepayers' Association had outpolled Sinn Féin, and STV was prescribed for elections by the Government of Ireland Act of 1920. The government had a simple logic: PR had already been introduced in Belgium and Denmark to block the advance of the left.[98] Nevertheless, at the Sinn Féin Árd Fheis of 1919 the party rejected a motion that it oppose the introduction of STV for the coming local elections. The vote was nearly unanimous. Sinn Féin's President de Valera stated that he was not going to ask whether PR benefited Sinn Féin or not, but favoured it, 'because it was justice'.[99] This was the clearest example of constitutional idealism in the Sinn Féin revolution. Predictably, Sinn Féin was damaged by the results of the 1920 local elections, especially in urban centres. STV had produced a more proportional result, with Labour and Unionist candidates doing well.[100]

At the Irish Convention in 1912 Griffith had proposed one all-Ireland constituency for Senate elections.[101] To Figgis, the Senate would derive its authority from its own prestige, rather than the functions accorded to it by the constitution.[102] This would require a special method of election, and the relevant provisions were influenced by Mr John Humphreys, secretary of the PR Society of Britain. He was asked to comment on the committee's plan for elections by STV from one all-island constituency. He thought these were quite 'practicable' and Humphreys supported combining two methods of election (by county and by chamber). This could be done first as an experiment, and the system refined through subsequent amendment to the constitution. (New South Wales was cited as the closest practical example.)[103] Humphreys's advice was followed, and he also shared the committee's predilection for the largest constituencies possible for Dáil elections. The committee's firm view that this would mean 'seven seaters' was reinforced by his analysis of the results of the Glasgow Education Authority elections of March 1922, in which the results of seven electoral divisions were collated in a single day.[104]

In the electoral schedule and maps of constituencies submitted to the committee by the PR Society of Ireland in February 1922, STV was proposed for both houses. Dublin City would be divided into three constituencies returning four members, in which one fifth of the vote would suffice for election to the Dáil. These elections would return 212 members from constituencies as small as Cavan (three seats), and as large as Mayo (nine seats). The Senate would be elected from six electoral areas returning eight senators each. The scheme had a crucial political aspect. Michael Collins hoped to avoid the necessity for a Boundary Commission, by drawing the unionists into a constituent assembly which would draft a constitution for the whole island. The newly formed Irish Constituent Assembly Movement specifically rejected the electoral arrangements of the 1920 Government of Ireland Act. In line with this, the PR Society of Ireland proposed to divide the North into a North-West and a North-East senate constituency of equal sizes, thus depriving the unionists of provincial representation.[105]

PR was eventually prescribed in the following way by the 1922 constitution:

Dáil Éireann shall be composed of members who represent constituencies determined by law. The number of members shall be fixed from time to time by the Oireachtas, but the total number of members of Dáil Éireann (exclusive of members for the Universities) shall not be fixed at less than one member for each thirty thousand of the population, or at more than one member for each twenty thousand of the population: Provided that the proportion between the number of members to be elected at any time for each constituency and the population of each constituency, as ascertained at the last preceding census, shall, so far as possible, be identical throughout the country. The members shall be elected upon principles of Proportional Representation. The Oireachtas shall revise the constituencies at least once in every ten years, with due regard to changes in distribution of the population, but any alterations in the constituencies shall not take effect during the life of Dáil Éireann sitting when such revision is made.

Prescribing the 'principles of PR', not a specific electoral system, gave the government leeway regarding the actual system to be used. The 1922 and 1923 general elections were conducted under STV, and the 1923 Electoral Act provided for STV for future elections. Its provisions for counting votes are still in force. The civil war had subsided in May 1923, and the August election which followed worked well enough. Less than four per cent of ballot papers were found invalid. It had not been necessary to give special voting instructions to voters because of their experience from 1920 and 1922.[106] The Provisional Government then opposed the Northern government's abolition of STV for local elections. This constituted a clear attempt to predetermine the outcome of the Boundary Commission. To Kennedy, the British government's reluctance to veto this abolition was a violation of a fundamental principle of the Treaty: that there not be two dominions in Ireland.[107] The unionists' argument was that the issue was about local rather than minority representation and, although Churchill accepted that Northern Ireland was not a dominion, a British veto was cynically rejected because it could be 'misconstrued by the powerful self-governing states of the British Commonwealth'.[108]

The prescription of PR reflected commitments made to the southern unionists during the Treaty negotiations. Griffith had promised them that ample representation and security would be provided by the new constitution. PR had not been written into the Treaty on this assumption. The constitutional committee were unanimous on the virtues of a single-chamber parliament, but conceded the need for a Senate to check hasty legislation and provide representation for Unionists.[109] At negotiations in May and June 1922, the Southern Unionists and the British government were jointly represented by Sir Francis Greer and Sir Frederick Liddell. Their need for special minority representation in the Senate, they argued, stemmed from the fact that the 350,000 unionists south of the border were too geographically scattered to be able to secure adequate representation during elections from small constituencies.[110] Lord Midleton had doubted that any minority figures in commerce, the universities, education, or the landed interest, would be elected from a constituency of 1,200,000 people. He considered the Provisional Government's proposals as they stood late in May a violation of Griffith's earlier pledge. During meetings on 13 and 14 June, the number of Senators, the period for consideration of bills in the Senate, and the Senate's power to independently request a referendum, were also discussed.[111] The British government urged that when nominating Senators the President should consult with representatives of the Chamber of Commerce, the Royal College of Physicians, the Royal College of Surgeons, the King's Inns, the Incorporated Law Society, and local government bodies.[112] It was later agreed that nomination to the first Senate be made on the advice of such bodies. With respect to these concessions the government considered itself bound to these agreements when the constituent assembly met in September.[113] To O'Higgins they were a way of showing the unionists that they were part of the Irish nation.[114]

A Senate had been seen as a way of providing for unionist representation since the second Home Rule bill in 1893. Yet, as in Europe, the constitutional committee wanted to protect minority rights primarily through PR, and differed over the Senate. Murnaghan and O'Rahilly wanted a Senate (in American nomenclature) composed of experts, with the power to call a referendum, but not independently elected. The authors of A and B wanted the first Senate to be nominated by the Dáil, and subsequent Senates elected by PR among electors nominated by the Dáil. This would give it greater independence. Draft B proposed giving two-fifths of the Dáil, or a majority of the Senate, the power to suspend legislation and create a referendum if a popular petition signed by no fewer than 30,000 voters demanded one. The 1922 constitution provided for a Senate of 60 members directly elected under STV from a single, nation-wide constituency. Half of the first Senate would be composed of Senators elected by the Dáil by STV, with the rest nominated by the President of the Executive Council. Cosgrave used this power to nominate twenty Protestants, three Quakers, and one Jewish member. Sixty per cent of the Senators could demand a referendum on any bill. The Senate was also allowed to appeal to voters directly if there was a disagreement between the two houses, and the Dáil attempted to override the Senate.

The 1922 constitution thus continued on the Home Rule tradition of seeing minority rights as integral to democracy. Indeed the Provisional Government sacrificed the idea of a 'vocational' Senate for such minority representation. All three of the committee's drafts had allowed for the establishment of councils representative of specific social functions. Moreover, a sub-committee of the PR Society of Ireland submitted an electoral scheme in March 1922 which envisaged a vocational senate. With large constituencies, the return of popular candidates with different qualities from those elected to the lower house, would be guaranteed.[115] Sinn Féin's thinking followed that of the British reformer, G. D. H. Cole, who wanted to divide legislative power between parliament, functional associations, and a joint council at the top of parliament representing the main functions of society. This council would be more like a Supreme Court than a second chamber. However, the 1922 constitutional committee did not believe that the life of the country was sufficiently developed to allow for functional representation straight away. Ernest Blythe remarked that PR would provide it in an indirect way in the meantime.[116] Citing the prestige of guilds in ancient Ireland, Figgis reflected that only when functional representation was achieved would all parts of the nation be brought within the constitution.[117]

On other issues, too, pragmatism inhibited a new beginning. A crucial factor in achieving proportional representation was constituency size, but the 1922 election was held from constituencies of very mixed sizes, some below the size (five) then thought necessary to achieve proportionality between the votes cast for a party and their number of seats in the Dáil. George O'Brien had urged the committee to limit the maximum and minimum size of constituencies, so as to prevent a dominant party from creating an unlimited number of seats in an area where they were popular.[118] His criticism was rejected by the committee.[119] Large constituencies would have made single-party government highly unlikely. In October 1922 the Ministry of Local Government submitted a memo to the government recommending the unification of entire administrative counties or boroughs, or a combination of different administrative areas, to create constituencies of sufficient size. It stated that the ideal size was five or seven seaters, but the government persisted with very mixed sizes.[120] There was no consistent attempt to realise 'the principles of PR'. All three drafts also allowed for federal tiers of government, as did the 1922 constitution. Representation in the Dáil was arranged on a population basis which would have given the North-East 50 out of 200 members.[121] In 1933 William Cosgrave recalled that the committee were aware of the Swiss example, particularly with regard to incorporating Northern Ireland, but felt that the imperative of political stability would be affected by following it.[122] The Free State would be highly centralised. The prescription, in all three drafts, of fundamental rights, mechanisms for judicial review, and special provisions for ratifying constitutional amendments, underscored the constitution's status as a higher law. Yet Figgis argued that its provisions should not be so rigid as to constrain a state in a time of crisis.[123] To Collins he reported that his draft was 'simple and flexible', and the 1922 constitution allowed amendments by ordinary legislation for an initial period of eight years.[124] This was consistent with Collins's 'stepping stone' approach to the Treaty, but would undermine the constitution's status as a higher law.

The constitution's introduction into a legal system for centuries based on judicial precedent and parliamentary supremacy was nonetheless a new beginning in itself.[125] Figgis believed that strong courts were the only way to guarantee the fundamental rights in the constitution.[126] The Irish judiciary would consist of a Supreme Court, the High Court, and any lower courts established by law. Draft B had proposed an *Árd Chúirt* (High Court of Appeal), and proposed that any law it found unconstitutional could be reworded as a constitutional amendment, and submitted to a referendum. The Supreme Court was conceived of as a court of appeal, with the power to declare any law to be in conflict with the constitution. This distinguished it from the Home Rule provisions.[127] Lijphart argues that if a special body is created for the exclusive purpose of reviewing the constitutionality of legislation, 'it is very likely to carry out this task with some vigour'.[128] Yet the Irish legal profession was steeped in British traditions, and strong judicial review did not follow. Moreover, the 1922 constitution allowed for a judicial appeal to the Privy Council of the House of Lords. Lord Hewart had insisted that this appeal was necessary in order that the constitution conform to the Treaty.[129] It also safeguarded the extensive British property rights in Ireland. Yet the original draft of the constitution had required the decision of the Irish Supreme Court to be 'final and conclusive', and 'shall not be reviewed, or capable of being reviewed by any other Court, Tribunal, or Authority whatsoever'. The tension between the two conceptions of constitutionalism remained, and the appeal indicated the supremacy of British legislation.

The model of government contained in the constitution was hybrid. The executive arrangements allowed for single-party government, but the checks and balances were strong for a non-federal state. The Free State had a substantial second chamber, written constitution, and judicial review, often associated with federal systems. Long seen as ways of reconciling majority and minority, these features were appropriate to a state in which Unionists remained influential, or one in which partition proved temporary. When partition became entrenched, this source of constitutional idealism dried up. After the civil war the checks and balances progressively weakened. A 'winner take all' mentality set in in 1922; strong party discipline followed. Giving Irish politicians experience of responsible government, as Lionel Curtis foresaw, changed their views on the constitution. Electoral polarisation (or 'civil war politics') continued on the pre-1921 pattern of electoral competition. Here formal constitutional analysis is insufficient, since the 'vision of democracy' in any country may predispose elites to govern in certain ways. This vision quickly returned the country to the traditions of party government Sinn Féin had revolted from in 1917.

AMENDING THE CONSTITUTION

Given its hybrid nature, amendments were inevitable. In inter-war Europe, as the new democracies proved unable to resolve their problems, experimentation gave way to strong government, or to various forms of authoritarianism. Proportional representation, multi-party systems and coalition government became associated with instability. Provisions for direct democracy lapsed into desuetude, and minority rights were rarely delivered upon. Constitutional orders generally began to dissolve. Irish attitudes to democracy quickly changed. In 1911 J. J. Horgan had published a pamphlet proposing radically new institutions as a means of safeguarding minority rights. In 1933 he derided the 1922 provisions as 'the radically anti-authoritarian postulates of Cromwell's levellers as translated into practice in France and America'.[130] The need for Irish governments to ratify constitutional amendments by referenda was circumvented by legislation in 1928, extending the original period in which they could amend the constitution by ordinary legislation for a further eight years. This extension further diminished the authority of the constitution.[131] Twenty-seven amendments were made, shared between Cumann na nGaedheal and Fianna Fáil, the civil war parties. By 1936 more than half of the articles had been amended. The process began in the constituent assembly with amendments to the provisions for university representation, the amendment procedure, and the executive.

A 'mechanical' conception of constitutionalism was soon expressed in the assembly. To Figgis the constitution provided the fundamental 'machinery' by which the Irish could achieve full freedom. It was both the organisational basis of the state, and a basis for evolution.[132] O'Higgins believed 'the Constitution is, after all, the mechanics of government'.[133] Cosgrave also later described the constitution as 'a machine', whose work depended on the skills of the operatives.[134] The mechanical analogy suggested amendments that would make the system more efficient, rather than provide for popular self-government. It returned the Irish to an evolutionary and British concept of the constitution as a building 'constantly added to, patched, and partially constructed, – but not razed to the ground and rebuilt on new foundations'.[135] As constitutionalism became an organising principle of government in this way, the alliance between Sinn Féin and Labour ended. In 1922 Labour's leader Thomas Johnson told the constituent assembly that the subjugation of Ireland had been economic, social, and cultural, and Sinn Féin's aim was to end it in all its forms. Institutions were a means of developing humanity and delivering on the promise of the revolution.[136]

Before 1921 many believed that Sinn Féin was not 'a mere political machine', but could grow as the scope of its work became wider.[137] Their premise had been that the public's potential was stunted by existing institutions, but the civil war confirmed suspicions that the Irish public was not really ready for self-government: O'Higgins lamented their 'irresponsibility', 'protest', 'negation', 'wantonness', 'waywardness', and 'destructiveness'.[138] It now fell to a responsible elite to raise them to the appropriate level. For O'Higgins independence brought 'very weighty responsibilities', and the need to reconcile political theories with the facts of life.[139] The principles of democracy were now to be solved in proportion to the qualities of 'the public men'.[140] Sinn Féin's 1917 constitution had been democratic 'down to the last comma', but also recognised 'a spiritual aristocracy'.[141] Two wings of this aristocracy were now engaged in civil war. The values of the 1919 Democratic Programme were not incorporated into the constitution. The assembly rejected amendments on children's rights, the right to a livelihood, and on private property.[142] Labour's Cathal O'Shannon proposed a new Article 63, which would prevent members of the Executive Council, TDs and Senators from being directors or representatives of business enterprises. Cosgrave was initially reported to be sympathetic, but the article did not materialise.[143] Pro-treaty Sinn Féin had not won an overall majority in the June election. Had the anti-treaty TDs been present, the government could have been outvoted on crucial issues.

The rights of women were not advanced by the assembly either. Hannah Sheehy-Skeffington, now the widowed chairwoman of the Irish Women's Franchise League, had received assurances from the constitutional committee that the constitution would guarantee 'equal rights of citizenship'. The committee had wanted to guarantee equality with respect to social and economic, not just political, rights.[144] Yet the 1922 election had reduced the number of female TDs – from six to two – and Irish feminism suffered from the identification of many prominent women with the anti-treaty cause. The British government had vetoed Article 2 of draft B which provided for equal socio-economic rights in an Irish 'Commonwealth', although commitments to equality remained in the citizenship and voting provisions. The constituent assembly amended the original clause saying that 'men and women have equal rights as citizens', to 'equal political rights'. Ministers had met some prominent women who had interpreted the broad equality guarantee to mean that all legislation in any way discriminatory on the basis of sex would be unconstitutional. Hugh Kennedy was worried that this would mean women would have equal employment rights in public service. Cosgrave thought that a broad guarantee would involve reconsideration of too much existing law, and proposed addressing existing anomalies on an *ad hoc* basis.[145] The Provisional Government's women supporters pointed to broad equality guarantees in the Austrian, German, and Polish constitutions as exemplars, to no avail. Discrimination in public employment, recruitment and jury service followed.

Westminster traditions were reasserted. The President of the Executive Council (William Cosgrave) was drawn from the largest party in the Dáil, he chose the cabinet, and the cabinet controlled the Dáil through party discipline. Single-party government became the norm. The civil war parties, Cumann na nGaedheal and Fianna Fáil, profited from a clause in the constitution which stated that 'Dáil Éireann may not at any time be dissolved except on the advice of the Executive Council'. The first extraordinary dissolution occurred in 1927, when the Attorney General, John A. Costello, advised Cosgrave's minority government, which had done badly in the June election, that the constitution did not prevent the Executive Council from dissolving the Dáil without its consent.[146] The September 1927 election returned Cumann na nGaedheal to power. Fianna Fáil governments also called 'snap elections' in 1933 and 1938, gaining an increase in seats which enabled them to form a single-party government. The civil war parties' share of the seats, less than 65 per cent in 1922, reached over 88 per cent by 1938. The first coalition government was formed in 1948.

Majority rule returned as the organising principle of political life. The results of the 1922 and 1923 general elections had enabled Cumann na nGaedheal to claim that the majority of the people supported the Treaty. For Collins it would stand unless the anti-treatyites became a majority in the country.[147] In 1927, after the assassination of Kevin O'Higgins, the government passed legislation forcing candidates to declare their willingness to take their Dáil seats if elected. As a result, Fianna Fáil, which split from Sinn Féin in 1926, abandoned its abstentionist policy, took the oath, and entered the Dáil. De Valera believed that 'the majority of the people were going to shape the future'.[148] Cumann na nGaedheal stood down from government after the 1932 general election, when Fianna Fáil emerged as the largest party. De Valera then gradually revised the Treaty on the basis of his parliamentary majority.[149] A pure system of majority rule requires only electoral limits to the legislative powers of the parliamentary majority. Brian Farrell writes:

> with two large parties competing for majority support, that parliament moved even closer to its Westminster origins. Many of the experimental and continental features of the Irish Free State were abandoned virtually without trial. Few of the 'extern' Ministers were ever appointed; all were staunch party men. Neither the referendum nor the initiative were ever used to ascertain the people's opinion; both were abolished when de Valera tried to invoke these constitutional provisions to jettison the Oath. The elaborate schemes to give the Senate some power and purpose were gradually modified. The constitution itself, although it was the fundamental law for fifteen years, remained throughout its life, like the British constitution, wholly flexible and subject to amendment simply by act of parliament.[150]

An 'Amendments to the Constitution Committee', appointed on 19 December 1924, met thirteen times. It consisted of senior ministers and two senators. Its remit was to use its experience of government to propose amendments before the eight-year transitory period elapsed.[151] All departments of state, the chairs of both houses, and the judiciary, were consulted. Decisions were by majority vote, and the recommendations were conveyed to the government on 6 May 1926. The report expressed the view that the constitution should provide only for fundamental matters, leaving questions of detail or of carrying out the principles of the constitution to ordinary legislation.[152] The Senate, the referendum, the electoral system, the manner of dissolving the Dáil, and the means of amending the constitution, had been considered. The final report recommended amendments which would remove the referendum and initiative for ordinary legislation, allow different forms of PR, give the government more freedom to dissolve the Dáil, reduce the powers of the Senate, and give the President the power to appoint more ministers. More 'elastic' arrangements were suggested for the executive.[153] There was no longer any interest in popular self-government. The committee considered the position of women, and thought an interpretation of Article 3 which would prevent women from being excluded from civil service examinations would give an extraordinary wide meaning to the expression 'privileges of citizenship'.[154]

In European states like Austria, Germany, Estonia, and Latvia, those excluded from the constitution-making process after the war subsequently rejected the constitutions when they came to power. Through amendments (or replacements) they strengthened executive powers, facilitating the emergence of authoritarian regimes.[155] In Ireland executive power was strengthened by both sides. Of the 27 amendments, most affected the powers of the Senate, culminating in de Valera's abolition of the House in 1936. The existence of a second chamber with significant powers was not necessary in a non-federal system, and its election from one constituency in 1925 had been problematic.[156] The abolition followed the Senate's controversial rejection of de Valera's 'Removal of the Oath Bill' in 1933. Taken together, the twenty seven amendments reduced the political system to three (British) cornerstones: 'parliamentary sovereignty untrammelled by reference to any higher law, a cabinet sustained by its parliamentary support, and a constitution as flexible as ordinary statute law'.[157]

One experiment that lasted was with PR/STV. Yet the pro-treaty elite grew impatient with it too. At a meeting of the government's constitution committee on 4 January 1926, an amendment was considered that would rule out only the single non-transferable vote system. Later, it decided to stick with the existing provisions.[158] Individuals pushed for change. Patrick McGilligan criticised the personalistic voting encouraged by STV. Ernest Blythe recommended a combination of single-member constituencies with the German system. Desmond FitzGerald's hostility was public knowledge. In October 1926 the Department of Local Government complained that STV was not providing PR, because of the variation in the number of votes needed to secure election, and the fact that a large minority of those elected in 1923 had failed to reach the quota.[159] In 1927 the press reported pro-Treaty feeling that STV had stunted political development by blurring the verdict of the public on the Treaty up to 1927.[160] The Department of Local Government complained that the electorate was restricted in its endorsement of the policy of a party to the number of candidates presented by the party in particular constituencies. It proposed a radical reform which would give more weight to first preference votes.[161]

Cosgrave told the Cumann na nGaedheal convention in 1927 that they would propose an electoral system more suited to the country after the June election. Yet the issue faded from view. In 1928 he reflected that there was no 'simple answer' to the issue of electoral reform, and that STV had worked 'satisfactorily enough' so far. He saw little prospect of change in the near future.[162] The arguments against change remained strong. The southern unionists were opposed, under the British system the republicans would have complete control of certain counties in the south and west, and the Dáil favoured a system which made electioneering easier.[163] The British PR society published a pamphlet on the highly polarised 1933 election, pointing out that Cumann na nGaedheal still obtained eight out of 27 seats in the strongly republican counties of Kerry, Limerick, Clare and Galway.[164] Ironically, Fine Gael made the abolition of PR a policy commitment in its election manifesto that year. However, at its first Árd Fheis in 1935 a motion supporting abolition was overruled, and the opponents of PR were hesitant about splitting the party so early in its career.[165]

By December 1922 the original provisions for the executive were radically diluted, and no extern ministers were ever appointed. In Britain 'Peelites' saw parliamentary control as an unstable basis for government, and believed that the executive, not parliament, nor through it the people, is responsible for public policy. A necessary condition for good government is that liberal mechanisms for enforcing governmental responsiveness are curtailed, or ineffective.[166] The Peelite mentality lent itself to a 'managerial' view of constitutionalism, which saw politics as a matter of executive leadership and rational administration within a hierarchical system.[167] The Cumann na nGaedheal elite also viewed politics as 'administration', but their emphasis on 'streamlined' government, strong executive control over government departments, and a meritocratic and hierarchical civil service, actually went back to the first Dáil's local government policy. The managerial approach would remain a strong 'undercurrent' in Irish public life, finding its clearest expression during conflicts between central and local government. It transcended the civil war divide.

In inter-war Europe many democratic constitutions proved fig leaves, and actual practice depended on conventions and informal traditions, such as (in Ireland) the doctrine of responsible government. Its importance was reflected in the decision to abolish the referendum in 1928. The 1924 amendment committee had recommended removing the requirements for mandatory referendums on constitutional amendments, depriving the Oireachtas of the power to initiate referendums on bills, and leaving the Seanad only with the same powers as the British House of Lords. Its May 1926 report noted that referendums were costly; the parties contesting them would be the same as those in a general election; it was difficult to find a clear issue for a referendum; and a defeat of the government might necessitate a general election.

All presupposed a strongly representative conception of democracy. However, the report did support the idea of giving two-fifths of the Dáil and three-fifths of the Senate the right to call a referendum on constitutional amendments. (This would materialise in 1937.) Referendums on ordinary legislation were rejected. The pretext for action was Fianna Fáil's attempt to initiate a referendum on the oath. To this end, it collected and presented the required 75,000 signatures in 1928. Fianna Fáil had not taken their seats in the Dáil when they first proposed the petition. Officials commented:

> I think it is abundantly clear that the power was intended to belong and could properly be held only by members who have undertaken the *responsibilities* of membership. It would be absurd to suggest that after a measure had been carefully considered in this House and in the Senate it should be open to persons who take such a light view of their *responsibilities* as public representatives as to absent themselves from the discussions of the House, to enjoy the privilege of obstructing the business of the nation by lightheartedly signing their names to a petition, and thus initiating machinery which would hold up important measures for nine months and put the country to the expense of a referendum.[168]

The decision to remove the referendum was taken in July 1927, while in May 1928 a further decision was taken to stop parliament from initiating referendums on constitutional amendments. The second followed logically from the first: once the referendum had been removed, Fianna Fáil could have used the surviving constitutional provisions to contest its removal in a referendum.

The first amendment was accompanied by legislation forcing Fianna Fáil candidates to promise to take their seats when standing for election. The phrase, 'for the immediate preservation of the public peace and safety', accompanied the cabinet decision.[169] The outcome – Fianna Fáil becoming a responsible parliamentary opposition in 1927 – reflected effective leadership by Cosgrave. Yet his government had also 'subverted the democratic framework adopted in 1922', in order to avoid an embarrassing defeat.[170] Patrick McGilligan told the Senate that they 'gave' the people rights in 1922 – with Articles 47 and 48 – and the people would not complain 'if those rights are taken away'.[171] Cosgrave asked: 'how are you going to have Government in the State if you are going to have that kind of nonsense?'[172] Officials thought the procedure could be easily manipulated 'by well organised minorities', thwarting the views of the majority.[173] O'Higgins thought direct democracy impossible on a large scale.[174] The move to abolish the provisions had begun even before Fianna Fáil was founded in 1926. Such elitist attitudes existed on both sides. De Valera later refused to resolve the oath issue by referendum in 1933, and used his parliamentary majority to justify removing it. In 1928 his opponents had maintained that the September 1927 election had given them a mandate to remove the referendum.

Constitutional flexibility was valued by both sides, for different reasons. Patrick McGilligan, Minister of Industry and Commerce, told the Senate in 1928 that, unlike the Americans, they were not in possession of a constitution in a final form. Outside its Treaty commitments the constitution should be flexible.[175] When the issue of whether some provisions were so fundamental that they could not be amended surfaced in *The State (Ryan)* v. *Lennon* in 1935, there was ambiguity. One argument was that the 17th amendment in 1931, which allowed for the establishment of military tribunals, involved interference with the underlying principles of the constitution that had been intended to be 'fundamental' and 'immovable'. It was countered that other constitutions specifically declared certain provisions 'non amendable' or 'fundamental', and the constitution made no such distinction among its articles.[176] This view suited de Valera. The transitory period in which governments could amend the constitution by ordinary legislation would have elapsed on 5 December 1930. The extension of the period by eight years followed an indirect request by him.[177] It enabled him to pass amendments after 1932, which were technically illegal, because the Supreme Court had ruled that the Treaty commitments made by the constituent assembly could not be overturned by ordinary legislation. De Valera could refer to the redefinition of the constitutional relations of the Commonwealth at imperial conferences in 1926 and 1930, as justification, but only this flexibility averted a more serious constitutional crisis after 1932.[178]

Nonetheless, the flexibility undermined the authority of the constitution. In 1930 Fianna Fáil's Seán Lemass stated that the two larger parties regarded the constitution as nothing more than 'a piece of paper'.[179] John Hearne, legal adviser to the Department of Foreign Affairs, later called it a 'forlorn' document.[180] The UCC political scientist, James Hogan, compared it to 'a football kicked around by the political parties'.[181] The insertion of Article 2A (the 17th amendment) in 1931 at the start of the document, giving the state permanent emergency powers, reflected the shift in attitudes since 1922. It was intended to show that no subsequent provisions could be used to override them. Hugh Kennedy, alone among High Court judges, found the 17th amendment unconstitutional. In 1931 he reflected that it was originally intended that any change affecting 'the fundamental law and framework of the state' should be given full and general consideration. This assumed a special procedure, but at the last moment it was decided that it could be amended by ordinary legislation for a limited duration. This clause was then used for making changes 'of a radical and far-reaching character', some far removed in principle from the ideas and ideals of the document's original authors.[182] In 1936 the government prepared an up-to-date copy of the constitution for members of the Oireachtas. There were black lines through parts of half the articles.

In some European states, where the initial constitution making had been participated in by all sides, the political system enjoyed a sufficient amount of loyalty on the part of political elites to overcome later periods of instability. This was absent in Ireland where the principal problems related to the constitution's lack of supremacy. If it was subordinate to the Treaty, the constitution could be amended to protect the Treaty. If the people were sovereign, they had the right to change its Treaty provisions. Both views weakened the constitution. In 1929 an observer wrote that if de Valera assumed office, 'he could plunge the country into chaos without being unconstitutional or doing anything unprecedented'. This situation would never have arisen 'had the spirit and the letter of the constitution been adhered to rigidly'.[183] After de Valera re-established military tribunals in 1934, Fine Gael's Richard Mulcahy asked: 'will the President say that there is any movement of violence in this country that can equal the Fianna Fáil party in practically wiping out the courts, and wiping out the Seanad, and imposing against the widespread opinion of the country, burdens that they are not able to bear'.[184] In his study of inter-war Europe, Karvonen stresses that 'the strengthening of executive power in an ongoing process of polarisation is a risky manoeuvre in a parliamentary system'.[185] In 1936 O'Rahilly complained that the constitution 'rivets every detail of the alleged Treaty around our necks', while leaving 'every other principle of rights and liberties' to the mercies of Dáil majorities.[186] By 1937 the amendments had given de Valera 'a classic opportunity to establish a dictatorship'.[187]

CONCLUSION

The passing of the 1922 constitution followed the rituals of a new beginning, but there was no constitutional moment. The supremacy of the Treaty, bitter divisions within Sinn Féin, and the exigencies of civil war, ruled out radical change. Instead, the Free State's constitutional order was gradually reduced to the basic structure of the Westminster system. This would remain its constitutional 'backbone' up to 1937 and beyond. The 1922 constitution did not and could not realise the constitutional committee's ambition to ground the political system in a basic law. In the context of civil war its experimental approach gave way to the coherence and resoluteness provided by responsible government. Yet responsible government was insufficient to generate a stable constitutional order. This was not surprising. The Treaty split had reflected the tension between the two forms of constitutionalism Ackerman outlines.

This tension had surfaced in the 1922 constituent assembly when Labour questioned the appropriateness of calling it a constituent assembly, since its sovereignty was limited by the Treaty commitments. The Free State wanted to present its constitution as one 'recognised as drawing its validity from adoption by the Irish people'.[188] This necessitated keeping the drafting process hidden from public view.

Indeed the encounter between the two forms of constitutionalism was not over. Successive Irish governments, pro and anti-treaty, would try to recover what was lost between 1920 and 1922. After joining the League of Nations in September 1923, the Irish Government overrode British objections, by registering the Treaty with the League's Treaty Registration Bureau, as an agreement between two states.[189] British officials were alarmed by the appearance on 11 November 1922, of an article in *The Irish Free State*, considered to be the official Irish organ in Britain. It summarised their conception of the relationship between the Treaty and the constitution:

> If we use this Constitution properly, and if we regard it not as a perfected edifice, but as a foundation on which to build, if we never fail in moments of conflict to take the strongest line of action to enforce our interpretation of the dispute we cannot fail to develop our present status into one of complete independence . . . We shall be able to ignore England so completely that her Monarch and his trappings will drop out of our Constitution unheeded.[190]

After their recovery from defeat in civil war, the anti-treaty view also came to matter. Here O'Rahilly was a guide to de Valera's thinking. Citing Collins's ambition to write a constitution from a 'purely Irish standpoint', in April 1922 he had told the constitutional committee that he would resign if he were instructed to embody the provisions of the Treaty into the constitution.[191] After being encouraged by the editor of *Studies*, he had wanted to publish draft C in August 1922, but was prevented by the government from doing so.[192] Complaining that the Provisional Government were rushing the constitution through the constituent assembly, and that it had not discussed his draft with him, O'Rahilly again threatened publication if his views were not put before it.[193] He was unsuccessful. In 1937, invoking 'Irish Law', he wanted another new beginning.[194] His 'organic' conception of the constitution contrasted with the 'mechanical' one, which some nationalists rejected as soulless and uninspiring. The challenge for de Valera was how to recreate this organic sense of community in a modern constitution, without jeopardising the freedoms it had to protect. Opinion has long been divided on his response to that challenge.

THREE

CONSOLIDATION

THE 1937 CONSTITUTION

—

The 1937 constitution repealed that of 1922, renamed the state Éire/Ireland, and was legitimised through a plebiscite. Its preamble ended with the phrase 'We the People of Éire do hereby give ourselves this constitution'. The constitution's most important principle was popular sovereignty, which had been overridden in the 1922 constitution by the clause which subordinated it to the Treaty.[1] The constitution repudiated the British past, but not the fifteen years that had elapsed since 1922. Introducing some new Irish names, it symbolised another transition, faithful to Sinn Féin's 'Ourselves Alone'. De Valera had kept to his promise to draft a constitution 'as if Great Britain were a million miles away'.[2] The constitution was intended to complete the process of gaining independence, but the 1922 clause on the validity of pre-1921 laws was still retained. Parts of the 1922 constitution were simply transposed into the new document. Thus while the symbolism pointed to a new beginning, the purpose was to consolidate rather than to experiment and start anew. This took on a broader significance in a Europe where the foundations of liberal democracy had been shaken. De Valera emphasised the Christian and democratic character of his constitution in response. So, while his civil war adversaries were first offended by the claims of his new beginning, after opposing it in the plebiscite they acquiesced in its content. Apart from de Valera's 'miserable "Year One" business', it was 'a conservative instrument'.[3]

THE DRAFTING PROCESS

The constitution was drafted in a decade of mounting crisis. Democracy was in retreat, Fascism established in Germany and Italy, and the successor states created after the First World War were struggling to survive. The 1922 committee, in a general mood of democratic idealism, had located the purpose of Irish statehood in the moral renewal of post-war Europe. By 1937 the Irish state was diplomatically isolated, dependent on protectionist economic policies, and culturally defensive. The emergence of mass politics had seen Fascist,

Social Democratic, and Communist political systems established after 1930, but some Catholic countries – Austria, Poland, and Portugal – simply became more authoritarian. With the striking exception of Finland, most post-war constitutional experiments had failed by 1937. Liberalism was challenged by the rise of collectivist philosophies on the left and right, leading many Irish Catholics to take an interest in corporatist thinking. A group of Irish Jesuit intellectuals formed a constitutional committee which submitted proposals to de Valera in 1936.

Pocock writes of 'Machiavellian moments', when constitution makers had to establish republics precisely at those moments when they had doubts about their durability. They wished to secure moral and political stability in the face of destructive and irrational events.[4] De Valera, conscious since 1921 of 'the temporal finitude' of his republic, and of the wider crisis, also wished to protect a set of values he associated with a virtuous society. His approach was an Irish variant of an older 'Whig' tradition brought to America by the first British and North-west European colonists. This tradition assumed a communitarian polity and stressed the importance of a virtuous citizenry. Individualism was tempered, and assemblies, as representatives of the community, could intervene and control behaviour in ways that would now be regarded as infringements of individual rights. The Whig tradition also placed emphasis on strong, direct, and continuous popular control over government and legislatures, and was marked by a general distrust of power.[5] All were true of the 1937 constitution.

De Valera did not distinguish between the ethical and political strands to constitutionalism.[6] The failure of European democracy, he argued, was not due to different constitutional arrangements, but to the failure of men 'to live by the obvious rule of their being'.[7] The protection of rights meant more to 'moral integrity' and 'the continuance of organised society' than the reorganisation of state institutions.[8] A new document which confined itself to the definition of legislative, executive, and judicial relations, would not inspire loyalty.[9] The inter-war crisis posed questions about the basis of good government, which the Irish, with their unique historical experience, had their own answer to. The constitution was thus a statement to the world of what they consisted of. This implied an expressive approach, which had not found full expression in 1922. His broadcast speech on the constitution on 15 June 1937 stated:

> This Constitution, for example, is presented for the approval of our people at a time such as this without parallel in history. The world is in the throes of a conflict of political philosophies which have divided it into two schools and bids fair to divide it also into two camps. The issues that hang on the outcome of that conflict relate to the most serious questions that can concern mankind. The question of the relation of the individual, and of the family to the state, the rights of the one

and of the other, the limitations upon the rights of each in respect of each other, the duties of each to each, and the responsibilities of them all for the discharge of their respective duties. All these questions and their answers are bound up with the answers we are prepared to give to the supreme question of all, namely, that of the origin and purpose of human life itself.[10]

The 1937 constitution thus reflected the values of a peripheral European society falling back on its own cultural resources during an era of crisis. De Valera thought that the Versailles settlement had collapsed because it tried to limit the right of peoples in domains in which only they were sovereign. This placed the Free State in the 'revisionist' camp of states defeated in the first World War, who were unhappy with the settlement.[11] By 1937 the doctrine of self-determination had become a nationalist instrument of these states, and was expressed in Article 1 of the 1937 constitution. In contrast to 1922, the drafting was a purely domestic process. Article 5 stated that 'Ireland is a sovereign, independent, democratic state'. Unlike some European constitutions drafted after 1945, the constitution did not allow international agreements to prevail over its provisions. It provided for the democratic control of foreign policy, requiring the Oireachtas to approve participation in a war. It also committed the state to the peaceful resolution of international disputes. Article 29, which committed the state to respect generally accepted principles of international law, was influenced by Article 12 of the League of Nations Covenant, an agreement supported by de Valera before independence.

It is difficult to identify exactly when de Valera decided to write a new constitution. The abolition of the oath was the only constitutional change Fianna Fáil sought a mandate for in the 1932 general election. That de Valera was unhappy with the Treaty settlement, however, was apparent from his Removal of the Oath Act the following year. The 1926 Imperial Conference had given equal status with Britain to the dominions, giving, it was argued, the Free State the legal right to remove the Treaty from the constitution. De Valera then took advantage of the 1931 Statute of Westminster, which established the principle of co-equality between Westminster and the dominions, to argue that he could remove the oath without violating any legal obligation towards Great Britain.[12] The oath stood in the way of national unity, and the courts should not be in a position to declare such legislation unconstitutional, simply because it conflicted with the Treaty.[13] The principle Collins articulated in 1922 – the freedom to frame Irish domestic institutions regardless of Treaty commitments – was again invoked.

After his 1933 electoral victory, de Valera formed a civil service committee in 1934, to assess what provisions of the 1922 constitution ought to be retained in the interests of democracy. One member, John Hearne, wrote a provisional constitutional draft on his advice in May 1935. Yet Hearne's 'draft heads' were to be inserted into the existing constitution, rather than being, 'at this stage', an effort to write a new constitution.[14] De Valera's desire for a new constitution reflected his dislike of the *source* of the 1922 constitution, and as the Treaty settlement unravelled, room for a new beginning emerged. This followed the severance of the last link with the Crown on 11 December 1936, when the office of Governor General was abolished. As the powers exercised by the King had become exercisable by the Governor General after 1921, the abolition of that office in 1936 led to them being transferred to the Executive Council by the 27th amendment. Hearne argued that since it was a question of policy whether these powers be given to the President, that office was not derived from the previous ones.[15] De Valera argued that the Crown had been a symbol of forced, not free association, and the new Presidency in 1937 symbolised a new beginning.[16]

One can represent both Cosgrave's and de Valera's amendments as part of a 'gradual' process of constitutional development through which the Irish state became sovereign.[17] Under more stable conditions, Kelly argued that a similar constitutional framework to that established in 1937 could have emerged within the framework of the 1922 constitution.[18] Yet there were fundamental differences over the connection between constitution and Treaty. The anti-treatyites argued that while the colonies enjoyed a gradual process of devolution, from 'treaty to constitution', Ireland had dominion status thrust upon it. This undermined the 1922 constitution in their eyes. The pro-treatyites regarded the Treaty as an international agreement, alterable only by agreement between the two governments. The Constituent Act of 1922 which gave it authority, could not be revised, except by convening another constituent assembly or a national plebiscite.[19] Thus its repudiation required a 'constitutional revolution', in which the constitution, and its manner of enactment, symbolised another new beginning. The link between constitution and Treaty was repudiated in 1937.

Yet the 1937 constitution still completed a 'treaty to constitution' process. The pro-treatyites had argued that the Treaty would prove not an impediment, but a basis for a process of constitutional enlargement (an aspect of Michael Collins's 'stepping-stone' approach to independence). The 1937 constitution fulfilled this vision. The legal history now being published by the Royal Irish Academy shows how a succession of legal decisions and developments in Commonwealth relations after 1922 created a space in which a new constitutional order could emerge.[20] These changes left concrete legal and philosophical problems for the 1937 drafters to resolve. Just as in the United States, where the colonial legal culture had hinged on the question of whether colonial law was *repugnant* to English law, in Ireland the doctrine (key to the 1922 constitution) reappeared in 1937, but the higher law to which legislation now had to conform was Bunreacht na hÉireann, not the 1921 Treaty. Ackerman's concept of a constitutional moment suggests that constitutional orders can come into existence quickly, but Ireland's post-1937 constitutional order was still gradually constructed.

Once the first draft was finalised on 16 March 1937, the civil servants' contribution was key. De Valera did not believe in open government, and of the 1922 committee only Kennedy and O'Rahilly had influence. The draft was circulated confidentially to members of the Executive Council, and to other experienced persons including Conor Maguire, President of the High Court, Gavan Duffy, Judge of the High Court, and James Geoghegan, Judge of the Supreme Court. On receipt of ministerial, departmental, and other comments, de Valera then appointed a committee to examine and revise the draft in light of these comments. It consisted of Maurice Moynihan, Secretary to the Executive Council, Michael McDunphy, Assistant Secretary to the Executive Council, Philip O'Donoghue, legal assistant to the Attorney General's department, and Hearne. The first revision of his draft was finalised on 1 April 1937. This was then sent to departments and individuals for further comment.[21] The drafts point to the importance of what didn't go into the constitution. The 1922 experimental approach was not continued with, and the civil servants wanted a short and precise constitution. Finance was worried that the rights provisions, and the commitments to welfare and justice, would raise expenditure. Thus extensive left-leaning clauses on private property in the first official draft, did not appear in the second. Yet de Valera had the final say on crucial issues. Articles 2 and 3, which claimed authority over the whole island, were retained against civil service complaints on the grounds that this was 'policy'. On 10 April, the second revised draft was circulated to ministers, and on 23 April a corrected copy was sent to the press. On 1 May the document was released to members of Dáil Éireann. Approval by it, a committee stage, and a successful plebiscite, awaited.

Keogh and McCarthy stress the broad political culture of de Valera and these civil servants.[22] The 1934 committee had been asked by de Valera to decide what provisions from 1922 were necessary for the protection of democratic rights, and to recommend how they could put in the position that they could not be altered by ordinary legislation. In May 1934 Fine Gael's John A. Costello, a former Attorney General, had proposed that some articles in the constitution be immune from the reach of ordinary legislation, which suggests that the existing safeguards were inadequate.[23] The committee held ten meetings between 28 May and its report on 3 July 1934. Recommended for immunity were those articles on personal rights, the national parliament, state revenues, the role of the comptroller and auditor general, and the courts. These were incorporated into the 1937 constitution, including those recommended to the committee by William Cosgrave, John A. Costello, and Patrick McGilligan of Fine Gael. De Valera had instructed the committee to ask them what provisions they regarded as essential to democracy, with a view to reaching agreement between the civil war parties. The provisions for personal rights, religious freedom, and an independent judiciary, were retained in 1937. Here there was substantial continuity.

In order to immunise fundamental rights from ordinary legislation, the 1934 committee had favoured judicial review and amendment by referendum, but differed on the value of a written constitution: Stephen Roche had invoked the spectre of a responsible executive saving the people from 'irresponsible courts'.[24] Few questioned ministerial responsibility, and the concept of extern ministers was dropped. Indeed the 1922 provisions for the popular initiative – PR, functional representation, and the Senate – were not considered fundamental to democracy by the three Fine Gael leaders in 1934. In contrast, the personal rights clauses, the requirement for amendments to be passed by referendums, and the court's power to decide on the constitutionality of legislation, *were*. Two of these were lawyers, so the concept of the constitution as a fundamental law transcended the civil war divide. De Valera's task was simply to retry what had been attempted in 1922.

Did the 1937 constitution indeed vindicate the 1922 approach? Kelly thought it a 'rebottling' of that of 1922, on the grounds that the state that existed in 1937 was substantially that which came into being in 1922.[25] Bunreacht na hÉireann was not a new beginning, but part of a gradual process by which a free constitution emerged from the Treaty settlement. In contrast, de Valera's supporters thought the 1922 constitution's Treaty ties 'hindered state development', and that it had failed to provide effective safeguards for those fundamental rights the 1922 drafters had been at pains to define. Only another new beginning could complete the process of gaining independence and secure rights. The crucial issue was whether a constitution tied to the Treaty could claim moral allegiance. De Valera disliked the *origins* of the Free State, stating in 1931 that the Crown was a symbol of forced not free association. This was his rationale for opposing the Treaty. It is fair to conclude that the civil war which followed the Treaty has lain behind 'the whole subsequent constitutional history of the state'.[26]

The distinction between evolutionary change and a new beginning is captured by the difference between 'amend' – to add to, correct, improve upon – and 'revolution': the repudiation of the past and the creation of something new. If the basic purpose of the constitution was to organise power, with the constitution simply the 'mechanics' of government, a complex amendment took place, since the mechanisms for voting, forming governments, and passing legislation, remained largely the same. In the British sense, de Valera's constitution could be considered a series of amendments, additions, and revisions, which left the constitutional backbone of the state intact. Kelly considered the new document 'a stabilising and reforming' continuation of that of 1922.[27] Yet Bunreacht na hÉireann still indicates an intention to ground the existing system in a new basic law. Finer credits the American revolution with six great constitutional inventions; federalism, the need for a written constitution, the desirability of a bill of rights, and judicial review, had all influenced the 1922 committee.[28] Behind the American model was the conviction that a legitimate government could only act within a framework of fundamental law, and this meant abandoning the cornerstone of British constitutional arrangements, parliamentary sovereignty. Bunreacht na hÉireann returned Ireland to popular sovereignty. In a Europe where many states were strongly resisting the encroachment of judges on the political process, the creation of a Supreme Court intended to act as a watchdog over the parliament represented a strong commitment to this principle.[29]

That the system's conceptual logic was changing is reflected by the references to 'organic laws' in the drafts. As laws which form the foundation of governments, in the United States they include the Declaration of Independence and the Articles of Confederation. In France, they refer to a fixed list of statutes, with constitutional force, which are not easily changed. 'Organic laws' in Ireland referred only to foundational laws of a system of government, not, significantly, the 1916 Proclamation, or the Democratic Programme in 1919. In de Valera's 'squared paper draft', the sovereign powers of the people would be 'exercised by the organs of Government set forth in this Constitution'. Article 1 of the transitional powers gave the next parliament the right to pass 'organic laws' with immediate effect, to be ratified by referendum. The section on the referendum wrote 'organic laws at discretion of President'. In the first unofficial draft, Article 5 refers to a Presidency 'to be regulated by Organic Laws'. An organic law is defined as 'a law to regulate any matter or thing relating to the exercise of powers of government, the regulation of which by Organic Law is required or authorised by this constitution'. A clear distinction between 'organic laws' and ordinary legislation is made. The draft from October 1936 stated that the powers of government are exercisable only through 'the Organs established by this Constitution' or 'established or recognised by Organic Laws made thereunder'. The phraseology was provisional, and the final text used only 'organs of government'.[30] The first official draft of March 1937 merely states that the powers of government 'are exercisable by or on authority of the Organs of State established by this Constitution'.[31] The change conceals a consistent conception of the constitution as a fundamental law.

As in 1922, constitutional rigidity, judicial review and the referendum were interconnected, but the Presidency now became central to how they worked.

Hearne's May 1935 draft did not give the President any power to question the constitutionality of legislation. The Oireachtas had the power to amend the constitution, but any amendment to its fundamental rights provisions, would require a two-thirds' majority of the voters, or a majority of the electorate to vote in favour of it in a referendum. De Valera's 'Squared Paper draft' scribbled down the more far-reaching principle that the people shall be 'the *ultimate court* for deciding *all* national and political questions', and that the constitution could only be amended by referendum. The first undated draft from late 1936 then allowed a majority of the Senate to petition the President to call a referendum on any bill passed. The President would have to give his decision, after consultation with the Council of State, within six days. The first unofficial draft then gave the President the power to submit to the people any 'organic law' after consultation with the Council of State.[32] The first official draft from March 1937 envisaged that the President could refer certain bills to the Supreme Court and to the people, and that all constitutional amendments would require referendums. The final provisions allowed Presidential referral of bills to the people after a petition signed by a majority of the Senate and four-ninths of the Dáil. This system of checks and balances was worked out without reliance on any dominant model, with the 1919 Weimar constitution a likely source.

The constitution's structure replicated O'Rahilly's draft C from 1922: with early sections on 'nation and state', a section on the machinery of government, a section on rights and social principles, and finally the amendment procedure. Hearne's 1935 draft began with articles on the state, citizenship and language. Irish was the 'national' language, and English 'equally recognised' as an official language. De Valera's 'Squared Paper Draft' indicated early articles on the name of the state, its territory, the source of sovereignty, the flag, language, and religion, but was not clearly structured either. There was a separate section, under 'organic laws', mainly covering the Presidency. This was later dropped. The first draft, from late 1936, contained a comprehensive structure, but was provisional. The first official draft began with distinct sections on Nation and State, and contained a section on 'Personal Rights and Social Policy'. Both drafts began with a declaration of the Irish nation's right to self-determination. In the unofficial draft this included the right to choose its own form of government, to determine its relations with other states, *and* the right to decide 'all disputed issues of national or public policy'.[33] In the first official draft, this third right was moved to Article 6 on popular sovereignty, and 'according to the requirements of the common good' qualified it.[34] *Éire* was substituted for *Saorstát Éireann* by de Valera at an early stage. The title Directive Principles of Social Policy appeared only in the final text. The Irish names: *Uachtarán, Tánaiste, Dáil Éireann, Oireachtas, Seanad Éireann* had also been proposed by the 1922 committee.[35]

This raises the question of O'Rahilly's influence. In 1932 Conor Maguire, the Attorney General, solicited his opinion on the constitutional implications of the Statute of Westminster, the Treaty and the Oath issue. John O'Hearne was also in touch. De Valera borrowed and returned copies of draft C from him.[36] In 1930 Warner Moss, a New York-based political scientist, had requested permission to examine the proceedings of the 1922 committee. He was told that it was 'contrary to public policy' to make the confidential documents available. Those pertaining to the negotiations with the British government were also withheld.[37] Publication of draft C was considered in 1936, but Hugh Kennedy, then Attorney General, was strongly opposed.[38] O'Rahilly had received legal advice that publication could be made the subject matter of a prosecution.[39] His 1937 collection of articles, *Thoughts on the Constitution*, diagnosed a state of constitutional limbo. Since the Treaty could be altered only through agreement of the two governments, this made for expediency not constitutionalism. The British had not recognised the 1922 assembly as sovereign, and its intention to pass a fundamental law had been violated by (*a*) the abolition of the referendum, (*b*) extending the period in which the constitution could be easily amended. It was time to fall back on first principles, and appeal directly to the people as the source of constitutional authority.[40]

So O'Rahilly articulated the logic of de Valera's new beginning, and he wanted no ambiguity on the name for a state, which was 'a new moral personality and international entity'. Complaining of 'elaborate paraphernalia for taking over the old State', he argued that the constitution should be clear about its Catholic nature. The battleground of the future would be over education, where the functions of the state should be reduced to supervision and support.[41] The acceptance of a territorial limitation to the state's jurisdiction should not be construed as an acknowledgement of partition. Draft C's provisions on the state's commitment to marriage, on constitutional protection for maternity, the question of industrial work for women, and the ban on divorce, were also reflected in the 1937 constitution.[42] Hearne and de Valera had drawn on his clauses on the family in their initial draft.[43] In this draft the Dáil was a 'House of Representatives' and the Seanad a 'Senate', as proposed by Murnaghan and O'Rahilly in 1922. O'Rahilly had also proposed *Cathaoirleach* for the chair of the Dáil in 1922.[44] O'Rahilly supported the new constitution, but wanted religious education to be obligatory in all state-aided educational establishments, and religious ministries to be guaranteed in all public institutions, such as hospitals and barracks.[45]

O'Rahilly wanted the constitution to be taught in schools 'without apology or reservation', which raises the issue of the general Catholic input.[46] De Valera had been in correspondence in 1936 with Edward Cahill, a Jesuit lecturer in sociology, and author of *The Framework of a Christian State*. To Cahill it was of paramount importance that the new constitution 'should mark a definite break with the liberal and non-Christian type of State'. Citing the Portuguese constitution, he proposed a directly elected President, with long tenure of office, an Executive independent of the legislature, and parish councils elected by heads of families, with priests as *ex-officio* members. The party system would disappear under these arrangements.[47] These suggestions were never adopted. De Valera stressed the difficulty of adopting Cahill's proposals into a formal constitution, but some 'might be set forth in the preamble'.[48] Cahill nonetheless served as intermediary between a committee of more senior Jesuits who made submissions for 'a Catholic Constitution'. This committee proposed a preamble on the Polish model, an article exhorting 'the State to aim at a wide distribution of private productive property especially in land', and an article acknowledging the special position of the Catholic faith as that of the majority of the nation'. [49] These did influence the final constitution.

By 1937 the position of the Catholic Church in primary and secondary education was so strong that the question for the drafters was how to secure the status quo through constitutional legislation. At the heart of the education system were two principles enunciated by canon law: (1) that Catholic parents should send their children to schools which provide a Catholic education; (2) that the State should provide the parents with the freedom to make such a choice.[50] Both were achieved under the 1937 constitution, which provided constitutional protection for a system of public funding of private schools. One saving grace was Article 44.2.4. which read:

> Legislation providing State aid for schools shall not discriminate between schools under the management of different religious denominations, nor be such as to affect prejudicially the right of any child to attend a school receiving public money without attending religious instruction at the school.

Such a provision, preventing religious discrimination in the admission of pupils to publicly funded schools, had several precedents, having been present, in different forms, in the 1922 constitution, the 1921 Anglo-Irish Treaty, and two of the Home Rule bills.[51] However, there was no provision requiring schools to attenuate the religious ethos of the school, or to establish the principle of non- discrimination in the appointment of teachers.

The most important Catholic influence was John Charles McQuaid, teacher at Blackrock College, de Valera's *alma mater*, and future Archbishop of Dublin. He was personally friendly with de Valera's family. From early 1937 de Valera was in frequent correspondence with him, sometimes twice a day.

McQuaid pressed the claims of Catholic social teaching, notably *Rerum Novarum*. To McQuaid, the constitution was 'a thesis of philosophy and theology', and he influenced the provisions on personal rights, the family, education, private property, religion, and the directive principles.[52] The *extent* of his influence is harder to establish, although he had a definite imprint on the personal rights and directive principles clauses.[53] He provided almost the exact wording for Article 42.3, which prevented the state from obliging parents to send their children to any class of school chosen by the state. His comment ended 'it would be better thus'.[54] Yet McQuaid's influence was not unqualified. For the Directive Principles, he proposed 'Fundamental Guarantees and Principles of Social Policy'. He insisted that the word 'right' be insisted in the text of these principles, since 'a personal right is a legal right'.[55] Yet the 'principles' in this section of the constitution are not 'guarantees', and remain unjusticiable. In March 1937 McQuaid also sent de Valera extracts on the 'Basis of Authority' from Papal Pronouncements. De Valera had in his possession a handwritten memo on 'Catholic Principles of Political Authority' which stated that God not the people was the primary source of political authority, while the people decided the form of government and their particular rulers.[56] This was not stated in the constitution. Article 6 stated that all powers of government derive, under God, from the people, whose right it is to designate the rulers of the state.

McQuaid could not divert de Valera's team from writing a constitution consistent with personal rights and civic freedoms.[57] The correspondence contains papal teachings on freedom of expression and of the press, but the relevant articles were still based on those from 1922. Article 40.6.1, however, specifically made the publication of blasphemous matter a legal offence. An early draft of Article 44 had given the Catholic Church the status of 'one true Church', and Catholic clerics wanted the Catholic Church recognised as the Church 'established by Christ'. The Vatican complained that the constitution's recognition of 'the special position' of the Catholic Church as 'the faith of the great majority' of citizens, had no value. This formula had Napoleonic precedents, and Article 44 stated that 'the state also recognises' other churches, including the Church of Ireland, a name considered a usurpation by some Catholic clerics. Later, de Valera received a letter from the Jewish rabbinate committee, thanking him for providing them with 'equal recognition' to the other religious bodies: Article 44.1.3. specifically mentioned the Jewish congregations.[58] The compromise was worked out at the last minute: more than 20 meetings between de Valera and the churches took place in April 1937 alone. The Catholic Church was not satisfied with the outcome, but any vestiges of secular republicanism among de Valera's ministers were also suppressed.[59]

Much of the debate about the 1937 constitution concerns its religious sources. Keogh and McCarthy have demonstrated that the Catholic input was tempered by other influences. The preamble, and the 'Directive Principles', suggest de Valera used religion to create loyalty and respect, without allowing itto contaminate the rest of the document. The first section was devoted to Nation and State, not Church and State. Yet the balance between religious and secular influences was not a case of either/or for the drafters. For example, Article 6 gave the people the right to 'designate' the rulers of the state. On the meaning of 'designation' officials were made aware of rival Scholastic (Jesuit and Dominican) and Designation theories.[60] Some of the drafters, like de Valera, saw no incompatibility between the specifically Christian and the democratic strands to Irish constitutionalism. Both required a set of fundamental rights to be put beyond the reach of parliament, both saw the constitution as 'a national code' which would express the values of Irish civilisation, and both were suspicious of the claims of the state, especially in education. The influence of draft C from 1922 raised the question of how minority rights would be respected in a constitution that expressed, and almost defined, a national self. The issue hinged on whether it was a Catholic or a Christian document, an issue which would dominate debate when the taken for granted version of that self was challenged. Before the 1960s the constitution's content, including its prohibition of divorce, was generally accepted.

INSTITUTIONAL ANALYSIS

It is commonly believed that the constitution's institutional provisions did not fundamentally shape the development of the polity, as opposed to the clauses defining the values of the political community. Only the Senate had been subject to serious public discussion in the 1930s. Whereas Cosgrave's amendments had brought the institutional structure into conformity with the Westminster model, de Valera's had largely focused on Anglo-Irish relations. He believed his predecessors had done a good job, and the constitution codified much of what had been developing in practice. Symbolically, it marked a break with the Free State, but less of a new beginning in institutional terms. Yet the commitment to a fundamental law still implied modification of the Westminster model. In 1922 most of the committee had tried to establish popular control of the executive by looking elsewhere. In 1937 de Valera's team assumed a strong executive on the British model, but wanted a strong system of checks and balances to control it. They produced a constitution based on the formal circumscription of power, as opposed to the 'power grab' attributed to de Valera by the Fine Gael opposition.[61]

The constitution provided for Westminster-style cabinet government. To de Valera, the Dáil was elected by the people not to govern, but to elect a government which must be allowed to govern.[62] 'The Executive Council' was renamed 'The Council of Ministers', and then 'the Government'. The constitution provided for a tripartite system, with a weak head of state, and a bicameral parliament with a very weak second house. The development of ministerial responsibility in the UK had occurred at the same time as the growth of disciplined political parties, and the emergence of the Irish civil war parties had the same effect. The 1922 committee had recognised problems with the system, and required election of the President of the Executive Council by the Dáil, and its express approval of his individual ministers. By 1937 there was little dissatisfaction with the British cabinet system, and the Free State had enjoyed the highest degree of executive stability in inter-war Europe. Debate focused on how to dissolve the Dáil, and the President was given the role formally enjoyed by the Governor General since 1922. This power was to be exercised only on the advice of a prime minister who controlled a majority in Dáil Éireann. Here, the constitution formalised what already existed in practice, and strengthened the position of the prime minister, who was now given the power to dismiss ministers. The UK and Ireland would remain the only two countries in western Europe where the government had exclusive power to determine the plenary agenda for the lower house.[63]

The challenge was to reconcile the concept of a fundamental law to this strong executive, and thus address a central tension in Sinn Féin's constitutional project since 1919. The 1922 provisions on judicial review, the amendment, the referendum, and the Senate, were revisited. Hearne's preliminary draft from May 1935 allowed constitutional amendments by the Oireachtas, except with regard to personal rights.[64] This was later disallowed. The President's powers, initially extensive, were quickly modified. Constitutional amendments, as in 1922, first required two-thirds of recorded votes or a majority on the register in a referendum, making it extremely difficult to change. Crucially, this was later changed to a bare majority of the voters. The first unofficial draft allowed the government to submit a bill to a referendum. This was changed too. A majority of the Senate was first given the power to petition a referendum on a topic of major importance if the President, after consultation with the Council of State, agreed. That power was later jointly given to a majority of the Senate and four ninths of the first chamber (roughly as suggested by the 1925 amendment committee). There was never any provision for the popular initiative.

If the task was to conjoin a strong system of checks and balances to the existing machinery of government, not all civil servants saw the need. Stephen Roche, secretary to the Department of Justice, disliked 'the whole idea of tying up the Dáil and the Government with all sorts of restrictions and putting the Supreme Court like a watch-dog over them for fear they may run wild'.[65] Patrick Lynch, the Attorney General, remarked that:

> It will be appreciated that the idea of a sovereign national parliament can only be approached by reducing to the narrowest limits any constitutional restrictions. It follows from this that the greater the number of matters expressly covered in the constitution, the greater will be the consequent limitation on the powers of the legislature under that Constitution.[66]

J. J. MacElligott, secretary of the Department of Finance, complained of the degree of 'uncertainty introduced to the legislative system' by concessions to the doctrine of repugnancy. He specifically criticised the President's power to refer bills to the Supreme Court, and the power given to the Senate and the Dáil to petition the President to call a referendum on bills.[67] The observations of the Department of the President, from 23 March 1937, contain the responses. On the right of final appeal to a referendum on any question of policy they read 'No leave it as it is'. On the suggestion that the constitution should make clear that it is the nomination of the Taoiseach which requires approval by Dáil Éireann, and not the appointment of the members of the Government, they read 'Agree. Change to be made'. On the proposal that the President should be required to consult the Council of State before refusing to dissolve the Dail, it reads 'No. Absolute discretion'. When the principle that the state should be committed to the distribution of material resources was questioned, these were 'merely' statements of 'moral principles', not 'positive rights'.[68] De Valera had the intellectual self-confidence to see beyond the standard civil service attitude, and worked with civil servants who shared his attitude.

The most important was John Hearne, who in a memo 'The Constitution and the National Life' provided an intellectual case for a new beginning. He thought that the people had a right to a legislative independence untrammelled by any foreign policy connection, or any theory of their relationship with another group of states. This meant the connection between constitution and Treaty should be broken. The 1937 constitution created a framework in which those opposed to the state (Sinn Féin and the IRA) could pursue any policy on Anglo-Irish Relations peacefully. The connection between the constitution and 'the national life' was organic, since the constitution would 'foster and reflect the social and political order of a distinct Irish commonwealth'. Even if the 1922 constitution was not 'the forlorn fragment that it has become', the Irish would have had to deal with the question of 'the relation of our national law to the whole of our national life'.[69] This assumed a strong expressive approach. To de Valera, the constitution should be 'a code of their own making, cast in the mould of their own history', and 'a covenant accepted by them in their own understanding of their own national ideals and the needs of their own land'. Independence was not just self-government, but about making laws 'reflecting the genius of their own civilisation'.[70]

The powers of the President were outlined near the start of the drafts. A semi-Presidential system on the model of the Weimar Republic was a possibility. Its 1919 constitution provided for a President, directly elected by the people for a term of seven years, and divided power between President, cabinet, and parliament. The Weimar President was obliged to sign bills into law, but had the power to refer them to the people for a referendum. In emergencies Article 48 gave the Weimar President the power to suspend the government, rule directly, and to suspend the constitutional protection of basic rights. In May 1935, de Valera instructed Hearne to 'provide for the suspension of the said articles during a state of emergency only'.[71] Here the Weimar precedent was important. The Irish President would also be elected by the people for a seven-year term, was given the power to refer bills to the people, and Article 10 of Hearne's preliminary draft stated that 'the Oireachtas shall be summoned and dissolved by the President'. Article 17 then stated that this power should be exercised on the advice of the Council of Ministers. The first draft of the constitution also proposed that the President could head a national government during a crisis, internal or international, if requested to do so, and Article 24 gave him the power to suspend the constitution temporarily, on the cabinet's advice, with the approval of the Dáil, in situations or districts where grave disorder exists.[72] These powers were quickly removed. When the cabinet discussed the draft in October 1936, the article concerning the national government had been deleted, the President could only summon and dissolve the Dáil on the advice of the Prime Minister, and the power to temporarily suspend the constitution was not specified, and subsequently dropped. Thus Article 48, which enabled Hitler to establish a dictatorship, was not replicated in Ireland.

In contrast to practice in most non-monarchical European systems, the choice of head of state was vested not in party leaders nor in parliament, but in the people.[73] De Valera initially told Hearne to provide only for a President who would fulfil all the functions exercised in 1935 by the King and the Governor General in internal affairs.[74] Article 4 of Hearne's draft, however, proposed a popularly elected office, while the election of the President in de Valera's 'squared paper draft' was covered by 'organic laws'. This was so in the draft constitution considered at cabinet in October 1936, and 'proportional representation' was written in handwriting beside it.[75] This document was strongly influenced by Hearne and Philip O'Donoghue, and had received the approval of the Fianna Fáil national executive and the executive council.[76] There is no record of disagreement, and STV was prescribed for Presidential elections in the first official draft. [77] The Presidency has subsequently allowed a distinction between state and government to be maintained, helped by the degree of political stability since 1937: refusing governments the power to dissolve the Dáil under such provisions would have been very controversial in the summer of 1927.[78]

Since 1937 the President has had the power, after consultation with the new Council of State, to refer any ordinary bill to the Supreme Court for a decision on its constitutionality. A decision of unconstitutionality prevents a bill becoming law. Once deemed constitutional by the Supreme Court, the constitutionality of the bill can never again be challenged in the courts. De Valera believed that the guiding principle was that the authority of the people's representatives was to be maintained, unless the people vetoed the proposed bill in a referendum.[79] The Presidency led to much opposition in 1937. Hearne stressed that the President's powers were confined to express constitutional functions, exercised mostly on the advice of the government. The President's referral of bills to the Supreme Court, and to the people for a referendum, were to be exercised in consultation with the Council of State. Many of the objections to the office missed out on the crucial fact that the power to refer bills to the people applied only to bills already passed by both houses of the Oireachtas. The operation of the safeguard rested on the Seanad, a substantial body of opinion in the Dáil, and the President, acting together. The right to refuse to dissolve the Dáil on the advice of a Taoiseach who had ceased to retain the support of a majority in the Dáil was nonetheless at his absolute discretion.[80]

The 1934 committee, like that of 1925, had recommended that the new constitution could only be amended by referendum. The 1937 provisions conceived of the referendum as a constitutional safeguard, not a popular veto. Referendums were not to be initiated by the people, were limited to certain bills considered by parliament to be 'of fundamental national importance', and only after its assent would the people's views be ascertained. This would happen if the President, after consulting with the Council of State, also gave his or her consent.[81] According to de Valera, the people would be 'masters' of their political system at the time of an election, and their 'mastery' maintained during the period between elections, by the President, who would be chosen to represent their interests The constitution distinguished between the mandatory constitutional referendum, and the ordinary referendum on government bills, and made the legislative initiative highly unlikely. The Senate's *independent* power to initiate referendums was removed in the drafting. Article 27.1 gives members of both houses the right to jointly request the President to decline to sign bills and call a referendum, on the grounds that the bill contains proposals 'of such national importance' that the will of the people ought to be ascertained. This power has never been exercised. The provisions reflected draft C from 1922, since the rejection of any bill by the Supreme Court could allow the President call a referendum on it.

The constitution prescribed STV for elections to the Dáil, the Seanad, and the Presidency. After the war Fianna Fáil would try to change the electoral system in two unsuccessful referendums, so its prescription in 1937 mattered. The significant differences between the first constitutional draft of 16 March 1937, and the first revised draft of 1 April 1937, did not extend to the electoral provisions. The preference was for continuity. Hearne's 1935 'proposed heads' simply stated that the election of TDs should be in accordance 'with the existing electoral law'. De Valera's 'squared paper draft' suggested a parliament elected by PR. The first draft from late 1936 specified that Dáil Éireann would be elected 'upon principles of Proportional Representation, the election to be by means of the single transferable vote'.[82] The first official draft extended this to Presidential and Seanad elections.

De Valera stuck with STV when European opinion had become generally hostile to PR. Indeed the three Fine Gael leaders had not considered PR an essential element of the democratic system in 1934. De Valera referred to the 1920s:

> After the Treaty when the Republican Party was out of power 'PR' saved us from political extinction and enabled us to retain a large number of seats. Now that we are in power, we retain the system, although it means that instead of having a two to one majority in the Dáil (as we would have if the three last elections had been held on the old system) we have a majority of only three over all the other parties combined. We believe that PR is a fairer system, it gives to every considerable group or nearly as possible the representation to which its numbers entitle it it, and that makes for contentment and stability.[83]

He was also keen to advertise his constitution as a democratic one, and the retention of PR could serve a useful propaganda purpose regarding Northern Ireland which had abolished PR in the 1920s. Yet this does not explain why he didn't just stick with the 1922 formula, which would have made it far easier to alter the system. De Valera also made an election issue of PR in 1938, at a time when his government was able to amend the constitution without a referendum. This was obviously a way of testing the water on the issue. Fine Gael's attitude had been expressed by the constitutional committee in 1928:

> The constitution should only set out general principles leaving to the Parliament as much liberty as possible for the settlement of details and systems. For example, it is quite proper that the Constitution should provide that election to the

parliament should be conducted on principles of proportional representation; but it is not desirable that the constitution should go on to provide that a particular system of PR should be adopted. The system of election under the principles of proportional representation and all the details of the election, should be settled by the electoral law.[84]

Yet de Valera argued that PR 'needed a foundation that could not be changed except by the expressed will of the people'.[85] There is no evidence that he envisaged referendums on STV, but some suggest he left it for future generations to amend.[86] Of course Fianna Fáil was on a roll in 1937, having increased its first preference vote from 44.5% in 1932 to 49.7% in 1933. Even under STV Fianna Fáil could be dominant.

Indeed the concession was not as great as it seemed. When asked why he did not just leave a flexible choice, as in 1922, de Valera replied that such a broad clause could easily be abused for party political purposes, resulting in a system far from PR.[87] Yet the constitution required that the minimum constituency size be not less than three seats, which was below the size (five) then believed necessary to achieve proportionality. A motion in the Dáil to make the minimum size five was defeated by 50 votes to 26. In 1913 James Meredith had warned what while the new electoral system under Home Rule could not be changed by the Irish House of Commons, its ability to reduce the size of the constituencies would have the same effect.[88] In 1935 a Fianna Fáil cabinet committee had radically reduced the number of constituencies of five or more, from two thirds to a third of the total, ensuring that they retained the ability to win parliamentary majorities.[89] The appointment of this committee in January 1933 followed rapidly from Fianna Fáil gaining a parliamentary majority which freed it from dependence on Labour. The result was that the number of three-seaters was increased by 6 to 20 (those of five or more decreased from 17 to 7). Figgis had requested a scheme for constituencies of no less than seven members in 1922.[90] Fianna Fáil had retreated from such idealism. Revealingly, the possibility of further electoral redistribution was revisited by the government in May 1937, while the constitution was being debated.[91]

A cornerstone of the Westminster model is the primacy of the lower house, and reference to the sovereign Irish parliament in 1937 was still implicitly to the lower house, founded as Dáil Éireann in 1919. The abolition of the Seanad in 1936, and of university representation in the Dáil meant that of the 1922 concessions to the southern unionists, only PR now remained. Nonetheless, the Senate was re-established in 1937, and the state again became one of few unitary democratic states with a second chamber. De Valera had argued that the Senate's opposition to his removal of the oath bill obstructed good government. Nonetheless, Conor Maguire, the Attorney General, stressed how much revision of bills passed by the Dáil was actually needed.[92] The Senate had also sent de Valera a conciliatory message, proposing a conference between the two houses on transitory arrangements should a new Senate be intended.[93] After the decision to abolish it was made on 12 May 1936, de Valera was mindful enough of opinion in favour of a second house to appoint a committee to review the issue.

This committee, with Hearne, Kennedy, and O'Rahilly among the members, met 27 times and reported on 30 September 1936. The majority report wanted a house with the power to delay bills for 90 days, and no power to delay money bills. It was divided over electing the Senators. Another proposal was to have them nominated by panels, representing a variety of cultural, economic, and educational interests, as proposed in 1922. Kennedy wanted a fully elected house which could help scrutinise legislation in committees. The other minority report proposed a Senate with the power to call referendums on government bills in order to protect democracy.[94] O'Rahilly believed its chief purpose should be to defend the people 'against a party-ridden Dáil', and wanted the referral of Dáil bills to the people to require only a majority of Senators' support.[95] Michael Tierney of Fine Gael later alluded to the danger of a single-chamber parliament leading to a Fianna Fáil dictatorship.[96] The final provisions were influenced by all three reports: the Senate was given the power to veto non-monetary bills within a three-month period, it had the right to call a referendum in conjunction with four-ninths of the Dáil on government bills, and the electoral system was mixed.[97] However, although most of the Senators would be elected from university and vocational panels, the Taoiseach would nominate eleven out of eighty senators. The house would be differently constituted, but not really independent. Its weakness stemmed from two factors. There is a strong correlation between second houses and federalism, and being a small homogeneous society, there was no need for federalism in Éire. Secondly, the idea of a second chamber providing a check on the more democratically elected lower house was discredited by the Treaty division, on which the Senate effectively took sides. Enthusiasm could only be revived if functional, vocational, or corporatist ideals were taken more seriously. De Valera's real attitude to the chamber was suggested by the note in the 'squared paper draft' stating that 'the legislature shall consist of Dáil Éireann selected by – proportional representation and Seanad (?)Éireann'.[98]

Minority rights had become less integral to European democracy by 1937, and the League of Nations proved ineffective in this area. The 1937 constitution was more accommodating of existing realities than that of 1922, and Labour, the ex-unionists, and women, had all declined in parliamentary representation. The referendum was no longer identified primarily with minority rights, the Seanad was less independent, and the popular initiative gone. STV remained, but with smaller constituencies. Minorities would best influence legislation when governments were dependent on independents or in coalitions. The protection of minority rights depended more on the fundamental rights, the Home Rule clauses, and the provisions for denominational education. Here judicial review was fundamental. Article 15.4.2 stated that 'every law enacted by the Oireachtas which is in any respect repugnant to this constitution or to any provision thereof, shall, but to the extent only of such repugnancy, be invalid'. In October 1936 Hearne had sent de Valera copies of the constitutions of Czechoslovakia, Austria, Spain, Poland, and the USA, showing the machinery established to determine the validity of laws and to resolve conflicts between the administrative authorities and the courts.[99] The next constitutional draft outlined the functions of a Supreme Court. After the first official draft was circulated, McQuaid had opposed allowing the Oireachtas to be a constitutional court, and recommended 'the safer method' of giving the Supreme Court the power to judge the constitutionality of legislation.[100] The first unofficial draft, from late 1936, referred to the Supreme Court as 'the court of Final Appeal'.[101] The concept of repugnancy logically entails judicial review, but in 1937 it was not foreseen how it would develop.

Ward argues that the constitution 'made no fundamental changes in the basic model of responsible government' practised since 1919.[102] Stronger executive dominance, and increased powers for the Taoiseach, brought the system more in line with practice in the Commonwealth. Yet the British model was fundamentally modified. De Valera 'retained a highly centralised structure, in a territorial sense', but also created 'a framework for the dispersal of power across autonomous institutions within it'.[103] After 1922 governing elites had understood the constitution in a mechanical way, making amendments which reinforced the basic Westminster structure. Constitutionalism became an organising principle, not a doctrine of political legitimacy which stressed the primacy of fundamental rights, and the need for a fundamental law to limit governmental power. This allowed them overcome repeated crises, but ultimately resulted in constitutional limbo. The 1937 approach, which sought to refound the state on the basis of first principles, was different. It spoke to an American tradition, conveyed by the phrase 'the people . . . give themselves this constitution fundamental organic law' in de Valera's first draft preamble. As before 1921, organic again invoked the idea of a constitution with a source of authority prior to the state. The British tradition favoured incremental change, with more democratic forms of rule gradually added to a previously existing structure, without fundamental change to its identity. In Ireland, constitutional identity and Irish constitutionalism changed in 1937. Unlike in 1922 Bunreacht na hÉireann was legitimised by a plebiscite, not an act of parliament. De Valera accurately called it 'the first free Constitution of the Irish People'.[104]

The language of a new beginning accompanied de Valera's public advocacy. The constitution was a 'renewed declaration of national independence', a 'firm foundation' for an ordered life, and 'a basic public law'. As in 1922, the preamble suggested that the unity of the country could be restored, and concord established with other nations. As a framework in which domestic peace could be assured, rights protected, and the people's 'mastery' of their system established, de Valera believed that the constitution ought to do more than define relations between institutions, if it wanted to inspire and elicit loyalty.[105] The expressive approach was evident in the preamble which began 'In the Name of the Most Holy Trinity' similar to the Greek 1827 constitution. The preamble to the Polish 1921 constitution began 'In the name of Almighty God', while that to the 1935 Polish April constitution began 'In the Name of the Most Holy Trinity'. De Valera introduced the constitution to the Dáil on 11 May 1937. Opposition focused on the Presidency and the position of women. The 'manifesto' qualities were less contentious. Fianna Fáil's Frank Aiken suggested that the principles behind the constitution were those that the vast majority of TDs had worked for at one time.[106]

In a series of interviews de Valera had stressed the democratic character of his new beginning. He thought the Irish state was the servant of the people, not the people the servant of the state, and like his civil war opponents he subscribed to the essential tenet of nineteenth-century British liberalism, which was that the principal function of the state was to protect individual rights and liberty. Europe's recent history had shown that only under a democratic government could such rights be protected, and in 1934 de Valera had predicted that the European countries which had succumbed to dictatorship would eventually return to democracy for this reason. Democracy was also the most stable form of government, since even though a gifted dictator might govern for a while, the people under a dictator had no means of disposing a less able or popular successor. There was no difference in this regard between communism and fascism. In democracies people may suffer from a bad government for a time, but have the remedy in their own hands when they go to the ballot box.[107] The constitution explicitly protected the principle of democracy, committed the state to the peaceful resolution of international disputes, and explicitly recognised the Jewish minority. In 1937 none of these were token gestures.

The Dáil made significant amendments to the number of times the President could be elected, the panels for Senate elections, the right to freely criticise public policy, and women's rights. The name of the state in English was changed from *Éire* to *Ireland*. De Valera treated the Dáil as nothing more than an advisory body, and stressed that the people were the source of authority. The plebiscite was held on the same day as a general election, presenting the public with 'a Hobson's choice' between a constitution from which all democratic safeguards had been removed, and the new document.[108] The difference between a plebiscite and a referendum was that the former was used following the First World War to denote popular votes held to resolve sovereignty conflicts over territories and boundaries.[109] In this respect the repudiation of the Treaty and Articles 2 and 3 were essential to the new beginning. Yet the result was close. The constitution passed by a small majority (56.5% of the poll), and only 38.5% of the electorate voted for it. On 29 December 1937, the British government announced that they were prepared to treat the constitution as not effecting 'a fundamental alteration' in the position of the Free State, now *Éire*, as a member of the British Commonwealth of Nations.[110] The constitution had not established a republic.

The constitution was opposed by Fine Gael who, in their spokesmen Costello and McGilligan had actually recommended some of its content in 1934. Cosgrave, while conceding that the constitution contained much of general appeal, thought its objectionable features – the powers of the President, the degradation of the status of women, control of the press – all pointed towards the end of parliamentary democracy.[111] De Valera argued that without a strong constitution, there was nothing to stop a minority government 'stampeding' the courts and establishing a party dictatorship in the way the Blueshirts had tried in 1934.[112] The civil war background was crucial. Fine Gael were worried about the Presidency being used to establish a dictatorship. The constitution stated that 'subject to this constitution, additional powers and functions may be conferred on the President by law'. Senator James Douglas thought this 'too drastic a power', and proposed a formula whereby any bill extending these powers would not come into operation for 60 days after the next election after the bill was passed.[113]

Doubts about de Valera's democratic credentials went back to 1922. Fine Gael's Tom O'Higgins claimed that the constitution would establish 'a throne' for 'the greatest political fanatic' in the country. Europe of the 1930s was dominated by strong men.[114] Fears of a dictatorship were real. The increased concentration of power since 1922 pointed in that direction. The *Manchester Guardian* thought the Presidency an 'incalculable force' in Free State politics. The *Daily Telegraph* declared that *Taoiseach* signified *Duce* or *Fuehrer*. The *Times* thought that a popularly elected head of state would lead to conflicts as in Latin America. The *Irish Independent* argued that a President claiming a direct popular authority 'can and will develop in power and prestige'. Where the President was directly elected, (the USA, Finland, Portugal, and Estonia), he was given substantial executive powers. In France, Czechoslovakia, Latvia and Lithuania, where executive power was vested in a cabinet, the President was not directly elected.[115] *The Leader* wanted responsible government:

> We have little liking for any personage who can be called 'the supreme guardian of the liberties of the people' or as the Irish Press puts it, the keystone of the Constitution. The power to rule should be in the hands of the responsible Executive of the Government chosen by the people and the liberties of the people should be safeguarded by the people's courts.[116]

These critics did not know that the President's powers had already been severely curtailed. 'On advice of government' had been written in handwriting beside the article on the President's powers in the first official draft of 16 March 1937. The power to temporarily suspend the constitution in situations where grave disorder existed was first limited, then dropped. The power to summon and dissolve the Dáil was to be exercised on the advice of a Prime Minister who controls a majority in the Dáil. The right to refuse a dissolution to a Taoiseach who had ceased to command the support of the majority in the Dáil, was the President's only absolute power. The *Irish Press* welcomed the Presidency as 'a brilliant solution' to the constitutional difficulty left over by the Free State, since the office was 'to prevent the people's rights being given away by tampering with the constitution without the people's consent'.[117]

The American press was nonetheless fixated on the possibility that an American system could develop. Yet de Valera told the *Boston American* that the office was an 'important' not a 'dictatorial' one. In only one case would the President actually decide an issue. He told the *New York Times* that the Irish President had no executive powers. To the International News Service he remarked that the system was altogether on a different basis from the US one.[118] In 1936 he had predicted that the new president would be 'a sort of referee', who did not make decisions himself, 'but who refers matters to others for decisions under certain clearly defined conditions'.[119] This is how it turned out. The first president nominated for election by de Valera, Douglas Hyde, founder of the Gaelic League and a Protestant, was elected with no opposition, after an agreement on his nomination was secured with Fine Gael.

The question remains whether a semi-presidential system was intended. While the drafters never considered permanent executive powers for the President, the office could potentially have acquired more powers during an emergency. The three-year period when the constitution could be amended by ordinary legislation ran into 'The Emergency' (1939–45) when the state acquired further emergency powers. The initial presidential oath, from October 1936, had pledged the President to defend the state against 'its enemies whomsoever domestic and external'.[120] In late 1936, it was proposed that the President could head a national government during a state of emergency. Hence the decision to give the Dáil the power to declare an emergency was crucial. The proposal that the President could head a national government was dropped in the first official draft from March 1937, in which the powers of the President in an emergency were outlined in a separate section from the article (12) on his regular powers. Even in a state of emergency, the office would function as a constitutional safeguard. Nonetheless, since it was envisaged that a semi-presidential system could strengthen government in a situation of serious crisis, Fine Gael's fears were not entirely groundless.

As in mainland Europe, Irish governments thought emergency powers necessary to counter the influence of movements that tried to exploit the freedoms guaranteed by the democratic system in order to undermine its fundamental bases.[121] The belief helped undermine one constitution in 1931, while providing an impetus for another six years later. De Valera believed that democracy had its limitations during moments of emergency, but that parliamentary government was the best way to protect rights.[122] The 1934 committee had recommended that the article which conferred special powers in 1931 should be replaced by a simple constitutional article which would allow parliament, by ordinary legislation, to empower the executive to counter any state of emergency not amounting to armed rebellion or a state of war. This could involve the temporary suspension of many articles, which under normal circumstances would be regarded as fundamental, and the constitution should provide that nothing within it could be invoked to invalidate any emergency legislation enacted.[123] Article 28.3.3 of the constitution precludes the possibility of a court challenge to the constitutionality of any legislation which the parliament considers necessary, 'for the purpose of securing the public safety and the preservation of the state' when a national emergency has been declared to exist by both houses of parliament.[124] The provisions put a gloss on what would be a more or less permanent state of emergency. The constitution's transitory provisions resulted in an amendment allowing for a state of emergency to continue indefinitely. Declared in 1939, this continued, after more declarations, until 1976. Such provisions, and the execution of six IRA men during the war, led Séan MacBride, leader of the new republican party, Clann na Poblachta, to ask in 1949 whether the framers had altered their views since 1937, or whether they were so cynical that they never intended the constitution's provisions to be taken seriously in the first place.[125]

Yet the constitution was also intended to reconcile republicans. In 1932 the IRA Army Council had stated that 'only a constitution in which are enshrined the rights and principle of the (1916 republican) Proclamation so fearlessly set forth can claim the allegiance of the Irish people'.[126] In October 1935 the Gardaí advised de Valera that a new constitution would succeed in 'demilitarising the IRA' and removing the organisation 'as a serious menace to democratic government'.[127] To de Valera the passing of the External Relations Act in December 1936, which limited crown authority to the sphere of external relations, meant that 'we have in this state, internally a Republic, and so long as we have an act of parliament associating us in certain respects with the states of the British Commonwealth, we will have that association, and no longer'.[128] Articles 2 and 3 were drafted with the republican position in mind: de Valera stated that the constitution provided a framework in which domestic peace could be assured, *and* Irish unity restored.[129] A common criticism is that Valera's constitution constructed a barrier to unity. Yet in 1938 he stated that Northern Ireland could come in under the existing provisions for a local parliament and for a certain association with the Commonwealth. The Belfast parliament would retain its existing area of jurisdiction, while an all-Ireland parliament, elected on the basis of PR, would assume the powers reserved by the British Imperial parliament.[130] Thus both federalism and PR would have provided for minority representation under his constitution. Yet six of the seven surviving members of the second Dáil from 1921, released a statement on 22 May 1937 stating that 'the people of the 26 counties are being asked to kill and bury the Republic under an avalanche of votes.[131]

There was nevertheless an underlying consensus on the constitution's 'manifesto' qualities. The sections on nation and state, including Articles 2 and 3, found general acceptance. Labour wanted a Republic declared, but the dominant view was that this should be attendant on the reunification of the country. The claim to Northern Ireland first appeared in the first draft from late 1936, which claimed the nation's 'absolute' and 'indefeasible' right to the whole of the national territory. In de Valera's 'squared paper draft', however, it had only been stated that 'the territory of Éire shall be such as from time to time may come within the jurisdiction of Éire'.[132] It also suggested that co-operation between the two entities would follow a common threat, such as invasion. The absence of guarantees for the family, education, and property rights in the 1922 constitution had reflected, not differences over values, but rather an affirmation of the untrammelled sovereignty of parliament in these domains.[133] This had not prevented the passing of legislation reflecting Catholic morality before 1932. Divorce, made illegal in 1925, was made unconstitutional in 1937. The debate about the Directive Principles in 1937 was not over their Catholic origins. Some questioned what guide they would provide to the

Oireachtas, while others wanted them to have legal force.[134] John A. Costello worried that they could be 'moulded to the idea and theories of the socialists and even of the Communists'.[135]

The opposition could not antagonise religious feelings during the plebiscite, even if it wanted to. This suited the Catholic Church. Dr Michael Browne, the Bishop of Galway, declared on 3 January 1938:

> There are some sections of it which deal with political machinery; in these there are grounds for differences of view; they may be amended later by peaceful and legal methods. But the important section is that which deals with fundamental rights. On these articles there is no substantial difference between the three political parties, and there can be no difference.[136]

Opinion differs on whether the constitution established a Catholic state. De Valera remarked that the influence of the Ten Commandments formed the basis of the different religious minorities' acceptance of the document.[137] On New Years Day 1938 Cardinal McRory, Archbishop of Armagh and Primate of all Ireland, declared the constitution 'a Christian document'.[138] Yet the political scientist James Hogan believed that the constitution 'makes no bones about being the Constitution of a Catholic people'.[139] O'Rahilly praised de Valera's 'courageous exposition of Catholic social principles'.[140] McQuaid thought its Catholicity was established by its commitment to legislate in accordance with natural law.[141] Pope Pius XII also later praised it for being 'grounded in the bedrock of natural law', and praised a pact between Church and State, 'independent each in its own sphere', but allied in defence of Catholic faith and doctrine.[142] These perspectives went back to the materialist case for Home Rule. The Irish Catholic Church later claimed the constitution as its own: Jeremiah Newman, later Bishop of Limerick, declared in 1954 that it was the philosophy of law behind the constitution, rather than the nature of the Constitution itself, which mattered in any country.[143]

Hearne's draft preamble from May 1935 had begun with 'In the Name of Almighty God', but was otherwise completely secular.[144] After the intervention of the Jesuit committee formed to submit proposals the following year, de Valera decided to use the preamble to the April 1935 Polish constitution as a template for a new preamble, which gave the nationalist version of Irish history a religious imprint, similar to draft B's in 1922.[145] It reads:

> In the name of the Most Holy Trinity, from whom is all authority and to whom, as our final end, all actions both of men and states must be referred, we, the people of Éire, humbly acknowledging all our obligations to our Divine Lord, Jesus Christ, who sustained our fathers through centuries of trial, gratefully remembering

their heroic and unremitting struggle to regain the rightful independence of our Nation, and seeking to promote the common good, with due observance of prudence, justice and charity, so that the dignity and freedom of the individual may be assured, true social order attained, the unity of our country restored, and concord established with other nations, do hereby adopt, enact, and give to ourselves this Constitution.

The longer the drafting went on, the more the Catholic influence. De Valera could not risk the opposition of the Catholic Church in the referendum along with that of the other parties. Yet neither had he a desire to abstain from religious commitment in his constitution. The Irish, he believed, were 'a conservative people', who for 1,500 years had preserved the traditions and practiced the rules of the Christian way of life. In a broadcast speech on 15 June 1937 he stated:

> We stand in the world for the public worship of God in the way in which he has shown to be his will, without trespassing on the freedom of the individual to protect and practise his religion according to his conscience. We stand for the institution of the family, the indissolubility of the marriage bond, the right of private ownership, and liberty of speech, assembly and association subject to the moral law, the lawful authority of the State, and the exigencies of the Common Good. If ever there was a time in which it was desirable for or people – whose whole spiritual history has been that of an uninterrupted spiritual crusade to record a solemn declaration of their adherence to these fundamental principles, it is the time in which we live.[146]

In invoking the common good, recognising prudence, justice, and charity as ends of the state, and employing natural law as a limit on government, the constitution reflected an older constitutional tradition, neither exclusively political nor religious, according to which its enactment was 'a covenant', freely entered into by a people for the purpose of giving direction to civil society, and establishing a framework of government. This covenant could be compared to a moral pact, made under God, on the basis of equality among citizens. After such a pact the legislation of a state would be guided by certain ethical principles. As in the United States, the propriety of this legislation was to be judged in terms of its 'constitutionality', namely its conformity to both the natural law and the covenant made by the people. The preamble, the Directive Principles, and the requirement that officials (President and Senior judges) take oaths under God, reflect such a covenanting tradition, rooted in the Judeo-Christian past, but strong in the United States.[147] Establishing 'a Commonwealth', an expression used by de Valera in 1937, was the language of the early New England puritan states. De Valera explicitly used 'covenant' as a description of the constitution in 1937, and had campaigned for a revision of the Covenant of the League of Nations during his tour of the United States in 1919.[148] He was well aware of its meaning. The League's Covenant, he had argued, was intended 'to confirm and perpetuate the political relationships and conditions' established by the Treaty.[149] In 1936, as President of the League, he had also protested against Japan's flouting of the Covenant.

To de Valera, constitutional orders required a virtuous social order to flourish. In 1937 Ireland this order was a very conservative one. The 'covenant' analogy suggested that the constitution established a civic and social framework in which certain widely accepted ethical ends could be pursued. Cardinal McRory thought it provided for 'the upholding and guidance of a Christian state'.[150] Since the ethical ends could only be those valued by Irish society at the time, the question of whether the constitution was 'essentially liberal' or not misses the point of the analogy. The type of liberty which allows people to do more or less what they please, and that enables people to pursue the moral purposes for which the covenant was made, differ in nature, and would come into conflict in the 1960s and 1970s.[151] The constitution also went into detail on the appropriate social relationships – between men and women, among the family, and between the different Churches – that was criticised when these social relationships changed. According to Elazar, 'a covenant is the constitutionalisation of a set of relationships of a particular kind'.[152]

The nature of power in any traditional society rests on 'Plough Sword and Book' – the specific combination of landed wealth, coercive power, and the appeal of religion.[153] With the 1937 constitution the state's coercive powers were undiminished, the appeal to religious identity emphatic, and the values of the land system codified. The three most important institutions south of the border were the Catholic Church, the State, and the Land Commission, which had implemented a major land reform immediately after the civil war in 1923. A succession of land reform acts under the Union had already established the small farmer as the backbone of rural society. De Valera believed that:

> The basic conditions that make for social stability exist in Ireland more than in most other countries. The most important element in our population is the small farmer, proprietor of his land, who values highly the advantages of ownership. Most even of our urban population derives from the same stock and share the same sentiment.[154]

In 1931 he had declared that the right to private property was accepted by his party as 'fundamental', and as far as Catholics were concerned, there was 'definite teaching' upon it.[155] Liberal theorists believed that this right generally followed from the principle of individualism, while in the Catholic tradition it was subordinate to a particular view of social order. *Rerum Novarum* had declared individual ownership of land a natural right, and Article 43 states that man, 'in virtue of his rational being', has the natural right to private property. The 1922 provisions had not been based on natural law, but Article 11 of the 1937 constitution reproduced Article 10 from 1922. Yet the overall conception had changed:

> The theory underlying the old article 11 and the new article 10 is that all natural resources should belong to the state and should be exploited for the benefit of the people and not for the private property of individuals; that theory has no application to land because all land is the subject of private ownership, and in so far as the State owns land it does so in the same way as a private individual. Therefore natural resources and land must be dealt with separately in the Article.[156]

The preliminary draft from March 1937 also had had left-leaning clauses on private property, twice as long as those in the final constitution. They contained a clause stating that 'the State shall use its best endeavour to provide that the material resources of the nation may be so *distributed* among private individuals and the various classes of the population as adequately to procure the common good of the community as a whole.[157] McQuaid wanted them to say that 'the ownership of the material resources of the Nation may be distributed'.[158] 'Distribution' was later dropped, alongside clauses concerning men receiving an adequate wage, opportunities to work, and industrial wage bargaining.[159] Labour had played no role in the drafting of the constitution, and remained neutral in the plebiscite. Unlike in 1922, at no stage did officials suggest incorporating the 1919 Democratic Programme into the constitution.

Alongside 'Plough Sword and Book' was the question of gender. Article 41.2 of the constitution read:

> 2.1 In particular, the State recognizes that by her life within the home, woman gives to the State a support without which the common good cannot be achieved.
> 2.2 The State shall, therefore, endeavour to ensure that mothers shall not be obliged by economic necessity to engage in labour to the neglect of their duties in the home.

The use of gender-specific language, and the paternalistic ethos, contrasted with the 1916 Proclamation, which stated that the Republic guarantees equal rights and equal opportunities to all its citizens, and Article 3 from 1922 which declared every person within the Free State, without distinction of sex, a citizen. Yet the 1922 provisions had not prevented discriminatory laws being passed, such as the Juries Act of 1927. A variety of women's groups opposed the new constitution. Concrete examples of the process of retrenchment from Article 3 of the 1922 constitution were highlighted. Ex civil servants were not automatically reinstated on becoming widows, as in Britain. No women were retained after marriage in the civil service. The Irish Women Workers Association complained that Article 50 would be used to further restrict rights and liberties, not only of women, but of workers in general.[160] Dorothy MacArdle, feminist and republican writer, warned de Valera that the language could restrict work opportunities for women, and was not counter-balanced by any specific guarantees for them.[161] She thus withdrew the strong support she had given to de Valera's constitutional project in 1933.[162]

De Valera received deputations from the Standing Committee on Legislation Affecting Women, the Joint Committee of Women's Societies and Social Workers, and the Women Graduates of the National University on 14 May 1937. The second group represented fifteen societies, and wanted female representation in the Senate, female Gardaí, and the restoration of jury service.[163] The latter suggested that functional representation should be used to nominate women Senators, that a special panel for public servants be established, and that at least four of the Taoiseach's nominees should be women.[164] De Valera said that the lack of women representatives was due to the state of public opinion at the time, and promised to 'consider' the idea of a women's panel, giving no grounds for optimism. The panel idea did not materialise. No women's group or woman had been involved in the drafting, and a broad organisation representing their interests had not emerged after the civil war. Only five female TDs had been elected since 1922, and vocal opposition to the constitution was provided by female Senators, who had actually been involved in the suffrage movement before 1918.[165] In response to protests, especially from opposition deputies, several of the relevant articles were amended, but the constitution retained a stereotyped image of women's place in society.[166]

MacCurtain stresses the paradox: women were free after 1922 in the area which they had struggled for, but remained subordinate in the society they helped to create.[167] Prominent Irish women found themselves on the wrong side of the civil war divide. During the truce, in November 1921, Síghle Humphries told the Cumann na mBan convention in her Presidential address that it was time for action not talk.[168] The organisation's leadership cadres rejected the Treaty, and banned women who were members of any organisation doing work for the Free State from membership. When women carried the burden of campaigning for Sinn Féin in the August 1923 general election, the party was derided as 'The Women and Childers party' (a reference to Erskine Childers, executed the previous year). Cumann na mBan continued to see women primarily as auxiliaries in the ongoing fight for the Republic.[169] Yet as in Greece after its civil war, most women retreated to the private realm.[170] Their activist pedigree was now primarily identified with republican women who did not recognise the Free State. Cumann na mBan continued to hark back to the 1916 Proclamation as a possible source of equal rights and opportunities. Eithne Coyle, who succeeded Countess Markievicz as President of Cumann na mBan in 1926, thought the organisation had been founded as an 'independent Revolutionary Organisation' in 1914.[171] Mary MacSwiney believed that the question at issue after 1923 was whether a nation could surrender its right to freedom at the ballot box.[172] This was the same language the surviving members of the Second Dáil used to reject the 1937 constitution.

The stereotyping of women reflected the state–society relationship expressed in the constitution. De Valera thought Irish democracy based on a specific social order. He believed that the lack of urban–rural divisions, the people's individualistic tendencies, the existence of voluntary organisations, as well as the Catholic religion, worked against an Irish dictatorship.[173] The Irish state was democratic, founded on reason and individualism: 'the only states where liberalism is possible'. He also claimed continuity with the nineteenth-century movement to widen opportunity to all and to eradicate class differences.[174] The two cornerstones of nineteenth-century liberalism, the protection of rights and the existence of a written document not easy to amend, *were* achieved by his constitution. Yet contemporary critics of liberalism maintained that the state–society dualism this tradition presupposed was no longer valid. The 'society turned state' resulted in Soviet, social democratic, or welfare states. The 'state as the self-organisation of society' intervened in all aspects of social life, and also ended the old dualism in corporatist states like Portugal.[175] The 1937 constitution also projected an image of 'the state as the self-organisation of society', expressing values which defined its fundamental social relations. Constitutional norms, religious and secular, supported a limited state, but the organic and corporatist themes reinforced this image of the state. Independent Ireland's democratic combination of 'plough sword and book' was unique for a Catholic country in 1930s Europe, but women were subordinate in each realm.

The state as 'the self organisation of society' image meant that the constitution was something of a public relations disaster. In 1939 the English political philosopher Michael Oakeshott published *The Social and Political Doctrines of Contemporary Europe*. In a Catholic section clearly demarcated from the democratic one, he placed passages from de Valera's constitution, and compared Éire to Salazar's Portugal. Ironically, the most novel feature of the 1934 Portuguese constitution, that of parish councils with *ex-officio* clerical representation, had been proposed by the Jesuit priest, Edward Cahill, for the

1937 constitution, but was rejected by de Valera.[176] Oakeshott quoted the papal encyclical *Quadragesimo Anno* of 1891, which stated that though individuals had a right to join associations, organisations should be suppressed by the state if people joined together for purposes which were unlawful, or dangerous to the state.[177] This provided religious sanction for repressive laws, but Article 9 of the 1922 constitution had stated that laws regulating the manner in which the right of forming associations, and the right of free speech may be exercised, 'shall contain no political, religious, or class distinction'. Article 40.6.2 of the 1937 constitution contains exactly the same formulation. This was not quoted in Oakeshott's book. To its critics, its 'manifesto' qualities, not its legal and institutional provisions, established the identity of the constitution. This has remained the case.

CONCLUSION

Since the impetus of the constitutional enterprise, as it began in 1934, was to secure rights, much legal appraisal of the document focuses here. Historians have been more critical of its 'manifesto' qualities. It is possible to see the constitution in an evolutionary way, as a document which protected a set of rights appropriate to the level of society that existed at that time. Since these rights, no less progressive for their earlier provenance, were relatively advanced, there is no reason to judge the constitution an illiberal document. There was essential continuity through the Home Rule clauses, the personal rights clauses from 1922, and the recommendations of the 1934 committee. The evolutionary view contrasts with that of Ackerman's constitutional moment, in which rights are established by the exercise of the popular will. Yet rights were later imputed from the presence in the constitution of abstract concepts, such as human dignity, personal honour and social justice, and from the 'Christian and democratic' character of the state itself. The constitution departed from the classical view of rights as principles which must be protected from the state, and conceives of a society where the individual sometimes needs the state to realise the freedom they want to enjoy.[178] The constitution specifically enjoined the state to 'vindicate' the rights of its citizens. The 'protective function' of the state was transformed, anticipating West European legal developments in this area.[179] The fact that 'the state' is mentioned more than twenty times, while virtually absent in 1922, points to a conceptual new beginning.

With institutions, the claims of innovation meet those of restoration. Responsible government remained an organising principle, and the strong centralised state assembled during the civil war endured. The Governor General was abolished, but many of his powers were taken on by the

President. The Senate, once defunct, was resurrected with a gesture to functional representation. 'The principles of PR' were rejected in favour of the prescription of a particular electoral system, STV, but the 1923 electoral law remained in force. Kelly suggests de Valera and his civil servants poured new wine into old bottles, and there was less room for experimentation than in 1922. Yet while 1922 promised much, the 1937 constitution delivered a system where the exercise of power reflected the fundamental norms of the constitution. These norms were valued by the 1922 constitutional committee, but the Free State struggled to reconcile its Treaty commitments with the claims of popular sovereignty. In contrast, Bunreacht na hÉireann reasserted the Sinn Féin constitutional tradition, reconciling strong government on the British model to the concept of a fundamental law. Indeed three experimental elements from 1922 – PR, the referendum, and the Supreme Court – were strengthened, not weakened, by the 1937 constitution.

The ratification of the constitution through a plebiscite suggested a new beginning, but 1937 produced a constitutional moment only symbolically. Little public deliberation had taken place, the drafting was secretive, and popular support lukewarm. The mood was for consolidation not transformation. Revolutionary times pull things apart, but at moments of crisis covenants 'reassemble them through conscious acts of consent'. The 1937 constitution reflected a need for the polity 'to reconstitute itself along more suitable lines', and brought southern Ireland's revolutionary era to a close.[180] As with other European constitutions, the 1922 constitution had been drawn up mainly by lawyers, they wanted to limit the power of the executive, and their choices were dictated by theory rather than political expediency. In contrast, de Valera took advice from clerics, civil servants, politicians, and lawyers, the British cabinet system was reinforced, and the emergency provisions reflected the prevailing view that in periods of crisis the state should be allowed to employ all available constitutional powers in order to preserve the substance of democracy.[181] Yet the difference was not simply between the claims of idealism and experience, since by 1937 a post-partition society had also taken shape. Constitutions do not arise 'out of right established by laws, but rather out of right established relations'.[182] The 1922 constitution, unsure of its geographical and social moorings, did not possess a social order peculiar to itself, and prioritised experiment rather than consolidation. A constitution must be established on the basis of some type of social order if it is not to prove a sham.[183] By 1937 such a social order had taken shape, and the constitution reflected this basis, giving it further stability. Its conservative cast has made for a diverse group of critics. Yet their voices would only begin to be heard when partition and the religious nature of Irish society began to unravel. This unravelling forms the subject of the next chapter.

FOUR

CHALLENGE

THE REFERENDUM PROCESS

—

If there was first consensus on the 'manifesto' qualities of de Valera's constitution, by 1972 this had evaporated. De Valera had written a constitution expressing Catholic and nationalist values deeply shared by the vast majority of Irish people in 1937, ensuring that the society could develop without major conflicts until the late 1960s. After 1969 differences over these values, tied to different conceptions of national identity, quickly emerged. In 1969 Northern Ireland was plunged into civil conflict, and any future reform of its governance could also involve change to the Irish constitution, notably to Articles 2 and 3. The case for reform became more compelling as southern politicians reconsidered the 32-county context, and argued for another new beginning. Fine Gael's Tom Higgins declared that if North and South could sit down to write a new constitution with the same fairness which marked the foundation of the state 50 years earlier, 'a new beginning' could be made.[1] Yet since the constitution could only be changed by referendum, the scope of the debate was amplified, and the ensuing referendums tell the story of how the self-identity of southern Irish society changed after 1969. The referendum protected the constitution by making it more rigid, but since any successful constitution also has to adapt to crises, the balance between flexibility and rigidity proved central to its fate.

THE CONSTITUTIONAL CHALLENGE

The constitution had always been vulnerable to the critique that it would never have been accepted by a 32-county electorate. It was natural therefore that when the Republic tried to redefine its relations with Northern Ireland the 'manifesto' qualities would come under scrutiny. The civil rights protests reached their peak in 1969, and civil war conditions soon emerged in Northern Ireland. In 1971 Fine Gael's Ritchie Ryan remarked that as the 32 counties did not vote for it, the 1937 constitution could not be a constitution for the whole island.[2] In ancient Greek the concept of 'crisis' invokes decision and the southern elite faced fundamental choices. Between 1969 and 1974, when the Sunningdale power-sharing experiment collapsed, a constitutional moment was emerging. Fianna Fáil wanted a meta-constitutional settlement on Northern Ireland as a prelude to changes to the 1937 constitution, but others wanted amendments in advance of such a settlement. The Committee on the Implication of Irish Unity, established in May 1972, and that on Irish Relations, set up in July 1973, were to consider steps required to create conditions conducive to a united Ireland. Both considered constitutional change.

A variety of government committees had already addressed constitutional reform. The first was the Attorney General's legal committee, formed in 1962, to consider the legal implications of accession to the EEC. It produced a report in October 1967 and was reconvened in September 1969, when the prospect of membership was revived. An informal committee to consider the constitution first met in September 1966, and an all-party Oireachtas Committee was then appointed to review the constitutional, legislative, and institutional bases of government. Its report was published in December 1967. After the collapse of the Stormont system in Northern Ireland in 1972, the All Party Committee on the Implications of Irish Unity was formed, which was supplemented by a permanent interdepartmental unit, with senior officers from the departments of An Taoiseach, External Affairs, and Finance. This unit was to examine all matters affecting North–South relations. All three committees pointed towards constitutional change. The Attorney General's legal committee concluded that accession to the EEC would require a referendum, since international agreements did not prevail over domestic law under the constitution. It specified changes to Articles 5, 15.2, and 62.[3] The Oireachtas committee on the constitution suggested that reform of the Seanad, for example, would require 'wholesale' changes to the constitution. The question of a completely new constitution fell within the remit of the committee on the implications of Irish Unity. Furthermore, the government's establishment of a Commission on the Status of Women in 1970 was followed by the commission making 49 recommendations for change, some requiring constitutional change.

The 1967 Oireachtas committee had been instigated by Fianna Fáil's Taoiseach Seán Lemass, and Fine Gael and Labour participated on the grounds that members need not endorse its recommendations. When he first met the Attorney General to discuss its role, Lemass indicated his dissatisfaction with STV, the Senate, the referendum, and the Presidency.[4] The committee was eventually divided on most of these issues. STV had not prevented single-party government, there had been only one referendum since 1937, and the Supreme Court was not assertive. The President was considered largely a 'figurehead'. Yet the committee did propose revision of some key provisions, with Lemass calling the constitution 'a straitjacket' in a rapidly changing world. Yet on the machinery of government, the claims of foreign models were resisted by the committee, and a value placed on adhering to provisions which had worked well in practice.[5]

Subsequent debate focused more on the 'manifesto' qualities. At its sixth meeting in March 1967, the committee determined to express its views on substantive issues which would be of significance for at least a generation. There was unanimous support for change to the divorce law, as Articles 41.3 and 44.2 were criticised for not paying heed to minority views. The constitution was intended for the whole island, and its Roman Catholic portion, though large, was not overwhelming. Deletion of Article 44 on the status of religions was urged, and unanimously supported, as it was a useful weapon in the hands of those wanting to preserve the Northern system. It was thought that the name 'Ireland' for the 26-county state might be construed as an acceptance that the Northern Ireland system was satisfactory A rewording of Articles 2 and 3 was also proposed, in order 'to face the reality of the situation', and to remove one of the causes of friction.[6] These recommendations were not acted upon. Lemass retired in 1966, remained on the committee on the constitution, but responsibility for change fell on his successor, Jack Lynch.

Since the constitution had attempted to blend two potentially contradictory value systems, Catholicism and liberalism, when the bonds between Irish civil and religious society loosened in the 1960s, constitutional divisions reflected confusion about the nature of Irish identity.[7] The 1960s had seen a recession in conservative social teaching, more interest in individual rights, and growing religious ecumenism. Constitutional reform was discussed in some legal articles.[8] At an address to the annual conference in October 1967, Labour's leader Brendan Corish argued for *A New Republic*, remarking that the Irish people had never made a choice about the type of society they wanted.[9] The view among the left was that Irish democracy had 'failed in every way'.[10] Fine Gael's *A Just Society* programme suggested that the machinery of government had been taken over 'uncritically ' at the foundation of the state, and proposed major institutional reform.[11] The *Just Society* programme was first deemed compatible with the social doctrines contained in the Papal Encyclicals. With the Northern Irish conflict this view changed. In 1969 the Northern civil rights activist, Bernadette Devlin, declared that her ambition was not just to free 'the Six Counties', but to start the national revolution all over again. She repeated the claim that the Southern Irish had replaced the British in 1922, but not their system.[12]

As with previous critics of Fianna Fáil nationalism, those wanting constitutional change were not rejecting nationalism as such, but trying to formulate a new vision of nationhood compatible with processes of modernity they believed 'would ultimately be beneficial to Ireland'.[13] In his 1968 'New

Republic' speech Corish had claimed Labour's membership of a tradition of brave struggle, including the eighteenth-century Defenders, Wolfe Tone, and the 1916 Rising.[14] At a Treaty anniversary meeting held in Leinster House on 6 December 1971, Fine Gael's leader Liam Cosgrave had declared that the constitution which replaced that of 1922 now stood in the way of achieving Wolfe Tone's idea of substituting the common name of Irishman for those of Catholic, Protestant, and Dissenter.[15] Fine Gael's advocacy of a more pluralist society to attract unionists was later placed in the tradition of Tone and Thomas Davis, two famous Protestant nationalists.[16] Garret FitzGerald, who became Minister of Foreign Affairs in 1973, thought that the Irish public were willing to solve the Northern conflict by creating a new kind of society, rather than attempting to impose the Republic's cultural values and Catholic ethos on Northern Ireland.[17] FitzGerald hoped for the repeal of Article 44 and of the ban on divorce, and changes, among others, in the law on contraception, obscene literature and censorship.

The criticism that the religious ethos of the South extended to issues considered by Protestants to be matters of private conscience applied to the status of women. The 1937 constitution had reflected the collapse of the state–society dualism of the nineteenth century, but now critics wanted some dualism restored. On some issues, contraception for example, legal reform was sufficient. On others, such as divorce, constitutional amendment was necessary. On denominational education, change would require structural transformation over many decades. The women's movement was successful in the area of legal reform, but such was the array of grievances, and so fraught the interface between liberal, republican and socialist feminism, that divisions quickly appeared. Sinn Féin came to see their cause as a 32-county one, and would later invoke a succession of feminist and socialist activists from the past with common ground in equality for all.[18] Others immediately questioned whether the women's cause could be served by Irish republicanism. Contraception, divorce and abortion were subject to different opinions, but no one doubted that the social roles of men and women were changing, and there had been no accommodation in the constitution 'of the fundamental shift in attitudes and behaviour relating to the equality of the sexes'.[19]

The 1960s had brought increased women's participation in education, more employment opportunities, and greater expectations about marriage.[20] In 1968 the Irish Housewives Association and the National Federation of Business and Professional Women's Clubs organised a meeting of women to discuss a UN directive of the previous year, which had asked the member states to examine the 'status' of women in their respective countries. This meeting asked the government to set up a Commission on the Status of Women, which was established by Lynch at the end of 1969.[21] Composed equally of

men and women, its 1970 report made 49 recommendations. In the background was an awareness that judicial review could improve the status of
women, the prospect of EEC membership, and a growth in the number of
women's organisations followed (eventually from 17 to 45 between 1970 and
1980).[22] The initial demands were for equal pay, equality before the law, equal
education, contraception, justice for deserted wives, for unmarried mothers
and for widows, as well as one house, one family.[23] Yet the issues quickly became
extra-legal. When Senator Mary Robinson introduced a contraception bill,
Cardinal Conway declared that the issue was not about private morality, but
about the type of society people wanted.[24]

The feminists shared much with other critical perspectives on the
constitution. The 1937 constitution, they argued, had made no advance on the
rights already granted to women in 1918 and 1922, and contained nothing to
counter the discriminatory legislation passed since 1922.[25] Since 1945 a succession of legal treaties had established the principle of non-discrimination, and
the Irish state had not incorporated them into its laws. The constitution was
couched in gender-specific language, it inhibited necessary legal reforms,
and contained no acknowledgement of the role of women in public life. As
social conditions improved, the problems multiplied. There was the residue
of previous legislation to deal with: such as the Censorship of Publications
Act (1929), originally intended to stop the flow of tabloids from Britain,
the Criminal Law (Amendment) Act 1935, which forbade the importation,
distribution, and advertisement of contraception, and the Censorship of
Publications Act (1946) intended to control information on birth control.
International norms had also to be incorporated into domestic legislation. In
its report, the Commission on the Status of Women referred to the
Proclamation of the United Nations International Conference on Human
Rights in 1968, and the United Nations Declaration on Social Progress and
Development 1969, both of which referred to the rights of parents to
determine freely the 'number and spacing' of their children.[26] To monitor
implementation of the commission's findings, a Council on the Status
of Women came into being, and in 1974 'A Women's Representative
Committee' was set up by the Minister for Labour, which would be replaced
in 1982 by a new Ministry for Women's Affairs.[27] Legal reform was achieved
more easily when required by supranational, especially European, legislation.
Most of the rights associated with citizenship, including equal pay and
treatment, job security for married women, and social security, eventually
emanated 'more from supra-national than national political institutions'.[28]
This left the constitution itself as an object of dispute. When the liberal
feminist, Nuala Fennell, published *Irish Marriage How Are You?* in 1974, it
began by quoting Article 41 on the status of marriage.[29]

In the 1960s, new thinking was also emerging on Northern Ireland. Lemass had proposed unification by agreement as Dublin's objective. In 1965 he proposed an all-Ireland federation, where Stormont would continue to exercise the same powers over the same territory. A Council of Ireland could help bring this about, as would co-operation on practical matters. An Irish Common Market might also make unity more attractive. Lemass, with a phrase used by Arthur Griffith to justify the 1921 Treaty, hoped to bring about the 'essential unity' of the Irish people, without revision to Articles 2 and 3.[30] In 1969 Fine Gael made a case for seeking, through closer relations with Britain, to persuade its government to move towards a solution of the Northern Ireland problem 'in conjunction' with the Republic.[31] The alternative to supporting the IRA, rejected by all parties in the Dáil, was to trade on Ireland's status as a sovereign state to get a settlement influenced by Dublin. In 1970 the legal adviser of the Department of External Affairs was asked to draft a general constitutional amendment that might get round specific constitutional difficulties with regard to the North by, perhaps, an international agreement with Britain.[32] So unity might involve another 'treaty to constitution' process. For T. K. Whitaker in 1969, unity would require guarantees that the North would not have to accept southern standards on divorce and censorship. The recommendations of the 1967 constitutional committee, on divorce and the special position of the Catholic Church, would have to be implemented. Article 3 would have also to be amended to remove the implication that Dublin had *de jure* control over Northern Ireland.[33]

Some leading southern politicians stressed the need to respond to the Northern conflict by accommodating various criticisms of the constitution. In September 1969 Labour's Conor Cruise O'Brien argued that if the Southern parties had agreed to achieve a united Ireland peacefully, as they had done, Articles 2 and 3 had to go.[34] Fine Gael issued a ten-point plan for peace and reconciliation, one of which proposed revising the constitution in consultation with groups from Northern Ireland.[35] The door was open to Northern groups to make proposals to the Dublin governments: the Alliance Party, the New Ulster Movement, the SDLP, and the Protestant churches, did so. Sinn Féin stressed the need to address the perception that Home Rule was Rome Rule.[36] Anthony Coughlan, of the civil rights organisation Solidarity, thought that constitutional change was needed both to ensure the civil liberties of Southern Protestants, and to dispel the fears of Northern Protestants.[37] The *Church of Ireland Gazette* thought more was required than revisions of some articles, since the teachings of the Catholic Church were also discernible in laws governing marriage and divorce, censorship and literature, and family planning.[38] In 1970 the Unionist leader, Brian Faulkner, implied that the Southern state did not have civil rights.[39] The line between liberal democracy and Catholicism in 1937 had been a thin one. Now critics questioned whether it existed.

Conor Cruise O'Brien was Minister of Posts and Telegraphs in the Fine Gael coalition government between 1973 and 1977. He remained Labour spokesperson on Northern Ireland in this period, and argued that the prospects for unity depended on changing the image of the Irish State in the eyes of Northern Protestants. In August 1969 O'Brien had signed a report on Northern Ireland, which stated that not only the B Specials, but the existence of the 'entire' Stormont regime was incompatible with socialist principles.[40] At that time the Irish Labour Party wanted Northern Ireland placed before the UN, a suspension of Stormont and, through local plebiscites, 'the abolition of the institutionalised caste system' on the road to a united Ireland.[41] O'Brien changed tack. In a confidential memorandum in 1970 he suggested that unity could be achieved only by agreement, and that the Irish government should not appeal to the British over the unionist heads. It should be made clear to the unionists that, having abolished one sectarian state, they were not trying to bring them into another. He thought that the unionists were being invited to join 'a Catholic state'. This pointed to amendments, notably to Article 44. Articles 2 and 3 he rejected as 'abstract legalistic or constitutional determinism'.[42]

A new constitution fell within the terms of reference of the Committee on Irish Relations. This committee had received the New Ulster Movement, Cardinal Conway of the Catholic Church, the SDLP, and the Church Committee of the Church of Ireland in both 1973 and 1974. It also met with the Alliance Party, the Northern Ireland Labour Party, the Irish Sovereignty Movement, the Methodist and Presbyterian Churches, the Irish Association, and the Northern Ireland committee of the Irish Congress of Trade Unions. The Ulster Unionist Party and the Vanguard Unionist Party were not interested in meeting the committee. On 10 July 1974 revision of the constitution was discussed, and the view expressed that only when the elected representatives of the North and South came together to discuss the island's future should constitutional change be considered.[43] This remained Fianna Fáil's position. Conor Cruise O'Brien thought the committee had been established as an excuse for inaction. In January 1974 he had urged Liam Cosgrave to try to get the committee to support a new constitution, to show that the whole epoch of Fianna Fáil domination, and 'their definition of what was national', had ended. O'Brien wanted such a constitution (like that of 1922) to be 'simpler, less grandiloquent, and less ecclesiastical in tone and language'. People would accept such a document in a referendum if shown it could serve the cause of peace and reconciliation.[44]

The Northern parties viewed the reform agenda through the prism of Northern interests. On 1 May 1974 delegates from the Alliance Party told the

Committee on the Implications of Irish Unity that it was not appropriate for them to comment on the constitution in general, but revision of Articles 2 and 3 would bolster unionist support for Sunningdale.[45] They were told that consensus between the main parties was necessary for amendment to them. The New Ulster Movement complained to the Committee on Irish Relations that the Cosgrave government's recognition, with Sunningdale, of Northern Ireland's *de facto* status as part of the UK, meant nothing until Articles 2 and 3 were removed.[46] The possibility of defeat in a referendum was again stressed. Seamus Mallon led an SDLP delegation on 18 January 1974. They suggested that the reform agenda be pursued in the context of Sunningdale. The aim should be the establishment of a pluralist society on the island, but the party was 'slow' to express a view on specific changes.[47] In the SDLP's 1972 *Towards a New Ireland*, the focus was on such new all-Ireland institutions, with nothing on the reform agenda south of the border.[48]

Lynch (Taoiseach first from 1966 to 1973) was accused of backtracking. In 1970 he had stated that the 1937 constitution reflected the deep and genuine religious outlook of the majority of the people at that time, but if some provisions were legitimately seen by people as infringements of their civil liberties, their voices should be accommodated. Article 44 on the status of religions would go if regarded as an obstacle to unity. Lynch was personally opposed to divorce, but thought the state should not legislate for private morality.[49] Lynch linked the case for reform to that of an all-island settlement, promising in February 1971 to 'grasp the nettle' if the result were to be a just and lasting peace. Yet at a meeting with the British Prime Minister Edward Heath and with Brian Faulkner at Chequers in August 1971, he made no commitments on divorce, contraception, or censorship laws. The meeting was dominated by the issue of internment. Instead, in December 1971, Lynch proposed the establishment of an all-party committee with the task of 'regulating a Constitution suitable for a united Ireland as part of an overall negotiation to achieve a united Ireland'. This committee was not established until May 1972. The worsening violence affected Lynch's attitude to reform, and he argued against changing the constitution in advance of a general settlement which would necessarily require further changes.[50] During his first period in office, southern opinion was influenced by the repression of Northern Catholics. On 16 July 1974 the Committee on Irish Unity agreed that it would be unwise to draft a new constitution, or to initiate a referendum on Articles 2 and 3. Instead it stressed the need to get the British Army under control, with a view to stopping harassment of Catholics in areas of Belfast and Derry.[51]

Fianna Fáil's George Colley remarked that the readiness to change the constitution would indicate the strength of republican sentiment, but the

Republic lacked a strong secular meaning for many nationalists.[52] Desmond Fennell reflected that many Irish intellectuals had seen the purpose of the Sinn Féin revolution to create a native and democratic state, radically different from the liberal capitalist state. Their thinking had been inspired, one way or another, by Catholicism.[53] In response to a request by Lynch for a definition of 'republic', officials had responded that it meant a state in which the power of government rested with the people, and was exercised on their behalf through their democratically elected representatives. This view was then published by Lynch in an article, 'Definitions of Irish republicanism', for the *Irish Independent*.[54] In 1972 Lynch declared a united Ireland inevitable, but unity should not mean the 'assimilation' of Northern Ireland into the existing structures of the Republic. He did not believe that the 1937 constitution was suitable for a new Ireland. A new constitution would be firm on rights and liberties, and these should relate to the individual citizen rather than to the institutions as such. Its drafters should take a 'minimal' approach – that is not start from 'broad philosophical assumptions' – but try to obtain broad agreement on what was necessary for government to function, while securing rights for the individual.[55] This implied a very different constitution.

The question of whether a Republic required a separation of Church and State remained. The 1937 constitution was criticised for being 'confessional'. Lynch objected to the depiction of Ireland as 'a Church-controlled State', since the Catholic Church played no role in the making or administration of laws.[56] His critics objected that the philosophy behind the constitution was at issue. The journalist Arthur Noonan argued that the constitution had soured the ideal of religious freedom by trying to spell it out. Listing the denominations in a particular order expressed a preference, however accidental.[57] Another journalist, John Horgan, observed that Lynch had not rejected de Valera's equation of Irishness with Catholicism, seeing change not as a new beginning suitable for a twentieth century state, but in terms of 'a see-saw' balancing act between Catholicism and Protestantism.[58] Lynch did believe that the Churches' collective views should be taken into account when changing the constitution.[59] Fine Gael's John Kelly objected to his emphasis on offering the North a constitutional deal first, and giving only secondary importance to assuaging fears by amending the constitution. He wanted a more secular preamble.[60] In 1966 the Attorney General's legal committee had suggested that the preamble could be amended by referendum, whether or not it was a provision of the constitution.[61]

Some stressed the constitution's stabilising qualities. The legal reformer John Temple Lang saw value in its fundamental purpose of taking the basic rules of the state out of the hands of temporary majorities.[62] Fianna Fáil's Minister of Justice Desmond O'Malley called it an 'admirable fundamental law', which was later copied in Burma and India.[63] Lemass, who recalled that some provisions were introduced in 1937 only to deflect opposition, later agreed that the constitution should only be changed by referendum.[64] Fr Desmond Faul, of St Patrick's Academy Dungannon, said that Northerners had the same views on the constitution as Southerners, and defended the appropriateness of expressing social values in it.[65] A constitutional committee of the Catholic Knights of Columbanus supported the idea of a new document, which would still express the religious views of the vast majority of Irish people.[66] The future President, Fianna Fáil's Erskine Childers, believed that that there had been little discrimination against Protestants under the constitution, although accepting that Article 44 would have to go with Irish unity.[67] Many who would later dominate the country's intellectual life found their voice in this debate. The feminist lawyer Mary Bourke (later Mary Robinson) stressed the need for the constitution to mature with the nation.[68] She wanted a debate on the nature of republicanism, and a new constitution in place of one whose provisions on the family and education 'obstructed' political reform.[69] Such a new beginning would result in 'a non-denominational state', and Bourke contrasted the slow pace of reform with the vigour with which the ground was prepared for EEC membership.[70]

As late as November 1975, Cosgrave was being asked in the Dáil about a new constitution. Yet during negotiations over Sunningdale he had reportedly told the Unionist leader Brian Faulkner that he could not offer revision of Articles 2 and 3 because of doubts whether the public would accept change in a referendum.[71] The next two decades would frustrate those wanting change. Fianna Fáil's support was crucial to any major amendment, but with a conservative support base it later opposed much of the liberal agenda. The Committee on Irish Relations had been intended to reach the maximum area of agreement, but its membership (Fianna Fáil 8, Fine Gael 5, Labour 3) put Fianna Fáil in a strong position. The party was deeply divided on the North. The committee had proposed consideration of Article 3. The 1967 committee had suggested a substitute clause stating that 'The Irish Nation hereby proclaims its firm will that its territory be re-united in harmony and brotherly affection between all Irishmen'.[72] Yet there was no consensus on change. In 1974 the committee discussed changes to the religious tone of the preamble, giving the English language equal status with Irish, denominational education, and minority representation in the Oireachtas. It was again unable to reach agreement. In a meeting held in August 1974 it was stated that the constitution stood in the way of change, and no suggestion had yet been made on the committee that would command 'widespread support' among the people. Reports in the press of divisions, and opposition from the Fianna Fáil members, forced the committee to drop constitutional issues, and focus on areas, such as

education, where there might be agreement.[73] The committee stopped
meeting in June 1975, with the parties blaming each other for its problems.

Frank O'Connor once said of Yeats that when a great man dies, not only
does a new era spring up, but 'a phase of reality ends'. The things which
happen after such a man dies may have been happening before then, but only
his death reveals their importance.[74] The challenge to de Valera's constitution
had its roots in the 1960s, but only later did 'de Valera's Ireland' itself become
'a phase of reality'. A hegemonic value system had lost its 'taken for granted'
nature. The role of the Irish Catholic Church in health and education, the
traditional gender roles, the connection between religious and national identity,
and specific laws reflecting Catholic morality, were not disputed with any
force before the 1970s. By not separating Church and State on the US model,
the constitution made conflict over such issues inevitable. In other young states,
such as Israel and Turkey, when new social forces emerged to challenge the
monopolistic nature of the post-independence value system in the 1990s, identity crises also followed. Values once thought harmonious became antagonistic,
as people were forced to emphasise the secular or the religious components of
their identity, or the sub-national versus the national identity.[75] A change in
the state–society relationship also took place in 1960s Ireland. The growth of
the mass media and the welfare state challenged the 'moral monopoly' of the
Catholic Church. The entry of women into the labour force upset traditional
gender roles. Church and State were facing an increasingly educated population. 'Identity crises' happen in a young person's life when an accepted and
unquestioned definition of self is no longer acceptable under a new set of
conditions. Such an analogy helps capture the constitutional challenge after
1969. Yet the referendum requirement was peculiar to Ireland. In Israel, with
no written constitution, the tensions between the democratic and religious
visions of the state were played out in the deliberations of its Supreme Court.
In Turkey the constitutional court has also been crucial. In Ireland the juxta-
position between an Oireachtas largely receptive to reform of a liberal nature,
and a traditionalist lobby very adept at using the device of the referendum for
its own ends, guaranteed the persistence of 'moralistic' politics into the 1990s
and beyond.[76]

THE REFERENDUMS

Constitutions are 'external' to the political system in that the things which
give them authority – their place in an independence struggle, their connection
with the founding fathers, the values they express – are outside the political
system. Yet constitutions are also 'internal' in that they shape the distribution

of power across government institutions.[77] As the nationalist, patriarchal, and religious values which first gave the Irish constitution 'external authority' have been challenged, the way the constitution distributes power across institutions has been fundamental to how these value conflicts worked themselves out. This explains the increased importance of the courts, the presidency, and the referendum, in recent decades. For a long period judges rarely found against the government, so respectful were they of the British concept of parliamentary sovereignty. After 1960 a more assertive attitude emerged. What followed was a 25-year period in which almost 100 separate statutory provisions and common law rules were either found unconstitutional, or radically modified in some way by the courts.[78] The President's referral of bills to the Supreme Court increased from once in the 1960s, to twice in the 1970s, to three times in the 1980s, to four times in the 1990s. The state gradually ceased to be a purely representative democracy. There was no referendum in the 1940s, one in the 1950s, two in both the 1960s and 1970s, but almost twenty after 1980. The constitution has been transformed from 'a background political document', to the central engine of legal development in the state.[79]

In the 1930s and 1940s the civil servants expected that referendums, constitutional and ordinary, would be inevitable. Article 51 provided for constitutional amendment by ordinary legislation, within the period of three years after the date upon which the President shall have entered office. On 29 January 1940, all government departments were asked to suggest desirable amendments, and these were reviewed by an interdepartmental committee after consultation with the Taoiseach. They resulted in the second amendment of the Constitution Bill 1941. Since the 1922 provisions had lapsed, the new referendum procedure had also to be refined. The Referendum Act of 1942 followed a series of exchanges between the Attorney General's Office, the government, and the Department of Local Government and Public Health, between August 1937 and February 1942.[80] On 3 September 1937 the Executive Council had decided for the simplest method of voting (in which the alternatives given to the voter would be *Tá* (for) or *Níl* (against)). On whether a referendum on a constitutional amendment was a matter for the government to decide there was disagreement, since it had first been assumed that any bill for the amendment of the constitution would automatically go to a referendum.[81] Not surprisingly, the government first wanted the right to defer the referendum, or to allow the amendment to elapse, but protests in the Dáil and Seanad followed. The Department of Local Government and Public Health warned that the government's powers in this area were 'equivalent to a veto', but the Fianna Fáil government stuck to them after its meeting on 23 March 1942.[82] They subsequently became law in the referendum Acts of 1942 and 1946, giving the constitutional referendum its discretionary quality.

This discretionary quality raises the question of the extent to which it is possible to speak of popular sovereignty, where the degree of involvement of the people in making constitutional decisions is the touchstone of their sovereignty.[83] The Irish state fits the pattern in which 'occasional' to 'frequent' users of the referendum have a mandatory or optional requirement in their laws.[84] Only Italy and Switzerland hold more referendums in Europe, but the Irish state has only held them on bills to amend the constitution. An ordinary referendum on government legislation has never taken place. This means that the people have been continually involved in making constitutional decisions. No amendment has been passed by any other means since 1941. The referendum is obviously integral to the constitution, generating a high degree of legitimacy for the new document in 1937, but also fostering co-ordination around this new set of rules since then.[85] This is because certain constitutional norms, not peculiar to Ireland, have been generally accepted by Irish elites since 1937.

Since the fall of communism the number of European states that have adopted their constitutions by referendum, and stipulate extraordinary mechanisms for amending them, has increased. As in Ireland, 'the mode of the '*pouvoir constituent*', as exercised at one instance, has the capacity to lock the constituent functions of the future to this same level, in the same way as provisions concerning amendments in established constitutions'.[86] This is firstly because subsequent amendments, to gain the same degree of constitutional legitimacy, have to be enacted through procedures enjoying the same or higher degrees of legitimacy as the adoption of the constitution. Secondly, the stability of any constitution relates to the special constraints that apply to its amendment, and these lend stability to its basic norms.[87] In February 1942 the department (Local Government) responsible for holding referendums outlined a similar logic:

> The Constitution is the fundamental law of the State and it is therefore essential that there should be no element of uncertainty with regard to amendments, passed or deemed to have been passed by both Houses of the Oireachtas. If such an amendment were passed and did not proceed to a referendum, the position of the bill proposal would be unstable, and it is considered that some provision should be made by law, within and subject to the Constitution, to deal with that position.[88]

The referendum thus makes for a relatively rigid constitution. On 25 March 1966, Seán Lemass declared that since the government was now entrusted with more responsibility for socio-economic progress, some constitutional provisions might be anachronistic. He did not wish to sacrifice, 'for the sake of democratic freedom', anything more 'in the way of efficiency than we have to'. He proposed a less 'costly' and 'cumbersome' method of constitutional amendment, when no serious divisions existed, such as requiring extraordinary parliamentary majorities.[89] His informal constitutional committee noted that the situation created by the Treaty of Rome meant that a more flexible method of constitutional amendment was required. Lemass's proposal was not accepted. Some objected that this would undermine the sanctity of the constitution, which was the citizens' bulwark between them and the parliament. The people were 'particularly attached to the idea that the Constitution is a charter which only they can adopt, enact, and give to themselves'.[90] The referendum could only be removed by referendum, and the issue was not put to the people.

The constitution makes major institutional change hard to achieve, especially if proposed by only one party. A republican constitution should provide for 'non-domination', whereby the power of the state is limited both by law and by institutional devices. It should not be easy to change laws that are important from a non-domination point of view, and the more important the change 'the more it should have to pass along a different route' from ordinary legislation.[91] The electorate's veto of two Fianna Fáil attempts to replace STV with the British electoral system (in 1959 and 1968) suggested the procedure worked in this way. The 1922 committee had clearly conceived of the referendum protecting the people from the practice of arbitrary rule. The removal of PR raised the spectre of even greater Fianna Fáil dominance, so the provisions still provided a popular veto in this sense. In 1996 Gallagher noted that of eighteen referendums that had taken place, of the six initiated by government without the support of the opposition only one was approved.[92] By 1970 the referendum had acquired the reputation for having a no bias.

Did this no bias apply to non-institutional issues? The case for constitutional change was strongest when framed in a 32-county context. When the Committee on the Implications of Irish Unity met on 2 February 1972, its chair Michael O'Kennedy noted that there was a real danger that the people would reject proposals for constitutional change on a 26-county basis.[93] The Knights of Colombanus, the Association of Irish Priests, the Irish Theological Association, the Archbishop of Tuam (Joseph Gunnane), and the Bishops of Kildare and Leighlin (Patrick Lennon), and Killaloe (Michael Harty), had originally supported the idea of a new constitution if a united Ireland emerged.[94] The constitution was first amended by referendum in 1972, when the deletion of Article 44 on the status of religions was approved, with the backing of the Catholic Church. Lynch argued that the proposed changes would contribute towards Irish unity, and be indicative of the 'outward-looking' approach of the government and the people towards Irish unity. The amendment was opposed by a small new movement called 'Defend 44', which saw change as the prelude to the introduction of the permissive society to Ireland. However, the opposition parties supported the amendment, accepted by over 70 per cent of voters. Nevertheless, Liam Cosgrave believed that an entirely new constitution was needed to attract the North, while Corish argued that de Valera's constitution should be replaced by 'a genuinely republican document without any taint of sectarianism'.[95]

With the collapse of Sunningdale in 1974, one source of constitutional idealism dried up, and differences over religion came to dominate the southern debate. In a throwback to the materialist case for Home Rule, some assumed the existence of a Catholic nation, north and south, entitled by their numbers, to a constitution expressing their values. In *Ireland Must Choose*, Jeremiah Newman, the Bishop of Limerick, quoted Pope John Paul II's 1979 admonition to Irish youth, to stay loyal to their Catholic faith. He thought it strange that the views of non-Catholic minorities should take precedence over the Catholic majority on constitutional issues.[96] Others saw change as a way of reaching out to the unionists. In the 1970s the impetus for constitutional change had been buried in two committees. In the 1980s the divisions were more in the open and were adjudicated by the referendum. At a speech delivered to the Irish-American Lawyers Association on 23 September 1981, the Attorney General Peter Sutherland declared it appropriate that the constitution be reviewed in certain respects. The report of the 1967 committee was outdated, and supervening developments in constitutional theory could produce a different approach. Sutherland spoke of the need for the constitution to protect the rights of the individual 'in the context of diverse beliefs', to promote a pluralist society, and to take cognisance of the rights and sensibilities of the majority of those resident in Northern Ireland.[97] Then, on 28 September 1981, on RTÉ's *This Week* programme, Garret FitzGerald committed Fine Gael to a 'constitutional crusade' to create 'a genuine Republic' on the principles 'of Tone and Davis'. This would involve removing the 'sectarian' element in the Republic's institutions and laws, and modifying Articles 2 and 3.[98] The Alliance Party welcomed this as 'historic'. The Ulster Unionist Party thought such reforms good for the South itself. Peter Robinson of the Democratic Unionist Party thought it an admission that the southern state had a sectarian basis.[99] Up to the Anglo-Irish Agreement of 1985, the door remained open to Northern parties to present their views to the Fine Gael-led coalition.[100] FitzGerald had hinted at amendments without the support of Fianna Fáil, who promised 'a crusade' in defence of Articles 2 and 3. FitzGerald was Taoiseach between 1981 and 1982, and between 1982 and 1987.

Differences extended to the form of Irish unity. The constitutional nationalist parties took part in the New Ireland Forum in 1983. Its 1984 report suggested that a new Ireland would require a new constitution, and that the needs of the diverse Irish traditions be met.[101] Yet while Fine Gael advocated a confederal structure for a united Ireland, Fianna Fáil proposed retaining a unitary structure. FitzGerald contrasted its 'single-ethos nationalism' with the 'instinctive pluralism' of the smaller parties.[102] Differences over Articles 2 and 3 went back to the 1970s. In 1974 the Committee on Irish Relations had told a deputation from Northern Ireland that there needed to be a consensus on the North before a referendum on these articles could be held, and a defeat in such a referendum would be worse than the present situation.[103] Labour's Conor Cruise O'Brien and Barry Desmond, and Fine Gael's Declan Costello and Paddy Harte, had strongly supported change. Fianna Fáil wanted the articles discussed only when North and South met to agree All-Ireland political arrangements.[104] De Valera had believed that the 1937 constitution had invested the southern state with a new legitimacy, and removed obstacles to the pursuit of Irish unity by constitutional means. Amending the articles would diminish Fianna Fáil's claim to be 'The Republican Party', and leave the state without a bargaining chip in subsequent negotiations.

On most moral issues, Fianna Fáil's opposition to liberalising amendments and its tacit alliance with the Catholic Church meant that one person's 'constitutional safeguard' became another's 'conservative device'. The referendums on PR had allowed minorities fearful of domination to protect their rights, but moral issues were determined by the views of the majority. The value of a constitutional safeguard is logically diminished when consensus about the content of the constitution becomes low. Labour's 1980 programme for government proposed a new constitution 'as a clear and unequivocal demonstration of our *bona fides* about the creation of a non-sectarian state'.[105] In his 1982 Dimbleby lecture, Garret FitzGerald envisaged a new constitutional order, 'purged' of 'accretions' which had obscured the common concern for liberty in the nationalist and unionist traditions.[106] The newly formed Progressive Democrats would publish 'a constitution for a New Republic' in 1988. On 1 October 1981 Peter Sutherland announced that he would conduct a wide review of the constitution.[107] He believed that the constitution 'must express in tangible and positive form the desire for reconciliation and peace on this island'.[108] When questioned on the appropriateness of the Attorney General entering into the constitutional debate, Sutherland argued that constitutional reform was a matter of law. Yet he believed the issues were both legal and political. The constitution ought to encourage pluralism, to reconcile rather than polarise the island's population, and this was an area where debate had been allowed to wane over the previous five years.[109] Dennis Kennedy caught the mood of the 1980s:

> What makes this so depressing in 1981 is that in the late 1960s when this particular Northerner took up residence in the Republic, it was possible to see breaks in the clouds all around. There was a strong liberal movement, and it seemed problems

like divorce and contraception, were going to be tackled. It was fashionable to advocate a pluralist society, and permissible to contemplate a secular one. It was even possible for some to see Mr George Colley as a radical, and to believe Mr Jack Lynch when he said nettles would have to be grasped. More than a decade on, there is no progress on divorce, little enough on contraception, and now a united rush to enshrine the Catholic view on abortion in the Constitution.[110]

The eighth amendment was introduced to make abortion, illegal before 1983, unconstitutional. The fear that abortion could be introduced into Ireland by the Dáil or the courts was at the heart of a campaign launched by the Pro-Life Amendment Campaign, formed after the Pope's visit in 1979. All parties were aware of the precedent of *Roe* v *Wade* in the USA, where the Supreme Court had found a right to abortion under the right to privacy in the constitution.[111] Both the larger parties wanted to protect a pro-life position, but a more economical amendment drawn up by Sutherland was rejected. His clause would have prevented the Supreme Court finding an unspecified right to abortion in the constitution, but otherwise leave the matter of abortion legislation to the Oireachtas.[112] Fianna Fáil proposed the following amendment:

> The state acknowledges the right to life of the unborn, and with due regard to the equal right of life of the mother, guarantees in its laws to protect, and as far as practicable, by its laws, to defend and vindicate that right.

This was subsequently opposed by Labour, Fine Gael, and the Church of Ireland. The Catholic Church became heavily involved in the campaign, stressing that Catholics had an obligation to vote, and highlighting the danger of abortion being introduced in Ireland. Fianna Fail's amendment was passed by a two to one majority, with 66.45 per cent voting yes. The result was clearly a vindication of the Catholic Church's authority, and demonstrated the vulnerability of the referendum to a campaign orchestrated by well-organised interest groups.

Progress on constitutional change was held up by the economic crisis of the 1980s, and the ongoing Northern Irish conflict. It was in such a context that another bitter referendum took place in 1986. Opinion polls had shown large majorities in favour of divorce under carefully defined circumstances.[113] Yet the activists of the Anti-Divorce Campaign were able to rely on the support of the Catholic clergy and members of Fianna Fáil in their efforts to frustrate change. The tactic of playing on the public's fears of what would happen to property rights if divorce were permitted proved decisive. By 63 to 37 per cent the amendment was rejected, leading many to doubt the viability of the whole liberal project. The 1983 campaign over abortion had quickly broadened to include arguments about the 'confessional' nature of the constitution: the independent TD Noel Browne declared Haughey's determination to have a referendum on abortion was in accord with the 'bigoted nationalists of the brand of republicanism favoured by his predecessor, Mr de Valera'.[114] Hesketh called the 1983 amendment *The Second Partitioning of Ireland*. The rejection of divorce in 1986 was the third.

The next amendments in 1992 were intended to qualify the right to life of the unborn, rather than to broaden the basis on which abortion would be permitted. The catalyst was 'the X case', that of a 14-year-old girl who in February 1992 was denied the legal right to travel to Britain to obtain an abortion as a result of a rape. This decision was then reversed by the Supreme Court which ruled that under the terms of the 1983 amendment abortion would be permissible in Ireland 'if it is established as a matter of probability that there is a real and substantial risk to the life as opposed to the health of the mother, which can only be avoided by the termination of her pregnancy'.[115] Since the 1983 contradiction amendment had provided no solution, the Catholic Church and the anti-abortion movement demanded a new referendum to reinforce its objective. While conceding the need to clarify issues left over by the Supreme Court decision, the parties shared a permissive attitude to freedom of travel and to freedom of information about abortion services, and were determined to exclude the interest groups from the policy-making process.

Opinion polls showed that in 1990 a majority of adults, and a huge majority of young adults, were prepared to accept abortion if the mother's health was at risk.[116] The election of Mary Robinson – who had opposed the 1983 amendment – as President in 1990 suggested a growing liberal constituency. The authority of the Catholic Church was also dented in 1992 by the revelation that the Bishop of Galway, Eamon Casey, had fathered a child and used Church funds to help raise it in America. Nevertheless, Fianna Fáil's Taoiseach Albert Reynolds, while accepting the Supreme Court judgement, was determined to legislate for it in the most conservative way possible. The proposed amendments distinguished between permitting abortion when the life as opposed to the health of the mother was at stake, the probability of suicide not being considered a basis for a threat to the life of the mother. By large margins, freedom to travel and of information were accepted by the electorate, but the new wording on abortion, where there were party differences, was rejected. The consequence was stalemate: although abortion was now legally permissible under certain conditions, in practice no abortions were likely to take place.[117]

When divorce was voted on again in December 1995, there was all-party consensus on an amendment to the article prohibiting divorce proposed by the 'rainbow coalition' of Fine-Gael, Labour, and Democratic Left. Fianna Fáil's support was partly due to the fact that the government had decided to write into the constitution the conditions under which divorce would be tolerated, specifying the number of years a couple had to be separated in order to qualify for divorce. Before the referendum, the government consulted opinion polls to decide what the public was willing to accept in advance of wording the amendment. Nevertheless, public support declined considerably during the campaign, and those opposed to divorce proved to be very successful in per-suading many to change their mind at the last minute. The Catholic Church opposed change, and the anti-divorce campaign again skilfully played on the public's anxieties over the implications for property rights. The slight margin of the victory for the government (less than one per cent) was remarkable considering how strongly supportive of divorce public opinion had been six months earlier. If it had not rained heavily in those conservative areas in the West of Ireland where the turnout was low, the no vote might have prevailed.

The 1992 and 1995 referendums occasioned less bitterness, and a pragmatic approach prevailed among the 1995 Constitutional Review Group, chosen by a Fine Gael-led government. Its report concluded that the constitution had stood the test of time well. Most were lawyers, and under the chairmanship of the pragmatic T. K. Whitaker, the group was determined to take the oppor-tunity to make changes, rather than become embroiled in the controversies of the past. They had learnt the lessons of the 1970s. The committee saw its task as legal rather than political. Articles 2 and 3, divorce, and votes for emigrants were beyond its remit. The issue of emergency powers hinged on progress in the peace process. The Senate was also discussed in this context, since its abolition would remove a chamber in which Northern politicians could be represented, as was Gordon Wilson, the father of a victim of the Enniskillen atrocity. On issues with past divisions, the committee either ignored them because they were too explosive (denominational education), or made a moderate argument for change (a new preamble would still express a Christian logos). The Directive Principles were considered not anachronistic, but there was majority support for equal recognition of English and Irish. There was nonetheless an acceptance of the three constitutional cornerstones: the fundamental rights provisions, their protection by judicial review, and the requirement that the constitution could only be changed by referendum. Judicial activism had not seen the courts become overly politicised, despite the political nature of legal appointments. Rather, judges went native when appointed, and since this was recognised by the people, the constitution was strengthened as a result. Professor Michael Laver, then of Trinity College, argued for constitutional recognition of local government, which was achieved in the twentieth amendment in 1999. The 17th amendment, dealing with cabinet confidentiality, and the 21st amendment, prohibiting the death penalty in all circumstances, also followed.

Those coming of age during the Celtic Tiger years did not experience the earlier culture wars. Rather the 1990s saw party consensus on the peace process, macro-economic policy, and European integration. Consensus on the constitution was natural in this context. The Catholic Church, after a succession of scandals, had lost much of its authority, and the social changes which had begun in the 1960s accelerated. A study of Irish social values published in 2005 showed that less than a third of adults then regarded Catholicism as an essential part of their national identity.[118] Yet the constitutional challenge had subsided. Even its critics acknowledged that there was much of value in the constitution. Differences over its 'manifesto' qualities obscured an underlying consensus on constitutional norms, dating back to the constitutional committee in 1934. Frustration with the referendum had been expressed by both sides, but there was general acceptance of its legitimacy.[119] For many, divorce completed the liberal agenda, and opinion polls also showed the public less secular, especially over abortion, than their West European counterparts. Successive governments have chosen to avoid the issue. In November 2001 an all-party Oireachtas committee on the referendum concluded that after the experience of 25 referendums it did not support any fundamental change to a procedure now 'a well-established feature of our political landscape'.[120] The referendum had inhibited change, but the constitution emerged unscathed from decades of criticism. Gallagher in 1999 remarked that at the start of the twentieth century 'the standing of the constitution has never been higher'.[121]

The constitutional moment, which existed only *in potentia* between 1969 and 1974, had passed. Indeed, by the time divorce was accepted, and Articles 2 and 3 were amended, three decades had elapsed since the 1967 Oireachtas committee recommended change in both these areas. The constitutional critique had undermined a hegemonic traditional value system, not the constitution. Instead a re-evaluation took place. Both Garret FitzGerald and Peter Sutherland had already stressed the constitution's achievement in creating a cohesive political community.[122] One member of the 1995 review group, the constitutional lawyer Gerard Hogan, questioned the basic premise of the 'constitutional crusade', stressing that changes to the constitution would have little effect on unionist attitudes.[123] He also rightly criticised historians for assuming that establishing the (Catholic) origin of a constitutional article was a sufficient commentary on its value. Too much focus on its manifesto qualities had prevented appreciation of the clear articulation of the separation of powers, the enhancement of the democratic process, the recognition of general principles of international law, and the articulation of important new rights.[124] This reflected a tendency to accept the 1937 constitution on its legal and institutional merits. The implication of the Good

Friday Agreement was that Irish unity could only come in two stages, with the establishment of a consensual democracy in the North the first step. This made constitutional change less urgent in the South. Just as after the bitter 1983 referendum, Fine Gael accepted that no major amendments, including on Articles 2 and 3, would be made without consensus between the largest parties, Fianna Fáil came to support the Anglo-Irish Agreement signed by FitzGerald in 1985.[125] It had taken the Northern crisis to exacerbate differences over the constitution, and now the peace process led to consensus. The 1995 Review Group had concluded that a new constitution would only be considered in 'a suitably inspirational context', such as a major change in Northern Ireland.

THE REFERENDUM AND THE CONSTITUTION

By making amendments difficult the referendum reinforced the authority of the constitution. It could have done so in two ways; by making amendments very difficult and preserving its identity, or by allowing changes to that identity so that the constitution became more reflective of a changing society. The survival of a constitutional order is closely bound up with the extent to which it accommodates change. Constitutional change occurs primarily through informal mechanisms (interpretive changes in the courts), and formal mechanisms to the text. A general objection to a rigid constitution is that it places some issues (like abortion) beyond normal politics, immunises them from public debate, and ties the present to past commitments. The issue is compounded when the constitution is identified with the values of one (dominant) party. Comparative analysis suggests that constitutions endure when they are flexible, balance the claims of *different* social forces and parties, and respond to shocks and crises.[126] To what extent was this true of the Irish constitution after 1969?

Where formal amendments are difficult to implement, responsibility for change falls on the courts or on supra-national institutions.[127] The Irish courts have generally been agents of change, making landmark decisions which have changed the identity of the constitution. Before the 1960s judges generally adopted a cautious approach to judicial interpretation, taking a 'literal' view of constitutional provisions. Reflecting West European developments, the judiciary has become more active since 1960. As a new generation emerged, influenced by liberalising trends, judges began to adopt a 'creative' approach, imputing meanings from the abstract concepts the constitution contained, or from the philosophy behind it.[128] The most significant article was Article 40.3.1, which stated that 'The State guarantees in its laws to respect, and as far as practicable, by its laws to defend and vindicate the personal rights of its citizens.' Initially judges thought that the constitution protected only specific 'personal rights', but subsequent judges have 'discovered' a large number of unspecified rights in the constitution. In a celebrated case in 1963 one judgement was that those rights included not only those specified in Article 40, but all those rights which result from 'the Christian and democratic nature of the state'.[129] Despite the power this creative approach gives to unelected judges, there has been little public criticism. Gallagher suggests that this may be due to the fact that judges, like those advocating amendments after 1969, were generally on the liberal end of the spectrum and, given that public opinion was becoming more liberal, judges were ahead of but not wildly out of step with public opinion.[130]

The judiciary outpaced the appetite for liberal reform in the Oireachtas. For example, governments had shown no willingness to grasp the nettle of reforming the contraception laws until the 1973 McGee case. The court's view in that case that married couples should have access to contraceptives 'was radical in 1973, but mainstream within ten years'.[131] Other judgements, such as the Crotty case in 1987, when the Supreme Court ruled that the state could not pass the Single European Act without a constitutional amendment, changed politics fundamentally. Over this period the public also became more assertive. Between 1937 and 1970 there were only 13 constitutional challenges to post-1937 statutory enactments: the figure for the period between 1971 and 1987 was a further 45.[132] The judicial 'discovery' of a more flexible, liberal, and nuanced document has resulted in a more positive appraisal. Hogan argues that the constitution, by strengthening judicial review and giving recognition to personal rights, provided the possibility for future constitutional development, while also containing provisions (such as those on the status of women) rooted in the 1930s. For some the constitution expresses traditional identity: for others it is a means of arriving at the future.

Constitutions are ultimately subject to a 'consequentialist' evaluation. Before the current economic crisis, most agreed that while the values may have been of those of 1937, the constitution's legal and institutional framework was sound. In 1981 Peter Sutherland remarked that the constitution had procured the separation of powers, protected the rights of individuals, and proved adequate in withstanding the stress of traumatic events. As 'the fundamental law of the State' it had been freely accepted by the people.[133] Also noting the substantial evolution of the constitution through the interpretation of the judges, Sutherland though it right that the 'accumulated wisdom' contained in their judgements should not be discarded. Rather, constitutional debate should be seen as protective of the authority of the constitution, since it would ensure that it remained a charter of individual rights and liberties.

However, there were changes which could not be brought about through the interpretations of judges, such as the need to express 'in tangible and positive form, the desire for reconciliation and peace on this island'.[134] The Belfast Agreement met this need, but the issue of pluralism takes on new significance after two decades of immigration, rapid secularisation, and the globalisation of culture. Questions now arise which were simply unthinkable in 1937.[135] They make future amendments inevitable.

If one branch of government comes to the fore in deciding constitutional matters, others will lose importance. As with the X case, when the politicians avoid an issue like abortion, it may come down to a court decision to highlight the inadequacies of the law. Yet referendums are sometimes necessary to pre-empt legal challenge to constitutional amendments, since the courts cannot reverse the outcome of a referendum. Judicial interpretation provides an evolutionary means of change, in contrast to the more democratic drama provided by referendums. Irish liberals would not have been content with the changes brought about by the courts had not certain landmark victories also been won in referendums. While the public might be vaguely aware of how rights are protected in the courts, they do (mostly) vote in referendums. Few people over 45 could forget the bitterness of the 1980 campaigns. Thus the question of whether the referendum has been 'a conservative device' has been central to the legitimacy of the constitution.

Crucially, there are no limits to substantive constitutional change through the referendum. In 1922 referendums were conceived of as a component of a system of checks and balances, triggered by the passing of an unpopular law. After 1937 judges saw them more as an expression of popular sovereignty, where the people had their sovereign status reaffirmed in each constitutional referendum. In some states certain constitutional provisions, (the federal and democratic character of the Federal Republic of Germany for example), are so essential to constitutional identity that they cannot be changed. In three cases in the 1980s the Irish Supreme Court ruled that there were no limitations on popular sovereignty when it came to amending the constitution. For example, the view that the people's sovereignty did not extend to breaching fundamental natural law principles was rejected by the court. Neither could the courts find a constitutional amendment, properly placed before the people, unconstitutional.[136] Judicial review can check the legislature *and* the people. Yet the case for judicial review abates in Ireland when it becomes clearer what the people preferred.[137] This left the road open to change.

Despite the referendum's no bias, the record has actually been one of the people accepting change. One can distinguish between *avoidance* (avoiding internal divisions), *addition* (legitimising change), and *contradiction* (blocking parliamentary legislation), as motivations for referendums.[138] De Valera's decision to restore the referendum to the constitution in 1937 had several motivations. He wanted a plebiscite to legitimise a new beginning: the invocation of popular sovereignty stressed the clear break with the past and the appearance of a new entity on the world scene. Contradiction was reflected by his statement that the constitution established a set of 'God Given rights' which the civil power could not 'invade'.[139] De Valera also later conceded that the compromise with the Catholic Church in 1937 had been intended to nullify the opposition (avoidance).[140] Since 1969 the motive has generally been addition, because the majority of amendments have legitimised changes bringing Irish law into step with changes in the wider world. Of more than twenty put to the people, seven were rejected, and three of these, divorce and the Nice and Lisbon treaties, were later accepted in a new form. A simple majority is sufficient for an amendment to pass. The fact that the vast majority – 22 out of 30 since 1941 – passed at the first vote, suggests that the constitution has become easier to change.

The 1980s nonetheless raised the question of whether the referendum was rather 'a majoritarian device', allowing change consistent only with the majority's preferences. The constitution satisfied two majoritarian criteria for Republican government: that the structure of day-to-day government – the Constitution – be derived from the people, and be legally alterable by a majority of them.[141] Compared to the 1922 provisions, in theory allowing minorities to force their concerns on parliamentary majorities, the 1937 provisions were majoritarian in the sense that the people, by majority vote, would rule as a court of final appeal, when other decision-making procedures had been exhausted.[142] The requirement for a majority also meant that any amendment, such as the pro-life amendment in 1983, be worded as a broad package acceptable to as many people as possible. Minority views could easily be discounted. Yet the referendum has slowed down change on moral issues, not prevented it. Since 1970 the liberal argument has been clearly defeated twice (1983 and 1986) in nine referendums on 'moral issues'. Changes in public opinion eventually resulted in constitutional amendments.

Neither has the referendum always been an extension of Fianna Fáil hegemony. In the 1980s Fianna Fáil's tacit alliance with the Catholic Church proved sufficient to block liberal change. Yet majorities tend to recompose themselves issue by issue. Proportional representation, Church–State relations and European integration were all issues related to the interests of parties. The first saw the smaller parties combine with civil society to defeat a dominant party's proposals for electoral change. The second saw that dominant party frustrate amendments proposed by smaller parties. The third saw the main parties support for European treaties challenged by a combination of single-issue groups and populist mobilisation. On two of these issues, neither majority rule nor the infringement of minority rights resulted. For a majority to rule it requires cohesiveness, which needs strong group or party identifiers such as religion or race.[143] Only on Church–State issues has such cohesiveness been present.

In one area, however, the rigidity of the constitution has the real potential to undermine the constitution. On EU treaties the coexistence of the referendum with judicial review makes for the most rigid constitution in Europe. In 1962 a legal committee had agreed that ratification of the EEC treaties before a referendum would be *ultra vires*, even with the approval of the Oireachtas, since agreement to them involved the exercise of power in a manner incompatible with the constitution.[144] Fianna Fáil's 1972 accession amendment could have been either a 'narrow' one, relating to the EEC in its then present form, or a 'broad' one giving constitutional authority to any future development in its form. At a meeting with officials on 5 November 1971, Lynch's government decided to present a narrow amendment.[145] It was not clear to them that future treaties would require referendum as a result of this decision. The 1972 amendment was carried by an 80 per cent plus majority. Yet ratification of European integration treaties now require a referendum if they go beyond measures necessitated by the obligations of EU membership. The need arose out of a challenge to the constitutionality of the government's attempt to pass the Single European Act without a referendum in 1987. The Supreme Court ruled that ratification without one was unconstitutional, because it interfered with the government's power to conduct foreign policy, and had the effect of altering the essential scope or objectives of the Communities to which the Irish had acceded in 1972.[146] This meant that the Maastricht, Amsterdam, Nice and Lisbon treaties were put to the referendum.

The first no votes on the Nice and Lisbon treaties were eventually overturned in second referendums held because the European Union would not accept an Irish veto on European integration. One problem was that the implications of the treaties were not clear to voters. This was supposedly addressed by the Referendum Act of 1998, which mandated the Referendum Commission to explain the issues to the electorate in a simple and effective way. Yet referendums on complex constitutional issues may have an inbuilt 'no bias', produce low turnouts, and are an inaccurate register of public opinion. This situation is compounded when the parties do not present rival positions. There is clearly a difference between voting on issues like PR or divorce, linked to minority/majority relationships, and such treaties. The emergence of single-issue groups, internal divisions within parties, and a general voting de-alignment, means that voting in referendums is less determined by party loyalties.[147] Fianna Fáil's stance has become less pivotal, which makes it difficult to co-ordinate expectations. One way of overcoming the no bias is to maximise the majority for change, as to Article 44 in 1972, and to Articles 2 and 3 in 1998. Here Switzerland provides a model. Given the cost of campaigns, and the importance of European treaties, governments can construct broad coalitions to introduce successful referendums, thus enlarging the size of the majority for change. The problem is that if this adds legitimacy, it also encourages the kind of populist mobilisation that derailed Lisbon and Nice. The second referendums have brought the procedure into disrepute, and occasioned the first constitutional crisis over the referendum since 1928. If the voters had voted for these treaties the first time round, there would have been no second referendum. It is this issue, not its manifesto qualities, that poses questions about the rigidity of the constitution.

We are no longer living in an era of Fianna Fáil hegemony. What makes a constitution effective or not is whether it establishes clear expectations about other actors' compliance with its provisions.[148] These expectations first converged in Ireland. 'De Valera's constitution' was clearly Fianna Fáil's, and would be respected as such by the dominant party. Yet since it could only be amended through the referendum, this brought into play the attitude of other parties. Thus the originating act, which grounded the constitution in a fundamental law, and the multi-party system imposing limits on the extent of changes to that law were mutually reinforcing factors, underscoring the authority of the constitution. The referendums on PR were classic examples. After 1972 when Fianna Fáil opposed liberal amendments, the referendum requirement was a more obvious expression of the party's hegemony. In 1990, a consensual approach allowed expectations to converge on a more liberal future. Now we are in uncertain territory. Fianna Fáil is no longer dominant, but when the opponents of the constitution (like the no camp in the Nice and Lisbon campaigns) represent such diverse views, the constitution may still survive simply because it is impossible to co-ordinate expectations around an alternative document.

CONCLUSION

The period between 1969 and 1974 promised a constitutional moment in many ways. The Northern conflict provided the crisis. Critics wanted radical change. Public deliberation of constitutional issues was greater than at any time since independence. Yet the impulse for radical change found its *dénouement* in two party committees and significant change came mainly through the courts. The way in which the referendum inhibited change after 1972 could be seen as an example of Irish nationalism failing to 'rise above' a narrow ethnic and religious base.[149] Those advocating change had underestimated the power of traditional nationalism, and the extent to which the constitution expressed its core values. In this sense the constitutional crusade was premature. To its critics, the rigidity of the 1937 constitution prevented Irish governments responding flexibly to the Northern crisis. Despite the 1967 committee's report, Lemass did not offer constitutional reform in his meeting with the Northern Irish premier Terence O'Neill in 1968. At that stage substituting 'Northern Ireland' for 'the six counties' in official correspondence was considered progress.

T. K. Whitaker thought it 'unfortunate' that Articles 2 and 3 made such a 'premature' and 'dogmatic' claim, but there was nothing they could do about them.[150] The truth is that the southern electorate was unlikely to have backed an amendment while the conflict lasted. Their inclusion in 1937 had suggested that nations, not just states or individuals, had rights, and the constitution repudiated the 1920 settlement which had violated the Irish nation's right to a unity superior to any positive law.[151] The historian Liam de Paor thought that they reflected the belief that British involvement in Irish affairs had never been productive of peace and prosperity, and the principle that 'Irish people should control the affairs of Ireland'.[152] The issue also became embroiled in Southern party politics. The New Ulster Movement complained that the Irish state had an 'aspiration to unity' rather than a 'commitment' to the North. The pragmatic spirit which had enabled it to overcome its own civil war differences was not applied to Northern Ireland.[153] Whitaker's criticism of Articles 2 and 3 was   that they were a claim 'without reservation as to form', and he wanted Irish governments to explore concepts such as federalism and condominium, rather than sticking to 'pre-conceived formulae' as part of their aspiration to unity.[154] Here were the seeds an approach that would eventually unlock decades of conflict.

The charge of inflexibility reaches the heart of the debate about the 1937 constitution. One position on the referendum requirement (for EU treaties especially) is that the norm of popular sovereignty is at odds with the needs of the political system: efficiency, legitimacy, and stability. Yet if the ability to meet major challenges is the acid test of efficiency, it is hard to maintain that the state has not done so over a long period of sweeping change. The overriding imperative behind most referendums has been legal reform, and the referendum has legitimised such changes. Changes to Church–State relations, where avoidance still predominates, have been slow, but this reflects a well-documented conservatism among the public. On domestic issues, the 1986 divorce decision was essentially put to the second vote and, like the negative votes on the Nice and Lisbon treaties, overturned. Articles 2 and 3 were changed in a consensual way when change would contribute to peace. If the durability of a state, without major alterations to its basic legal framework and governance structures, is the touchstone of stability, the referendum has enhanced this quality, since it rules out those casual changes to state institutions consistently and sometimes cynically being proposed since the 1950s. As a constitutional safeguard, the referendum revolves not so much on when and why referendums are held, but whether the government's actions are restricted by them.[155] The consequence is that Irish governments have generally had their hands tied when contemplating major institutional reform. Where the system of government has fundamentally changed is with respect to the EU, and here the tension between efficiency and legitimacy is clear.

The 1996 constitutional review group and the 2001 Oireachtas committee on the referendum expressed satisfaction with the referendum. The view expressed by some members of the 1967 committee that the referendum was a logical extension of the principle of popular sovereignty, and of the people's power to give themselves a constitution, still prevails. The record since 1969 has been a classic example of a system maintaining institutional continuity while accommodating crises and change.[156] Those provisions which produced most conflict have been altered by referendum, without fundamental change to the major institutions, yet alone a new constitution. While the 1980 campaigns produced bitterness, the referendums' long-term role in strengthening the solidarity of the political community should also be acknowledged. Yet the range of topics has widened, and in the 1990s alone ten amendments were voted on. The procedure has moved from being an 'auxiliary procedure' to a component of a system in which its use, or possible use, is fully integrated into the decision-making apparatus of Irish democracy. Hence the Irish state has slipped, quite unselfconsciously, into being 'a referendum democracy'.[157] The concept of a constitutional safeguard presupposes a distinction between ordinary and constitutional politics. If constitutional politics occurs only at significant turning points, the mandatory constitutional referendum should take place rarely. When it becomes assimilated into normal decision-making processes, the distinction between the two types of politics breaks down. A safeguard should 'supplement' not replace representative democracy. Nonetheless, the public will not vote away their right to reject constitutional changes in a referendum. Trying to differentiate between fundamental from non-fundamental constitutional changes which would not require referendums runs the risk of undermining the authority of the constitution, and was rejected by the 1996 committee. Ultimately, the Irish experience of the referendum has been determined by that constitution, and while its norms remain respected, a purely representative system will not return.

FIVE

CO-ORDINATION

—

The first paragraph of the Belfast Agreement signed on 10 April 1998 spoke of a 'truly historic opportunity for a new beginning' in Northern Ireland. It went on to say that the victims of past violence could best be honoured by a 'fresh start' with a commitment to reconciliation, tolerance, trust, and human rights. The Agreement pointed to 'a new beginning' in three sets of relationships, within Northern Ireland, across the Irish border, and between the peoples of the two islands. The Agreement also promised 'a new beginning' in the contentious area of policing. The latest in a series of agreements aimed at providing a basis for co-existence in Ireland, the Agreement was comprehensive, imaginative and subtle. It was legitimised by two concurrent referendums held in Ireland on 26 May 2008. Yet it returned Ireland to the pre-1921 world when relationships between Dublin and London were absolutely crucial. Twelve years on, the two governments still act as its 'fundamental guarantors'. At each successive crisis in the implementation process, they co-ordinate to facilitate consensus between the Northern Irish parties, but the Agreement's ability to generate a working constitutional order for Northern Ireland has been in doubt. A 'treaty to constitution' process has yet to succeed.

A GRADUAL INSTALMENT

The complexity of the Agreement is reflected by its different names. The 'Good Friday Agreement' could invoke a religiously inspired new beginning. The 'Belfast Agreement' is preferable to the Stormont Agreement, seat of half a century one-party rule by the Ulster Unionist Party (UUP). The 'British-Irish Agreement' points to its international aspects. The Belfast Agreement is used here, since much hinges on the success of power-sharing within Northern Ireland. Strand one of the Agreement focused on new democratic institutions for Northern Ireland; strand two on the North–South Ministerial Council, and strand three on the British–Irish Council and the

British–Irish Intergovernmental Conference. There were also at the end, specific sections on 'Rights, Safeguards and Equality of Opportunity', 'Decommissioning', 'Security, and Policing and Justice'.

Part of the problem for politicians had been in deciding what kind of a conflict Northern Ireland's was. Primarily it was 'a self-determination dispute spanning two states'.[1] Since the Anglo-Irish Agreement of 1985, it had been accepted by the British government that a solution required the transformation of all the relationships between the peoples of Britain and Ireland.[2] The Sunningdale Agreement of 1973 had established a power-sharing executive, but the Council of Ireland never materialised. The Anglo-Irish Agreement gave the Dublin government a consultative role in the affairs of Northern Ireland, without devolution. The Belfast Agreement could better claim to have addressed 'the totality of relationships' at issue.[3] There were two bottom-lines in the negotiations. Nationalists wanted a power-sharing assembly supplemented by North–South bodies. For Unionists the Agreement had to recognise the principle that the future of the region within the UK, or as part of a united Ireland, would be decided by the majority of voters in Northern Ireland. Thus the Agreement covered international as well as domestic issues. Under 'Constitutional Issues' the participants to the talks endorsed the commitment of the two governments to recognise certain fundamentals, including the right of the majority of the people of Northern Ireland to continue to support the union, or to choose a sovereign united Ireland.

The Agreement, which came into force on 2 December 1999, combined Ackerman's two forms of constitutionalism in ways no previous document had done. For Irish nationalists who voted in the concurrent referendums on 23 May 1998, it was the first meaningful exercise in Irish self-determination since 1918. For Northern Ireland the vote represented a commitment to principles that could draw a line on decades of conflict and division. The Agreement also broke new ground in British and Irish constitutional theory. Yet the older form of constitutionalism returned. The decisive victory of Tony Blair's New Labour in the 1997 parliamentary election had freed the British government from dependence on Unionist votes at Westminster, and heralded a process of devolving power to Scotland, Wales, and eventually Northern Ireland. The Agreement was signed within a year of Blair's election victory. Devolution established a new relationship between Belfast and London, and the 'North–South' body would involve co-operation between Belfast and Dublin. Since unionists received 'east–west' links in exchange, intensive co-ordination between different power centres was provided for. As these links had the potential for growth, monitoring respective spheres of competence would follow. Yet the Agreement was more democratic than the Home Rule bills. Co-ordination – like super-ordination and subordination –

speaks to the 'vertical' dimension of politics, concerned with the hierarchical organisation of political units. Referendums, like elections, relate to its 'horizontal' dimension.[4] The Home Rule bills would have acquired their legal standing solely from Acts of Parliament. The vertical aspects of the Belfast Agreement were legitimised from below.

Co-ordination between different power centres was intended to be both cause *and* consequence of the Agreement, since the arenas in which it was to develop were to expand. The Agreement's clauses on the North–South Ministerial Council, the British–Irish Council, and the British–Irish Inter-governmental Conference repeatedly use the terms co-ordination, co-operation, and common interests. Co-ordination is necessitated by the Agreement's three-stranded nature. The first strand provided for a democratically elected assembly at Stormont with executive and legislative authority. The assembly would have primary responsibilities for all matters devolved to Northern Ireland, subject to judicial review by the courts. The Secretary of State would remain responsible for Northern Ireland Office matters not devolved to the Assembly. Strand two provided for a North–South Ministerial Council, a forum in which ministers from Dublin and Belfast could meet to co-ordinate policy in areas of common interest. This Council, nationalists hope, will demonstrate the benefits of an all- Ireland administration.[5] The Council meets in plenary format twice a year, and in small groups to discuss concrete policy areas more frequently. The Agreement also provides for cross-border implementation bodies for at least six policy areas.[6] Strand three is provided by 'the Council of the Isles'. This will consist of representatives of the Oireachtas and Westminster, of all the devolved assemblies, and of the non-extraneous islands dependent on the UK, such as Jersey. The council can meet to agree to delegate functions and develop common policies.

The language of the Agreement suggested a new beginning. The second clause of 'the declaration of support' speaks of a tragic past, and a 'fresh start' for all. Yet without co-ordination between Dublin and London there would have been no new beginning. Well before 1998 the two governments had responded to the failure of the internal Brook–Mayhew talks with the Downing Street Declaration in 1993. This sent a clear message to the unionists of Britain's determination to deepen co-operation with Dublin. It also indicated to the republicans that they would not be able to bomb Britain into reversing its position on the consent principle.[7] The new institutions were outlined in 'The Framework Documents' agreed by the governments in February 1995, and the overall contours of a settlement firmly established when the governments published their 'Propositions of Heads of Agreement' for discussion between the parties on 12 January 1998. This document proposed consideration of a Northern Ireland Assembly, a North–South Ministerial Council, a

British–Irish intergovernmental conference, and North–South implementation bodies.[8] The Agreement's roots in earlier agreements meant that the local parties could compromise on fundamentals, reassured that their vital interests would be respected, and that future conflict would be regulated by institutions.[9]

Yet not only was co-ordination the axis, but the Agreement reflected previous inter-governmental agreements. The 'power sharing' assembly at Stormont harked back to the Sunningdale Agreement in 1973. The British commitment to withdraw from Northern Ireland and facilitate unity was prefigured in 1973 and 1985. The Irish government's recognition of the consent principle superseded that made in the Anglo-Irish Agreement in 1985.[10] The Belfast Agreement actually replaced the Anglo-Irish Agreement, which had given Dublin a consultative role in Northern Ireland. The provisions for Irish self-determination in 1998 were verbatim those laid out in the 1993 Downing Street Declaration. The Agreement thus resembled many other democratising settlements in being 'a gradual instalment' rather than a dramatic event.[11] A new beginning usually involves the negation of something in the past.[12] Yet the process of negation emerged only gradually, reaching back to Sunningdale. What was negated was not only Northern Ireland's divided past, but the models of democracy previously practised.[13] Instead of a new beginning, the series of international agreements since 1973, pointing to a more consociational future, were a *gradual* moving away from the past, clearing the way for a new 'bi national' constitutional order.

Behind this negation was the earlier experience of Stormont rule. Constitutional settlements do not simply express hopes for the future: a more powerful motivation is 'fear originating in and related to the previous regime'.[14] Article 5 of the Agreement spelt out safeguards that would accompany the return of devolution. These established the principle of proportionality in the allocations of Committee memberships, Committee Chairs, and Ministerial positions, the conformity of legislation to international Human Rights standards, and the establishment of Human Rights and Equality Commissions. This section envisaged the incorporation of the European Convention on Human Rights (ECHR) (and any bill of rights for Northern Ireland supplementing it) into Northern Irish Law. A double negation thus took place in 1998: of the Northern Irish past, and of the sovereign and indivisible nation-state model.[15] Indeed the Agreement forms part of a recent constitutional tradition, represented by Spain in 1978, which modified the traditional nation-state model, and set a framework for a multi-ethnic polity. The Agreement established the concept of 'double protection' for minorities. This envisages a 'bi-national' future whereby the identity, ethos and aspirations of both communities would be respected, and the right of the people of Northern Ireland to choose either British or Irish citizenship would be unaffected by

any future change in the status of Northern Ireland. Hence the two
governments are tied into a standard of minority rights protection in each
other's jurisdictions.[16]

   In terms of the basic principles that mark radical moments in constitution
making, one key aspect of the Irish government's approach at Sunningdale
resurfaced in 1998. This was the search for a constitutional formula recognising the right of the Northern majority not to be coerced into a united
Ireland, as distinct from their absolute right to self-determination, while the
Northern majority, for their part, also conceded the right of the minority to
seek national unity by every lawful means. The Social Democratic and
Labour Party (SDLP) leader John Hume provided a paradigm in which both
traditions were severed from their majoritarian premise in 1998. Unionists
would have the principle of majority consent respected, but lose a veto on the
wider governance of Northern Ireland. Nationalists would revise their
traditional case for unity, but were left with a framework within which unity
could be realistically achieved. The purpose of talks was for the parties to sit
down and decide how to 'share' the island.[17] The key concept was that of self-
determination. The dual referendum would signify the consent of all the Irish
people to share the island in the manner specified in the Agreement,
generating a new legitimacy for Northern Ireland. Hume helped to redefine
the Northern Irish problem in a way appealing to those who were willing to
address 'the totality of relationships', the most important being between the
unionists and the rest of the island.[18] Hume's was a redefinition, not a rejection,
of nationalism, and made sense in a Europe where borders were becoming
less firm. Indeed Hume had once proposed that the EU would share with the
British and Irish governments in the joint government of Northern Ireland.[19]
The Agreement authorised both the North–South Council and the British–
Irish Council to co-operate on EU matters.

   The importance of co-ordination reflected this wider European context. The Agreement was described by Seamus Mallon of the SDLP as
'Sunningdale for slow learners'. Sunningdale, signed on 9 December 1973, had
proposed a Council of Ireland, consisting of an all-Ireland Council of Ministers
and a consultative assembly. This Council would have seven members from
the Irish government, and seven from the Northern Irish Executive. With
'executive' and 'harmonising' functions it became the focus of unionist opposition who were strong enough to collapse the Agreement. Yet Sunningdale
showed how co-ordination could provide a basis for conflict-regulation. The
SDLP had consulted closely with the Irish government over Sunningdale. It
proposed joint policing of border areas by the Gardaí and the Royal Ulster
Constabulary (RUC), the incorporation of the European Convention of
Human Rights into Northern Irish law, a judicial role for the Council of

Ireland, and an all-Ireland police authority.[20] The Irish government's legal committee on Northern Ireland, which first met on 29 May 1973, hoped that the Council of Ireland could act as a Commission for Human Rights in both jurisdictions, and as a constitutional court to which legislation concerning human rights would be referred in similar fashion to that in which the European court functions.[21] Euro-enthusiasm was thus wedded to traditional nationalist objectives. The interdepartmental unit on Northern Ireland, set up on 28 May 1970 to act as an advisory group to the Taoiseach, concluded that the objectives were to further general reconciliation, and establish an institution with the potential 'for development into a legislature and a Government for the whole island'. The European system provided a 'skeleton structure' for such an institution.[22]

The EU thus provided a framework in which co-ordination could replace competition between rival nationalisms. As early as 1973 the Irish Minister of Foreign Affairs hoped that the EEC model would be 'intrinsically attractive to Unionists'.[23] He underestimated the traditionalism of their position. In October 1973 the Irish ambassador was asked to convey to the British government the proposal that the human rights specified in the European Convention be incorporated into the domestic law of both Irish jurisdictions, and that a Council of Ireland Court of Human Rights deal with issues arising from this. These were rejected by the UUP leader, Brian Faulkner, who thought the existing safeguards already adequate. The British government believed that human rights were better protected in Northern Ireland than anywhere else in the world. At official talks on 28 and 29 November 1973, the British rejected the Irish suggestions for reform, and wanted to stick to conventional legal systems, with the Secretary of State having exclusive authority over policing.[24] This raises the question of who the 'slow learners' were in 1998. The limits of economic nationalism, the potential of the European Community, and the spread of international legal norms, were grasped quicker by nationalists than by their British or unionist counterparts.

Explaining the sea change in British–Irish relations since 1973 has become a major issue for Irish political science.[25] One approach is to explain it as an offshoot of their increasing co-operation in the European Community. Europe provided an arena in which British and Irish elites got to know each other. Garret FitzGerald thought that relationships improved when a new generation of British civil servants emerged, with less memory of Ireland's neutrality in the war.[26] A post-imperial Britain and a Celtic Tiger Ireland began to regard each other as partners, resulting in the compromise on their rival sovereignty claims in 1998.[27] This perspective cannot, however, explain the compromises on sovereignty that both have been unable to make in other areas. The Belfast Agreement was characterised by asymmetry, in that the largest security benefits were gained by Britain which did not change its fundamental position on Northern Ireland. Yet the Agreement found greater favour among nationalists than among unionists. One explanation is that the end of the Cold War made American intervention in Britain's domestic politics possible, and once President Bill Clinton supported moves to bring Sinn Féin in from the cold, the British acquiesced. Both governments eventually welcomed the contribution of the United States, because it was seen as a way of achieving common objectives. A final possibility is that official circles simply came to realise that Northern Ireland was not a case for national liberation nor of defending law and order, but a complex conflict to be managed in the same way comparable conflicts have been. Brendan O'Leary suggests that the British Conservatives came to understand the 'bi-national' nature of the conflict, and that knowledge of how to resolve it 'has come from the experience of protracted war and conflict; from the understanding that no one can win outright, and that the opponents are political, with identities as well as interests and passions'.[28]

A CO-ORDINATING DEVICE

Constitutions can stabilise democratic politics if their enactment symbolises a general commitment to their underlying norms and rules. In the absence of such commitment, co-ordination, where parties find it in their interests to follow these rules, can be hoped for. Such a constitutional order will be less a binding contract than 'a co-ordination device' upheld by the two governments. This has been true for the Belfast Agreement. Those aspects which envisaged co-ordination between different power centres have been working, while power-sharing at Stormont has proven enormously difficult. Some suggest that the Northern Irish parties ('Scorpions in a Bottle') remain locked into an adversarial relationship, while relationships between the governments are much better than before.[29] Article 5 of the Agreement expressed a hope for reconciliation and rapprochement to take place within the framework of democratic and 'agreed' arrangements. Yet post-conflict constitutions can take two forms. They can remain equivalent to truces, and reflect the balance of power between the parties as it stood at the termination of hostilities. Alternatively, such constitutions can work as 'gentlemen's agreements' whereby the two sides compromise on fundamental issues, with the intention of moving on to issues over which there can be consensus. Up to now the Agreement has worked only in the first sense. Yet the deal reached between the Democratic Unionist Party (DUP) and Sinn Féin in February 2010 on the devolution of policing and justice powers resolved one more hurdle in the implementation process. The text suggested 'a fresh start', and a shared future based on better relationships.

Power sharing is key to this hope. By 1993 both governments' assumption had been that every party with a mandate, regardless of its violent past, would be entitled to share power. They believed that peace required power sharing, and the experience of power sharing would solidify peace. This reflects a history of conflict where control over institutions and the power to rule over others were central issues.[30] British governments' interest in power sharing went back to 1972, when officials began to look to foreign models, such as the Lebanon, for inspiration. For example, in 1975 the British government asked two political scientists, Professors Richard Rose and Bernard Crick, to advise the Northern Irish Office and all parties to the Northern Irish Convention on the different constitutional possibilities open to them.[31] In 1998 there was a range of models. The minority voting provisions, which required members to identify their group identification (nationalist, unionist, or other), are similar to those recently adopted in Belgium. The status of the assembly in relation to the European Convention on Human Rights was identical to that of the Scottish and Welsh assemblies. The formal structure of the North–South bodies was similar to those of the European Union.[32] The Council of the Isles had similarities to the Nordic Council. 'Parity of esteem' was a concept used in the South African transition from apartheid.

The Agreement was a new departure for the Ulster Unionist Party. Unionist attitudes to power sharing had always been lukewarm, with the prospect typically fragmenting their community. They remain united on their constitutional priority, but differed on how best to secure the union. When, in March 1973, the British Prime Minister Edward Heath produced *Northern Ireland Constitutional Proposals*, its proposals for a power-sharing executive and a role for the Irish government in Northern Ireland affairs produced deep divisions within unionism.[33] With a general election looming, the United Ulster Unionist Council adopted the slogan of 'Dublin is just a Sunningdale away'. The election, on 28 February 1974, damaged the moderate Unionist leadership of Brian Faulkner, chief executive of the devolved administration. Anti-Sunningdale candidates won eleven of the twelve Westminster seats. On 14 May 1974, the Ulster Workers Council, with loyalist paramilitaries, began a strike which threatened to paralyse the region. The British government caved in, and two weeks later Faulkner's resignation brought power sharing to an end. Unionist opposition to power sharing lasted into the 1990s. In the 1998 Agreement, the UUP committed itself to power sharing with nationalists, including Sinn Féin, attendant on the decommissioning of paramilitary weapons. The DUP opposed the Agreement.

Northern nationalism's internal divisions, the 'physical force' tradition represented by Sinn Féin and the IRA, and the SDLP's 'constitutional nationalism', are deeply rooted in Irish nationalist political culture. Both want justice and equality for the Catholic minority, but differ as to whether these could be achieved under partition. Not party to Sunningdale, Sinn Féin had opposed the 1985 Anglo-Irish Agreement, and rejected the 1993 Downing Street Declaration for setting no timetable for a united Ireland.[34] A number of factors explain Sinn Féin's entry into inclusive negotiations following the IRA ceasefires in August 1994 and July 1997, and their acceptance of an internal settlement. The Anglo-Irish Agreement had showed that the British government were willing to accept 'an Irish dimension' in spite of unionist opposition. There was no prospect that the IRA's 'long war' would lead to a British withdrawal. A series of clandestine meetings, which began in 1988 and resumed in the 1990s, between Sinn Féin's President, Gerry Adams, and the SDLP leader, John Hume, helped to establish some common ground. Sinn Féin was growing electorally, and further electoral success followed its participation in the talks process. This participation was encouraged by the British government, which maintained secret channels of communication with the IRA from October 1990 to late 1993, and earlier. In November 1990, Peter Brooke, Secretary of State for Northern Ireland, had publicly declared that Britain had no selfish or strategic or economic interest in Northern Ireland.

Power sharing is a means by which parties can signal a *mutual* commitment to democracy.[35] Only power sharing can reconcile the nationalist minority to Northern Ireland, and allow unionists to show that they accept equality. The requirement that the First and Deputy First Ministers are elected and removable only together ensures that executive leadership is jointly exercised.[36] The other ministers will be selected proportionally according to the d'Hondt rule, which guarantees any party with a significant share of the assembly seats some executive power if it wants it.[37] These arrangements allow for the sharing of power between (realistically) the four largest parties, without the need for a formal coalition agreement.[38] The Agreement's 'consociational' nature enables both communities to share in the governance of Northern Ireland as communities of equal standing. Decisions taken by the assembly will require either of two forms of 'cross community' support. The first, 'parallel consent' requires, of those voting, both an overall majority of the Assembly and a majority of both nationalist and unionist members to back a law. The second, a 'weighted majority', requires the support (from those voting) of 60 per cent of members, and at least 40 per cent of both nationalist and unionist members.[39] Under either rule, both nationalist and unionist sides will have a veto on legislation. The Agreement also committed the British government to a reformed police force aimed at a representative balance between the two communities.[40]

Thus far the Agreement has secured peace. It provides a stable institutional framework within which co-operation can develop. Yet its implementation has been repeatedly stalled. After the parties made the initial constitutional compromises in 1998, other issues continued to polarise relations. Unionists insisted that IRA decommissioning should be a precondition for Sinn Féin's entry into government, while Sinn Féin argued that it could take place only in the context of the overall implementation of the Agreement. Unionists were unconvinced of republican commitment to exclusively peaceful means. Nationalists were convinced that the unionists were looking for pretexts to avoid sharing power. The issue led to the resignation of the UUP's First Minister David Trimble in 2001, and the suspension of the Executive by the Secretary of State Peter Mandelson. The assembly was suspended on 11 February 2000, restored on 20 May 2000, and suspended again on 14 October 2002. The final decommissioning of IRA weapons in September 2005 did not resolve the impasse. Policing, prisoner releases, parades, also proved 'wedge issues', polarising opinion because, touching on relations between the two communities, they symbolised attitudes to the whole process.[41] Ruane and Todd asked a searching question in 1999:

> What if the depth and intensity of the conflict, which the Agreement is meant to contain and ultimately to resolve, prevent it ever being fully implemented or operating in the way intended? Here there is a real danger and it is already evident in the controversies surrounding decommissioning, reform of the police, marches and other human rights issues. These issues, which the Agreement left to commissions precisely because of their complexity and divisiveness, are already threatening its smooth implementation. They are issues which very potently symbolise and bring to the fore those general aspects of the communal conflict that the Agreement has not (yet) tackled – they relate directly to the long term interests of both communities and symbolically raise the issues of the past and present legitimacy of Northern Ireland.[42]

This polarisation has meant that co-ordination remained the axis on which the Agreement stands. The Agreement has been 'a device for co-ordination' in two senses: the choice of its content was itself a matter of co-ordination, and it has worked by successfully co-ordinating actions under it.[43] After 1998, externalising responsibility for the implementation of the Agreement became a constant tactic of the British government. A working assumption of international actors in conflict zones like Bosnia and Mozambique had been that some issues were so important that they needed to be decided by external arbiters. Crucial to the success of the Agreement in creating peace was Tony Blair's insistence that the administration of justice, police reform, and demilitarisation would be decided over the heads of the political parties.[44] This necessitated co-ordination. The decommissioning of paramilitary weapons was overseen by an international commission, headed by Canadian general Sir John de Chastelain. The task of overseeing police reform was given to an American, Tom Constantine, who reported to both governments. The four-person body tasked with monitoring paramilitary activity was nominated by the British, Irish, and American governments. Realistically, any constitutional settlement will reflect the balance of power within society. Yet a dual balance of power has not been possible since no common principle of legitimacy exists between the main actors. The objective was clearly the creation of a multiple balance of power, which required creating external sources of authority. This also involves co-ordination.

So the Agreement has worked thus far by successfully co-ordinating actions under it. Indeed, co-ordination has deepened. After the DUP emerged as the largest unionist party following the 2003 Assembly elections, the implementation process stalled. When the parties met in Armagh in April 2006 to announce a programme for the restoration of power sharing, they were presented with the same choice: share power and participate in the cross-border bodies, or watch passively as the two governments develop their own 'partnership government' over their heads.[45] For the unionists this threatened greater co-operation between Dublin and London. The agreement of the DUP and Sinn Féin to share power, reached at St Andrews in 2007, involved Sinn Féin committing itself to policing, and the DUP accepting sharing power with republicans. In February 2010 the Secretary of State for Northern Ireland, Shaun Woodward, and the Irish Minister for Foreign Affairs, Micheál Martin, jointly chaired eleven days of intensive crisis negotiations between the parties over the devolution of justice and policing powers. Northern Ireland's was a conflict spanning two states, so the issue was partly about the degree to which power should be dispersed across borders.[46] The devolution of justice and policing powers was an issue of this kind, requiring a joint approach. The two governments now refer to themselves as the 'fundamental guarantors' of the Agreement.

The devolution of justice and policing powers resolved what seemed to be the last major obstacle in the implementation process. Yet critics argue that the Agreement can only function as a truce, and that there will be no shift to more mundane issues.[47] They dislike the Agreement's assumption of equal but separate communities. They specifically argue that the cross-community voting procedures, which require parties to designate themselves as nationalist, unionist, or other, make the 'other' position unequal and institutionalise sectarianism. McGarry and O'Leary counter that of the 108 assembly members elected in 1998, 2003 and 2007, some 100, 101 and 100 respectively were from nationalist or unionist parties, representing over 90 per cent of the vote.[48] McGarry argues that an extended period of power sharing could actually reduce the depth of the divisions, and shift emphasis to those socio-economic issues that smaller parties like the Workers Party and the Alliance Party are concerned about.[49] The debate resembles the response of the US political science establishment to the Watergate crisis. The 'Americanists' (like our consociationalists) accepted the overall political framework, while trying to rectify abuses of power through novel institutional arrangements, but the 'Anglicans' hoped to transform the party system in order to create a new political culture. Since 1998 the vote shares of the DUP and Sinn Féin have grown significantly, and fears are that the process will again stall should Sinn Féin become the largest party and be entitled to choose the First Minister.

FROM TREATY TO CONSTITUTION?

The debate about the Agreement should not be confined to the issue of consociationalism. It should extend to whether an agreement sustained by co-ordination could develop into a viable form of constitutionalism. After the historic meeting between the DUP's Ian Paisley, and Sinn Féin's Gerry Adams on 26 March 2007, the Secretary of State for Northern Ireland Peter Hain said that if they were to find a way of agreeing, then they would be able to 'lock in their own form of power-sharing government, rather than me, as past governments have done, imposing something'.[50] The hope of the two governments is for a shift from treaty to constitution. The Agreement promotes a 'treaty to constitution' process in three ways. Should power sharing work, and a shared sense of responsibility emerge, Northern Ireland will itself acquire a stronger constitutional identity within the UK, or as part of a united Ireland. In the absence of violence, and with no divisions over Articles 2 and 3, the southern polity is free to contemplate further constitutional change consensually.[51] Should both developments occur, and a vote for unification takes place, the possibility of a new 'all-Ireland' constitution could emerge.

The difference between a treaty and a constitution was debated in the context of the proposed European constitution in 2003 and 2004. Originally, to the European Council in June 2003, its full name was 'Draft Treaty establishing a Constitution for Europe'. There are two possibilities for Northern Ireland. The word 'Treaty' could be highlighted and the Belfast Agreement read in the same way EU treaties have been: that is, as agreements between states that are equal to each other, and pool some of their powers for common purposes. Alternatively, the Agreementcould be viewed through the familiar lens of constitutional law, as a text that establishes a coherent set of institutions, laying out in a comprehensive way the relations between the citizens of Northern Ireland and their new system of government. The Agreement has all the essential features of modern constitutions: it establishes an institutional framework for the exercise of power, it strengthens the rule of law basis of this system, and it provides for fundamental rights.[52] It could be treaty in form, constitution in substance.

Can the Agreement combine these treaty and constitutional elements to make it functionally equivalent to a constitution for Northern Ireland? History shows Irish nationalists usually struggling to reconcile the two forms of constitutionalism and sustain a 'treaty to constitution' process. In 1996, Mallie and McKittrick wrote of 'the eternal, cultural psychological and temperamental gap' which exists between British and Irish nationalism.[53] The Agreement has the advantage over Home Rule in having been signed by two states of comparable status.[54] Yet they are not equal in size. An Irish government representing fewer than 5 m. people depends on co-ordinating with a neighbouring isle of 60 m. Two wider contexts have allowed this gap to be overcome. Co-ordination is best practised when states are of relatively equal status, as they are in the European Union. Since 1985 the Irish government has been able to trade on its status as a sovereign state to co-ordinate with Britain, at times going over the heads of the unionists. Secondly, the Agreement is in part a 'reordered union'. Devolution ended the old unionist position that London's options faced with minority nationalism were simply allowing for separation, or the retention of power at Westminster. Other aspects of constitutional reform – interest in PR, use of referendums to legitimise constitutional change, Human Rights Act, stronger judicial review – have also been applied to Northern Ireland. Nairn sees devolution as part of the decline of the UK state by instalment, with the Council of the Isles the model of the future. His vision of 'an archipelago system of effectively independent polities, meeting regularly to discuss or decide questions of common interest', actually returns us to the themes of the Gaelic Revival.[55] He anticipates too much change, but points to the context in which co-ordination could further develop.

These two wider contexts suggest different ways in which a treaty to constitution process could succeed. Stressing the Agreement's treaty character, one could hope that the stability provided by the Dublin/London axis would soften divisions and result in the local parties internalising its values. Some have argued that the two governments have an obligation to adhere to the Agreement's provisions similar to their other responsibilities under international law. Moreover, a clear difference between a treaty-based relationship among states and a domestic constitution is that the latter depends much more on confidence. Those unionists who compromised (David Trimble, Ian Paisley and Peter Robinson) faced the challenge of outflanking parties. In contrast, the two governments have benefited from a bi-partisan approach in their parliaments. Co-ordination rests on a more secure political footing. Alternatively, one could hope that British and unionist elites would regard the Agreement as part of a reordered union and stick to it for that reason. One can be sceptical about both arguments. O'Leary suggests that everything in the Agreement, including the commitment to facilitate Irish unity, is revocable by an act of any future parliament, irrespective of international law, or any promises made in 1998 as part of the negotiations.[56] Neither was the Agreement a simple extension of British constitutional reform. There is no part of the UK as divided as Northern Ireland and no settlement requiring such international dimensions. What is crucial to co-ordination is the fact that the two states have complementary interests. Since 1920 Britain has wanted to keep the Irish Question out of its domestic politics, while defending the right of the local majority to reject reunification. These objectives have been secured by the Agreement. Since 1974 Dublin has seen Irish unity as a two-stage process, with the creation of a consensual democracy in the North the first stage. This allows Dublin to derive obvious security benefits from partition, while hoping that unity might be achieved peacefully. While both governments' objectives remain complementary, they should stick to the Agreement. After all, a treaty is a way of maintaining peace.

Co-ordination will also remain necessary because of the absence of a strong sense of the 'we' subject to the Agreement. This makes it difficult to have any 'Northern Irish constitution'. The European constitutional project failed, partly because of its ambiguous constitution/treaty character, but mainly because of the absence, as in Northern Ireland, of a unified constitutional subject. When the EU tried to ratify this constitution through a procedure signifying a much stronger conception of political community – the referendum – it backfired. The 1998 Agreement follows a 'regulative' approach to constitutional issues, interested primarily in regulating an established range of conflicts, not a 'constitutive' approach, interested in more substantially defining the nature of the political community created by the document.[57] There is no preamble expressing a link between a specific people and the document, and no attempt to use public policy to forge a Northern Irish identity. Morison suggests that the Agreement departs from ideas of popular sovereignty which appear universally to be the foundations of constitutionalism.[58] Two questions – Who were the people in whose name the Agreement was adopted? and Whom does the new system of government represent? – were laced with ambiguity.

In 1998 the Agreement's drafters subtly reworked the functions of language so that fixed meanings became supple and fluid, and definitions open and ambiguous.[59] The question changed from being to whom does Northern

Ireland belong?' to one of co-existence'.[60] The emphasis of politics shifted away from ends and foundational issues – about which there is no agreement – to means.[61] Critics complained that this required 'an illusion': the Agreement strives to make the border seem more fixed for unionists, and more permeable for nationalists.[62] Aughey stresses its internal logic. In place of ownership of the new Northern Ireland, Catholics will put Irish unity on the back burner. In return for constitutional security unionists will make Northern Ireland 'a warmer place for Catholics'.[63] Yet this ambiguity, key to the Agreement's initial success, may prove its undoing. The Agreement confirms Northern Ireland's place within the UK, while also specifying mechanisms by which Irish unity can be achieved. It thus tries to accommodate two conflicting visions of the future. Sinn Féin sold the Agreement to their followers as a transitional settlement, while the UUP justified its role in the negotiations on the grounds that they settled the status of Northern Ireland. The decision on the ultimate status of Northern Ireland has been deferred not resolved. Popular sovereignty has not been rejected as a constitutional norm: it has been finessed. Both governments have explicitly recognised 'the legitimacy of whatever choice is freely exercised by a majority of the people of Northern Ireland with regard to its status, whether they prefer to support the Union with Great Britain or a sovereign united Ireland'.[64] The right of the 'majority' to determine its fate is limited to two options, with independence ruled out. In contrast, the Downing Street Declaration explicitly recognised the right of the Irish people as a whole to self-determination, but the mechanism by which this can be exercised is specified (joint referendums, North and South). The tension between the majority principle and the concept of a sovereign people is at the heart of unionist ambivalence about the Agreement. While in the majority, they exercise *de facto* sovereignty, but if that majority changes, their veto on Irish unity disappears entirely.

By deferring constitutional choices regarding the foundational aspects of the polity (i.e. partition), an 'incrementalist approach to foundational decisions was thus employed.[65] Yet demographics add uncertainty. Catholics are expected to become a majority in Northern Ireland in the next three decades. In November 2002 Senator George Mitchell recalled that during the negotiations the demand that a bare electoral majority should determine the future status of Northern Ireland was the bottom line of the unionist negotiating team. He added that this might have been 'a strategic error' on their part.[66] With Sinn Féin now the largest nationalist party, the issue of status is not going to go away. A comparison could be made with the Spanish constitution of 1978, whose provisions on regional autonomy are still being challenged by Basque and Catalan nationalists. Bourke argues that the Agreement simply reverts 'to the problematic principle which provoked the original crisis in Northern Ireland'.[67] Before 1920 Ulster Unionists had claimed exemption from Home Rule on the grounds that they were the local majority, and they proceeded to govern Northern Ireland as if that status gave them ownership of the state. Bourke contends that majority rule and popular sovereignty are again opposed under the terms of the Agreement, since 'a simple majority' is still entitled to decide the ultimate status 'of the community as a whole'.[68]

The Agreement can only work as 'a co-ordination device' while both nationalists and unionists feel they can pursue their interests under it. Yet the demographics point to a problem with many constitutional bargains: that of incomplete information.[69] When the UUP and Sinn Féin agreed to the settlement in 1998, they did so employing two different timeframes. Republicans could accept partition for now, hopeful that the demographics would help them overturn it later. Unionists could settle for the status quo, hopeful that this demographic shift will either not occur, or should it occur, not result in all Catholics wanting Irish unity. Both had first responded positively to the problem of uncertain payoffs. Yet should the payoff for Sinn Féin be deferred in the long run, their support for the Agreement might falter. Should it become obvious to the unionists that there is no long-term pay off, they could press for renegotiation. Over time it will become apparent whose judgement of the pay offs was more accurate. Calculations will be affected by extraneous factors: attitudes in the Irish Republic, Scotland's potential independence, immigration to Northern Ireland. Moreover, neither side has perfect information about each other's values. Is Sinn Féin's commitment to making Northern Ireland work conditional on the Agreement delivering Irish unity? Have Unionists accepted that Irish unity can be a legitimate outcome of the Agreement? When such information becomes clearer, support for the settlement may waver.

The weakness of such a 'co-ordination device', as opposed to a traditional constitution, is clear. Since the 1937 constitution conceived of an independent Irish polity in a way acceptable to most nationalists, it mattered less who benefited from it in partisan terms. In Northern Ireland, it matters a great deal whose interest is served by the Agreement in the long run. The 1937 constitution brought conflict over the 1921 Treaty to a close, and constitutional politics subsequently focused on issues to do with the distribution of power in the state, like PR/STV. In Northern Ireland there has been no settlement of the overall constitutional question, and the partisan interests of the parties cannot be viewed in isolation from this overarching issue. Since defection from the Agreement, or its revision, remains possible, only outside actors can enforce its rules. As these outside actors are 'kin states', identified with by the two communities in Northern Ireland, this enforcement will have to be a joint exercise to be accepted as impartial. This means continued co-ordination of the kind we have seen so far. A shift from treaty to constitution may never be complete. Nevertheless, compared to past agreements there are reasons for optimism. Any future decision on the fate of Northern Ireland will take place in a context where the two communities have been sharing power as partners of equal standing, and where partition is addressed by two states that have become partners with common interests. The partition issue may ultimately be decided by majority vote, but if not all Catholics want Irish unity, and if equality between the two communities gives decisive influence to smaller parties, then politics may be less zero sum than it has been in the past.

CONCLUSION

With the concurrent referendum producing the only occasion in modern Irish history where a constitutional package received the support of a majority of nationalists and of unionists, 1998 has some claim to be a constitutional moment. Although the new system of government was a gradual instalment, the referendum provided a 'post-national' exercise in popular sovereignty. The model of governance broke new ground in British and Irish constitutional theory. The Agreement could transform three sets of relationships and open new avenues for constitutionalism to develop. The old question of whether it was 'unconstitutional' for Westminster to legislate against the wishes of the Northern Ireland executive, on matters for which responsibility had been transferred, will surely return.[70] McCrudden compares the 'ideological' approach to constitutional issues in Northern Ireland, based on the development of explicitly normative principles, with the traditional pragmatic British approach.[71] This approach leaves Northern Ireland to the left of the spectrum, as with Scotland. Ideals of substantive equality, participatory democracy, community identification, and the role of government in limiting the operations of the market have less purchase in England.[72] Imputing rights from general principles could encourage a distinct Northern Irish constitutionalism, as in the Irish Republic.

The Agreement returned Ireland to the constitutionalism of Home Rule, but also reminds us of the weakness of the Home Rule cause. One unionist objection to Home Rule had been that it would always be provisional: a staging post on the way to independence. This meant that Irish politics remained focused on ends not means, and practical compromises were opposed by Conservatives and Unionists as concessions on vital constitutional issues. Electoral polarisation continued until partition. The same spectre haunts post-Agreement Northern Ireland. The Agreement has redirected its politics towards defining or 'spelling out' fundamental points of constitutional interpretation in a manner usually dismissed as unnecessary at Westminster.[73] Sinn Féin's leader Gerry Adams declares a united Ireland 'inevitable'. Just as pre-1914 constitutional thinkers saw the need for institutions such as STV to soften the main line of political division, much of the debate is about whether consociational institutions soften or entrench divisions. Yet the Agreement's treaty dimension has itself redirected politics on to constitutional issues, and there is only a certain period of time within which a 'treaty to constitution' process can develop. The hope must be that the successful operation of the institutions will create a consensual culture which facilitates an agreed move to unity, or another agreement on the status quo.

Hardin cites the US constitution as an example of a viable constitution which first rested on co-ordination.[74] Nevertheless, by 1860 the slavery issue proved irrepressible. The United States' venerable constitutional order could not prevent civil war. Yet if the issue of slavery was fudged when the founders wrote the US constitution, the Agreement has specified a route to Irish reunification. The parties have incompatible goals, but the two states have committed themselves to principles and procedures according to which the unity issue will be adjudicated. For this reason, the Agreement's treaty aspects remain vital. The 1920 Government of Ireland Act had also envisaged a possible movement towards a united Ireland, via the Council of Ireland, but only with the consent of each parliament. What is different is that Britain is implementing the 1998 Agreement, a factor not unrelated to the decline of the Conservative/Unionist alliance at Westminster. So perhaps 1998 represents a return to 'the priorities and intentions (but not the reality) of the 1920 Partition Act'.[75] Alternatively, if a treaty to constitution process were to succeed, the Northern parties could agree their future together. Were they to agree to stick with the Agreement, or to another halfway house between it and Irish unity, it is unlikely that the British or Southern Irish public would complain. Without a treaty to constitution process, like all previous treaties the Agreement will be superseded. A vote in favour of reunification could necessitate a new Irish constitution, perhaps another treaty, although elements of the Agreement would surely survive.

SIX

CONCLUSION

—

Once a constitution is accepted as an expression of national identity, when people feel a society is at a turning point its constitutional arrangements will come under scrutiny. This book has been organised around five such moments: 1919, 1922, 1937, 1969 and 1998. Yet if such moments gave the Irish public the opportunity to participate in higher law making, they have not always resulted in a transformation of the constitutional order. The centre-piece remains the 1937 constitution, and it has survived two major official reviews, while being prefigured by another in 1934. Thus while the economic crisis which began in 2008 has led to arguments for change, there is no *a priori* reason to assume we are now experiencing a constitutional moment, nor that the economic crisis is necessarily a constitutional one. Indeed the current constitution survived two major economic crises in the 1950s and the 1980s. A distinction must be drawn between the performance of the Irish state, which has varied, and the stability provided by the constitution, which is impressive. The latter is vital to the former, but constitutional change will not necessarily improve economic performance. The crisis is about performance not stability, and about the corruption of parliamentary institutions by party politics.

THE SECOND CRISIS OF LIBERALISM

Irish society is going through its second crisis of liberalism. Disillusionment with party politics, anger at corruption, and interest in new forms of represen-tation have returned. Given the vast cultural and social changes that have taken place, the concern is again to reconnect people to their political system, and to prevent elites, elected and unelected, manipulating public institutions for their own benefit. The first crisis of liberalism was produced by the emergence of industrial society. The second follows the absorption of Ireland into the world of global capitalism. Generational change has never been enough to produce a constitutional moment. The link with crisis is key. When the state's legitimacy is primarily bound up with its role in the economy, such crises will result in a loss of faith in the manner with which the state involved itself in capitalist development.[1] Brown envelopes, runaway development projects, golden circles of businessmen and politicians, together with a huge bailout of the banks by the taxpayer, are symptoms of a legitimation crisis in which the public interest was devoured by private ones. Yet the connection made between this crisis and the constitution is tenuous. The global crisis has impacted similarly on Britain, Ireland and the USA, with three different constitutions. The factor differentiating Ireland from more successful states is a particular model of capitalist development that made the state more vulnerable to the downturn. It is not clear what negative forms of economic behaviour the constitution encourages, nor what positive forms it disallows. It also not clear what alternative model of development the constitutional critics are proposing.[2]

The constitution has not caused this economic crisis, but there is a need for greater accountability, oversight and transparency in public life. Just as the first crisis of liberalism was motivated by the fact that the traditional Westminster model was unable to make the new financial elites and special interests accountable, the second crisis reflects similar concerns. The integration of the state into the world of global capitalism since the 1960s has produced affluence, but has brought bankers, businessmen and developers closer to the centre of power. What is noteworthy is that both crises of liberalism have resulted in a *constitutional* debate in Ireland. The shortcomings of the British model are very much those of the Irish system, but only in Ireland is the blame now put on 'the political system'. Nonetheless, there are parallels. In both Britain and Ireland the Westminster model concentrates power, and if those with that power pursue destructive economic policies, there is very little parliament or the opposition can do about it. The Irish response reflects a society where people traditionally thought of the state as something not quite their own. Their ability to externalise the state, to blame outcomes on elites rather than on those who elected them, is a form of 'constitutional populism'. Populism is an anti-status quo discourse that simplifies the political space by symbolically dividing society between the people (as the underdogs), and the elite. One consequence of this simplification is to forget the fact that Fianna Fáil elites were elected through a very representative electoral system, and implemented economic policies consistently endorsed by the electorate.

Populism thrives on an anti-politics appeal and, while not the highest form of democracy, provides a mirror with which democracy can contemplate itself, warts and all.[3] The examination this mirror provides is overdue, and may have emerged earlier had not the economic crisis of the 1980s been ended by the Celtic Tiger. 'Constitutional populism', particularly, emerges when the constitutional order has been unable to regulate politics, as during the last phases of the Celtic Tiger, where the boundaries between business interests and public authority became completely blurred. Yet constitutional populism also returns us to the origins of the Irish state, as do the issues of accountability, corruption and greed. Then Sinn Féin wanted real 'Government by the People', with no need to rely on 'pull' and 'influence' to get state services, no need for TDs to provide gifts for individual districts in order to get re-elected, and an emphasis on promotion by merit throughout the public services. Sinn Féin specifically proposed constituency committees to take the onus for dealing with local issues away from TDs.[4] Like many today Sinn Féin saw a need to rescue institutions from a corrupting political culture, a task which fell to Cumann na nGaedheal after 1922. Centralised control of local government was one response.

One of the early casualties of the current economic crisis was the consensus on the value of the constitution which emerged in the 1990s. Some traditional cornerstones – ministerial responsibility, strong judicial review, and the mandatory referendum – have been challenged. The rigidity of the system is contrasted with the nimbleness successful small economies need to deal with the global market. [5] A consistent theme is the need for parliamentary politics to focus not on local, but on 'big picture' national and international issues, and here a strengthening of local government, or some revival of the extern ministers idea from 1922, might help.[6] Long-standing concerns, the effects of STV, the necessity for the Seanad, and the weakness of the Dáil, have also resurfaced in Fine Gael's current proposals for major amendments. Such amendments would take us back to Lemass's 1967 committee, when his concern was to provide a system of government fit for economic development in an era of greater international integration. Yet the smaller parties' support for reforms to strengthen the Dáil has not been sufficient up to now.[7] Much will depend on the decline of Fianna Fáil. Other suggestions – for a Council of Economic Advisers or a Department of Public Service Reform – are new.

Fine Gael has committed itself to the abolition of the Seanad, a stronger committee system, a reduction in the number of TDs, and a shorter term for the President.[8] Labour's leader Eamon Gilmore has also promised a new constitution, to be produced by a Constitutional Convention, by the anniversary of the 1916 Rising. Fine Gael wants to establish a 'New Politics', a phrase which also reflects the general disillusionment with party politics. The *Irish Times* ran an opinion series, *Renewing the Republic*, with some articles in favour of a new constitution and others opposed. The Irish Political Studies Association launched a website providing expert commentary on many aspects of political reform, electoral reform being again a central issue. No one doubts that STV promotes localism: what is less clear is whether any other electoral system could eliminate it. Thus there are three identifiable themes in the constitutional critique: the need for better governance in an era of globalisation, disillusionment with party politics, and a feeling that the identity of the constitution is outmoded. I can think of no other time since 1921 that these themes emerged simultaneously.

Yet arguments for reform of the 1937 constitution again use the language of a Second, New, or Renewed Republic. The 1916 Proclamation and the 1919 Democratic Programme are invoked as moral yardsticks against which the failings of the state can be evaluated.[9] There is little effort to explain in concrete legal terms where the 1937 constitution falls short, but the constitution suffers from the comparison with 1916 and 1919. Constitutional identity is established by how a constitution fits within the social and cultural environment it operates in. Constitutions can take a *militant* approach expressing values impatient with existing social relationships, as with the 1916 Proclamation or the Democratic Programme, or an *acquiescent* approach aiming for a harmonious fit with existing social norms and structures.[10] In comparison with the idealism of 1916 or 1919, for some the constitution represents too much acquiescence in the shortcomings of Irish society as they were in 1937. Thus we now have calls for a new Preamble, for the constitutional protection of social and economic rights, and for a Republic of equality. The 1995 report on the constitution also called for elimination of the gender-specific language, and gender quotas for parliamentary elections are being discussed. Here there is a paradox. Since the 1960s the constitution has been criticised for being too acquiescent but, ironically, if society has changed so much that a new constitution would be more in harmony with these values, an acquiescent logic could justify its replacement.

Fine Gael and Labour's commitments raise the question of whether this particular moment will see expectations co-ordinated around a new document or a new value system. There are two possible responses to the economic crisis: a rejection of the values of the wider context (that of global capitalism), or a desire for new institutions which will allow Ireland to integrate better into that context. If there has been a loss of economic sovereignty, one could blame either global capitalism, or just the Irish elites who allowed it to happen. The values of 1916 or 1919 will not be served by the second approach, and Labour and Fine Gael are likely to differ on socio-economic rights. A joint commitment to changing only the identity of the constitution will take us back to the 1980s, when constitutional debates did little to address the ongoing economic crises. Rather, the constitutional crusade diverted energy into campaigns that required public opinion to change before they could be accepted. The record since 1970 suggests that similar amendments will follow incrementally anyway. Alternatively, if the constitution could be presented by these parties as an extension of Fianna Fáil's hegemony, co-ordination could simply follow from disillusionment with a party that was ostensibly in power for decades. If the party has lost its stature so might the constitution.

In 1937 three factors gave Fianna Fáil the opportunity to create an enduring constitution: the Westminster model, the Sinn Féin constitutional tradition, and the weakening of the Treaty. Has there been change to these three factors such that the constitution is no longer an extension of Fianna Fáil hegemony? The Westminster model, based on the doctrine of parliamentary sovereignty, gives legislative majorities extraordinary powers, and can be expected to entrench a dominant party. The situation prevailing in 1937 was one where there was 'absolutely no limit on the untrammelled power of the executive'.[11] The constitution addressed this anomaly by reasserting a fundamental law tradition ahead of its time in 1937. There seems to have been a genuine belief among TDs after 1937 that the Dáil (not the Oireachtas) was sovereign, and a lack of enthusiasm for judicial review.[12] In retrospect the two referendums on PR/STV were turning points. In September 1968 Jack Lynch told a referendum rally that the 'Fine Gael reactionaries' and 'dissident factions' wanted to establish 'a political permissiveness' which would ultimately destroy responsible government.[13] That the electoral change could mean constant Fianna Fáil government was the weakness of the argument. The constitution dictated that the issue be put (twice) to the people, who vetoed the change. In this way the constitution limited Fianna Fail's dominance.

The constitution also reconciled the British doctrine of responsible government with the fundamental law concept. The tension between them was manifest in the divergence of outlook between the 1922 constitutional committee and the Provisional Government, in the furore over the abolition of the referendum in 1928, and in the elite resistance to the concept of repugnancy during the drafting of the 1937 constitution. Nonetheless, this elite resistance failed, and by reconciling these two sources of limited government the constitution provided a stronger system of checks and balances than that provided by the Westminster model. This system had its origins in the 1922 constitution and in the work of the 1934 constitutional committee, which had suggested cross-party support for fundamental rights, their protection by judicial review, and a rigid constitution amendable only by referendum. These cornerstones were those of Sinn Féin and were also valued by the 1922 constitutional committee. They were not specifically Fianna Fáil's.

Institutions often 'drift' from the intentions of the drafters, and this system of checks and balances eventually created a constitutionalism distinct from that provided by the Westminster model. All democratic governments depend on the people as the fundamental limit to their power, but experience has shown the need for 'auxiliary precautions' as well. To these we give the name constitutionalism.[14] In Ireland these 'auxiliary precautions' – judicial review, the referendum, and the Presidency – have grown in importance, becoming less 'auxiliary'. Only up to the 1970s was it possible to argue that the political system was still based on the Westminster model. Since then frequent (now constant) coalitions (among other changes) have created a less majoritarian system creating a greater dispersal of power than that provided by the Westminster model.[15] As Fianna Fáil loses more electoral support, a more consensual democracy favouring the smaller parties could emerge under the current constitution. Yet the problem of a very weak parliament will remain. O'Halloran locates the alleged decline of the Houses in an era of so-called 'post parliamentary governance', where key decisions become made in arenas other than the parliamentary one.[16] Yet the first crisis of liberalism saw similar concerns, but such was the grip of party politics that a different model was stillborn in 1922. The case for a stronger parliament is strong, but is attendant on the emergence of a genuine multi-party system. The Irish system has been slowly evolving away from its Westminster roots, but it is up to the smaller parties to capitalise on the recent changes in voter loyalties to create a parliament on European models.

The Sinn Féin constitutional tradition assumed a strong connection between constitutional and national identity, a connection which made Fianna Fáil's constitution more hegemonic. Fine Gael is now proposing the amendment, not the replacement, of the constitution. Does this imply that the *identity* of the constitution is secure, either in the sense that its value commitments are not anachronistic, or in the sense that changes have altered the identity of the constitution in a way more reflective of contemporary Irish national identity? There is no doubt that Irish culture has changed enormously since 1937. The 1937 constitution had a 'covenanting' character, which suggested that its ethical and political dimensions were interconnected. The preamble saw Justice, Prudence and Charity as ends of the state. Natural law was as a source of limited government. Catholic social teaching provided 'guidelines' for the Oireachtas. Many of these ideas are outmoded. De Valera believed Irish democracy needed ethical values, and wanted to protect the way of life which nurtured them in his constitution. His covenanting approach assumed a morally informed constitutionalism, but the morals for a state called 'a global innovation hub' by a Fianna Fáil Taoiseach, Brian Cowen, in his St Patrick's Day speech in March 2010, have surely changed.[17] The expressive function of law can involve making a statement or prescribing behaviour. Were a new constitution written today, the values that would inform such a statement, and the behaviour it would prescribe, have changed. De Valera's constitution has survived, not de Valera's Ireland. Fíach MacConghail asks 'How can we accept as a multi-cultural, secular society that all actions of our people and the State should derive from the most Holy Trinity?'[18]

There is a connection between the covenanting and nationalist approaches to constitutionalism since – as Aristotle believed – the specific ends towards which the community aspires is essential to the concept of identity.[19] It fell to de Valera to make the connection clear, and he did so assuming that the exercise of writing a constitution was about defining a national self. Yet three crucial aspects of that self – religion, territory and sovereignty – have changed. One can now look back nostalgically at the social cohesion the constitution assumes, but welcome a transitional logic borne out by the successive amendments. This logic obtains especially in a partitioned island, and has meant that the constitution was stripped of some of its 'sacral' and absolutist aspects. It has becomes less of a covenant guided by fixed principles than an evolving framework in which those principles are modified according to the needs of the present. Opinion differs about whether judicial review should be guided by the principles of the constitution. Hogan cautions that too historical an approach would tend to 'fossilise' the constitution by applying the values and ideas of 1937 to the very different Ireland of today.[20] Just as we can have nations without nationalism, we can have de Valera's constitution without a covenanting constitutionalism. Just as identity is a fixed obsession of Irish constitutional life, the plasticity of Irish national identity allows some distance from the constitution's historical identity.[21]

The constitution's 'dialogic' logic hinges on the tension between commitments expressive of a nation's past, and the determination of those who in some ways seek to transcend the past.[22] In 1919 P. S. O'Hegarty wrote:

> There have been in Ireland two traditions, one that of the ancient historic Irish nation, with its separate language, culture, history, and mentality, and the other, dating from the creation of the eighteenth century, of an artificial state, based upon the subjection of the historic Irish nation, having its origins in the English invasion of Ireland, deriving its authority from the decrees of the English language, and accepting the status of an English colony, with no rights not subject to withdrawal by the English Parliament.[23]

The 1937 constitution closed the gap between these two traditions, but did so assuming that constitutional and national identity were equivalent. More than 70 years later that assumption looks untenable. Instead those who now want to vindicate the constitutional status quo can try to bridge the gap between the constitution and the classical precepts of constitutionalism, and thus reconcile its identity to the needs of the present. They can argue that the constitution was very democratic for the 1930s, its institutional design was sound, and it has nurtured a legal culture conducive to the protection of rights. Its negative aspects were a small price to pay for its fundamental achievement in the healing of civil war divisions.[24] In contrast, critics can still invoke alternative ideas of constitutional identity to show how the constitution constrained or constrains other identities.[25] This approach emerged in the late 1960s when the counterfactual possibilities of the New Republic, the 1922 constitution, or of a pluralist island, were invoked to criticise the constitution. There is something to say for each approach. The constitution has provided democratic stability, but some elements, the preamble for example, have become 'disharmonic'. The question is not whether these rival conceptions of identity have become more mainstream (they have!). It is whether they justify the replacement as opposed to the further amendment of the constitution.

The third factor making for a hegemonic constitution was the repudiation of treaty based law. Constitutions may be milestones in the history of independence, but are also mechanisms of international integration; influenced by model constitutions, universal conceptions of rights, and treaties. If international integration requires a 'treaty to constitution' process, how can a constitution which renounced a treaty enable such a process? How can its stress on popular sovereignty be reconciled with the need to co-ordinate with other governments and international institutions? History shows Irish nationalists usually failing to reconcile constitution and treaty. In the Home Rule period Irish nationalist preferences proved secondary to those of Ulster Unionists. The Versailles settlement could have provided a favourable context for Sinn Féin's 'national internationalism', but Britain's victory in the war closed down that route. The 1921 Treaty opened up another 'treaty to constitution' process. Northern Ireland had the right to opt out of the Free State, but pro-treatyites hoped that by meeting their Treaty obligations and passing a democratic constitution partition would prove temporary. The approach failed with respect to partition. De Valera rejected the Treaty, restated the anti-partitionist principle in emphatic terms, and his preference for autarchy reflected the collapse of international order in the 1930s.

Yet traditional anti-partitionism also achieved little. In 1969 Fianna Fáil's Seán MacEntee wrote to Jack Lynch complaining that the 'frontal attack' on partition had failed. Partition reflected not British interests but the 'deeply held' convictions of the Northern majority. MacEntee referred to de Valera's willingness in 1921 to accept the de facto position of Northern Ireland, if the unionists were willing to co-operate across the border in areas of common interest.[26] This pointed to a 'technocratic anti-partitionism' which eventually became government policy, and led to another 'treaty to constitution' process. In 1968 T. K. Whitaker submitted a paper to the Department of External Affairs discussing possible modes of reunification. He explored the merits of Federation, Confederation, Condominium and OECD/Council of Europe arrangements.[27] As early as 1972 Whitaker believed a treaty desirable:

> I think that, to clear away present ambiguities and causes of dissension and start with a cleaner sheet, there would be merit in a new Treaty or Agreement between the two Sovereign States governing the relationship of each to Northern Ireland and confirming whatever provisions are made for regional administration there, assuming these leave an opening for movement for agreement towards a united Ireland. A new Agreement would be more meaningful and acceptable than the other links such as recognising the Commonwealth or joining NATO. It could be founded on the fact that both countries share an urgent concern that conditions should be established which would enable all the people of Northern Ireland to work together in peace and justice for their social and economic progress. It would recognise that the imminent entry of both countries to the EEC renders their co operation to this end not only desirable but essential . . . The United Kingdom (Government and Parliament) would acknowledge that, while Northern Ireland would remain within the United Kingdom as long as that is the wish of the majority of the population of Northern Ireland, the UK would, on the other hand, in no way impede any arrangements, agreed by the majority in Northern Ireland, which looked towards participation in an united Ireland.[28]

The Belfast Agreement fulfils his vision of a 'treaty to constitution' process. Sunningdale was its first test, but clearly lacked the international dimensions of the 1998 agreement. Between 1974 and 1998 'an official redefinition' of the island of Ireland had occurred. Hayward shows how both European integration and the Belfast Agreement have been presented by the Irish elite as new ways of pursuing old (nationalist) objectives, an approach conceived of in the 1960s.[29] Neither the constitution nor Fianna Fáil has prevented this redefinition, which has permanently altered attitudes to reunification. Compared to the Belfast Agreement, the 1937 constitution does not lend itself to a 'binational' reading, but has adapted to international legal influences, such as on human rights, consociationalism, or European legislation. Indeed there *has* been a multi-pronged 'treaty to constitution' process since the 1960s. If the Belfast Agreement works, another will have succeeded.

In summary the three factors which produced an Irish constitutional moment in 1937 have changed. The constitution is no longer an extension of

Fianna Fáil's hegemony, but *De Valera's Constitution and Ours*.[30] The Westminster legacy provides the spine of the state, not the organising principle of Irish democracy. The equivalence of constitutional with national identity has been broken, with the constitution neither a *fait accompli* nor a totally open road to the future. In the current crisis of *representative* democracy, little has been said about the referendum, which will determine the scope of future change. The constitution renounced the 1921 Treaty, but has adapted to most aspects of international integration since then. Would a new constitution be anything other than an elaborate amendment of the current one, with a fresh statement of Irish values? It would still have to reconcile the machinery of government to the concept of a fundamental law. It would provide the same system of checks and balances. Articles 2 and 3 will remain as amended for the foreseeable future. New rights could be provided for, but not at the expense of those already found valuable by the courts. It is a mistake to regard the provisions of the constitution as predominantly Fianna Fáil's. Its commitments to the principles of international law, for example, were not included in the 1922 constitution, but similar clauses were found in many of the new *Select Constitutions of the World* presented to the Dáil in September 1922. The first crisis of liberalism proved of consequence in Ireland only when its innovative ideas were grafted on to the existing political machinery. This has been the Irish mode of constitutional change since 1922. Indeed many ideas thrown up in the first crisis of liberalism, and between 1969 and 1974, did find their way into the 1922 and 1937 constitutions. This can happen in the future. No matter how great the disillusionment, those wanting change have to act within existing institutions, and accept those 'mechanical' aspects of government each crisis of liberalism has been alienated by. If a constitutional moment presents itself (as in Finland in 2000), the new constitution would largely be a continuation of Bunreacht na hÉireann. As an exercise in reconstruction it would be unlikely to transform Irish democracy.

CONSTITUTIONALISM AND DEMOCRACY

In many ways 1922 was the acid test of the Irish constitutional moment. It tested whether the democratic credentials of the independence movement were sufficiently original to transform prevailing conceptions of democracy. The outcome was conservative, and the unmaking of the 1922 constitution part of a wider process of retrenchment in which the basic functions of the state were reduced to the protection of life and private property. The first crisis of liberalism ended in a more existential one in 1922. With the civil war the wheel turned full circle and, give or take its Catholic ethos, Cumann naGaedheal were largely faithful to the older nineteenth-century liberalism. The dramatic wave of democratisation around 1918, found its nemesis in the managerial view of constitutionalism, and Sinn Féin's project proved 'a constitutional revolution that never was'. Since then, Irish constitutionalism has not been about democratic transformation, but about organising the state more effectively or, in the case of Northern Ireland, regulating a conflict which most people accept as more or less immutable.

Yet each episode discussed in this book addressed the relationship between constitutionalism and democracy in a different way. During the first crisis of liberalism advanced nationalists wanted to reconstitute the connection between state and society, from one where elites manipulated institutions to dominate society, to one providing a more organic fit between state and society. The 1922 constitutional committee wanted to make institutions conform to the most advanced principles of democracy, but underestimated the resilience of the traditional parliamentary model. The 1937 moment was an exercise in *re*construction: it consolidated existing institutions on the basis of first principles valued by Sinn Féin before 1921, but succeeded as a reorganisation not a transformation of Irish democracy. Since the 1960s the case for institutional reform was a minor theme in a liberal and pluralist movement that wanted to redefine constitutional identity to make it more inclusive of those outside the *de facto* Catholic majority. The Belfast Agreement was also an exercise in reconstruction. It provides an institutional basis for co-existence in a society with no common national identity, but the constitution-making process was more a gradual instalment than a new beginning.

The current constitutional debate shares a dilemma with the first crisis of liberalism. Irish elites may profit and hide behind existing institutions, but responsibility for change still falls on them. As Upton Sinclair commented, 'It is difficult to get a man to understand something when his salary depends on his not understanding it.'[31] What stands out about the post-1921 experience is the rapidity with which party government reasserted itself after the crisis of liberalism ended. The use of the term 'the mechanics of government' for the constitution in 1922 was very revealing. The influence of international finance, the mass media, and golden circles of business and political elites, now creates a context where the traditional sources of democratic accountability, and parliament itself, have again been proven insufficient. Those arguing for better 'governance' may recognise this new context as a problem for Irish democracy, or just want different elites to manage it better. An interest only in institutional reform often assumes consensus on the ends of government, but it is the absence of such consensus that marks a genuine crisis. Where political reform can take place is though creating institutions, like the Supreme

Court, able to act independently of parties. Reforms requiring change in party culture are another matter.

The truth is that the current crisis is as much ethical as institutional, and has discredited clerical alongside political authority.[32] The question that needs to be asked is whether there could be effective and responsible government under the current institutions were civic values strong enough. A combination of clerical obsession with sexual morality and the passing of the revolutionary generation has clearly eroded what vestiges of public morality existed in the 1960s.[33] Although the economic crisis is global, there is something Irish about the way we conceive it. On the one hand, elites and 'the system' are blamed for the economic collapse. Yet the reason given for their failings is that they were a product of Irish political culture. This confusion about whether to internalise or externalise blame reflects an old dualism between culture and institutions made by the Irish political mind. The British state had to implant its institutions in a traditional culture, and at this confused interface between culture and institutions many of the current issues lie. It is no accident that the debate about clientelism represented one clear occasion when Irish political science debates actually impacted on Irish public life. It raised the question of whether institutional change could change culture, and the current case for electoral reform hinges on this issue. Since the mechanics of democracy – elections, interests groups, and parties – lie at the intersection between culture and institutions, it is hard to foresee huge change in the nature of our representatives without major cultural change. A New Republic requires new values, but this political culture is very enduring. Before 1921 Sinn Féin was also disenchanted with localism, appalled by corruption, and wanted the traditional parliamentary model to be supplemented by new structures. Yet theirs was 'a mental revolution', creating new identities rather than new structures.[34] By 1932 localism in electoral politics, a weak parliament, and excessive centralism, had returned as hallmarks of the new state. In May 1924 William Cosgrave, the President of the Executive Council, commented that the Dáil was only 'a time absorber' to him and his colleagues.[35]

If old institutions have been undermined by culture (not to mention the values of global capitalism), the same can happen to new institutions. With or without a fresh constitutional moment, the Irish clearly face what de Valera said of the anti-treatyites at the end of the civil war: a long patient process of reorganisation and re-education.[36] Better governance requires cultural change. Greek constitutional thought did not assume that the success of a constitutional order depended on institutional design. Rather, constitutional thinkers, employing 'a moral vocabulary', thought education, virtue, and general morality, key to the rise and fall of states. A constitution could help with fostering these virtues, but could not produce them.[37] Ireland also requires new 'post-capitalist' values, which cannot be produced overnight. The late Tony Judt thought the current crisis required changing the language of politics, so that the criteria by which people evaluate leaders and policies could change. This differs from an emphasis on better governance, which generally reduces the issues to how Ireland can become a profitable 'hub' in the chain of global capitalism, without asking questions about the price to be paid in terms of democratic self-government. On the one hand, reforms which have been considered for decades cannot be expected to deliver much change when responsibility for implementing them falls on the very people responsible for the current problems.[38] On the other, creating new institutions will empower new elites, creating the same problems of accountability and democratic control resulting from the power elites acquired during the Celtic Tiger. And it was primarily these elites, not Fianna Fail backbenchers, that created the financial mess Ireland is in today.

Much of the current debate assumes a dualism between culture and institutions. Yet the stability of the Irish state followed its reconciliation of the two.[39] The positive aspect of this reconciliation in the 1930s was the end of a long history of Irish alienation from the state. Its price was to give undue permanence to those aspects of the society which guaranteed a stable social order in 1937. Both judgements apply to the constitution. Sinn Féin was both spiritual aristocracy and political machine, and the question in 1919, 1922 and 1937 was how to combine these two tendencies. Only Bunreacht na hÉireann has done so successfully, and should remain the constitution. Indeed, it is precisely because of its success in integrating the political community, and its reinforcing of constitutional with national identity, that we are now having a *constitutional* debate in the midst of an existential financial crisis. The question of whether the 1937 constitution fulfilled hopes once placed in the Irish national revolution ultimately comes down to personal values. On the one hand, the new state largely failed to follow through on Sinn Féin's 'mental revolution' missing an opportunity to create a new type of state. On the other, the democratic credentials of the constitution were outstanding for 1937. Ultimately, the new beginnings documented in this book show the existence of a native constitutional imagination, not how its ideals can be converted into institutional reality.

Notes

———

INTRODUCTION

1 B. Chubb, *The Politics of the Irish Constitution* (Dublin, 1991), p. 117.

2 J. Elster, 'Introduction' in J. Elster and R. Slagstad (eds), *Constitutionalism and Democracy* (Cambridge, 1997), p. 1.

3 D. Figgis, *The Irish Constitution: Explained by Darrell Figgis* (Dublin, 1922).

4 See M. Loughlin, *The Idea of Public Law* (Oxford, 2004), p. 105.

5 R. Bellamy, *Political Constitutionalism: A Republican Defence of the Constitutionality of Democracy* (Cambridge, 2007), p. 91.

6 B. Ackerman, *We The People Vol. 1: Foundations* (Cambridge MA, 1991).

7 N. Walker, *After the Constitutional Moment* (online paper, London, 2003).

8 'President's broadcast speech', 15 June 1937, P150/2435, National Archives of Ireland (NAI hereafter).

9 G. Jacobsohn, *Constitutional Identity* (Cambridge MA, 2010), ch. 1.

10 See B. Ackerman, 'The rise of world constitutionalism', *Virginia Law Review* 83: 4. (1997), pp. 771–97.

11 'President's broadcast on the constitution', 30 Apr. 1937, P150/2341, University College Dublin Archives (UCDA hereafter).

12 J. Carey, 'Does it matter how a constitution is created?' in Z. Barany and R. G. Moser (eds), *Is Democracy Exportable?* (Cambridge, 2009), p. 160, p. 176.

13 Ibid., p. 160.

14 Z. Elchins, T. Ginsburg, and J. Melton (eds), *The Endurance of National Constitutions* (Cambridge, 2009), pp. 93–109.

15 P. Daly, 'A sound constitution', *Dublin Review of Books*, 25 Sept. 2008.

16 B. Kissane, 'De Valera, the 1937 constitution, and proportional representation' in E. Carolan and O Doyle (eds), *The Irish Constitution: Governance and Values* (Dublin, 2008), pp. 35–53.

17 E. Kedourie, *Nationalism* (London, 1994), introduction.

18 T. Garvin, *An Irish Republican Tradition?*, Working Papers in British-Irish Studies (Dublin, 2004), p. 39. J. Kelly, 'The constitution: law and manifesto' in B. Farrell (ed.), *De Valera's Constitution and Ours* (Dublin, 1988), pp. 208–17; Basil Chubb, *The Government and Politics of Ireland* (2nd edn, Oxford, 1982).

ONE: IDEALS

1 Chubb, *Government and Politics of Ireland*, p. 6.

2 See A. Ward, *The Irish Constitutional Tradition: Responsible Government and Modern Ireland 1782–1992* (Dublin, 1994), p. 52.

3   See L. Barrow and I Bullock, *Democratic Ideas and the British Labour Movement 1880–1914* (Cambridge, 1996); A. Chadwick, *Augmenting Democracy: Political Movements and Constitutional Reform During the Rise of Labour 1900–1924* (Aldershot, 1999).

4   E. F. Biagini, *British Democracy and Irish Nationalism 1876–1906* (Cambridge, 2007), pp. 1–50.

5   Ibid., p. 30, p. 127, p. 130, p. 139.

6   Ward, *Irish Constitutional Tradition*, p. 69.

7   Ibid., p. 207, p. 79, p. 85.

8   J. J. Horgan, *Home Rule: A Critical Consideration* (Dublin, 1911), p. 14.

9   Ward, *Irish Constitutional Tradition*, p. 51, quotation p. 63, pp. 63–9.

10   See D. McCartney, *Democracy and its Nineteenth Century Irish Critics* (Dublin, 1979).

11   B. Ackerman, 'The rise of world constitutionalism', *Virginia Law Review* 83: 4 (1997), pp. 771–97.

12   See J. H. Morgan (ed.), *The New Irish Constitution: An Exposition and Some Arguments: edited on behalf of the Eighty Club* (London, 1912).

13   See A. O'Day, *Irish Home Rule 1867–1921* (Manchester, 1998), p. 317.

14   Biagini, *British Democracy*, pp. 161–8.

15   Ibid., p. 4.

16   Seanacus, 'The question of Catholic organisation, *Irish Rosary* VI (1902), p. 729.

17   O'Day, *Irish Home Rule*, p. 309.

18   Ibid., p. 4.

19   F. Ashtown, *The Unknown Power Behind the Irish Nationalist Party: Its Present Work. . . and Criminal History* (London, 1907).

20   Biagini, *British Democracy*, p. 121.

21   D. Nugent, *The AOH and its Critics* (Dublin, 1911), p. 19.

22   See McCartney, *Democracy and its Nineteenth Century Irish Critics*, p. 19.

23   G. J. McCarthy, *A Plea for the Home Government of Ireland* (London, 1871); Sir John MacDonnell, 'The constitutional limitations upon the powers of the Irish legislation' in Morgan (ed.), *The New Irish Constitution*, p. 108.

24   *Catholic Bulletin* VIII: 5 (May 1918), pp. 214–15; E. Childers, *The Framework of Home Rule* (London, 1911).

25   Richard Hazleton, 'The Irish Senate', *United Irishman*, 9 Nov. 1912, p. 304.

26   Horgan, *Home Rule*, pp. 82–6; *Irish Citizen*, 9 Nov. 1912; M. MacDonagh, *The Life of William O'Brien: The Irish Nationalist: A Biographical Study of Irish Nationalism, Constitutional and Revolutionary* (London, 1928), p. 190; *Sinn Féin*, 10 Jan.1914; D. Figgis, *The Gaelic State in the Past and Future* (London, 1917), p. 73; 'Memo to be submitted by Griffith as basis of proposals to Ulster Unionists at Convention', Dublin 18 Apr. 1912 (NLI).

27   *The Leader*, 11 Oct. 1913.

28   Fred Ryan, 'Empire and liberty', *Dana* 4 (1904), pp.111–17; O'Day, *Irish Home Rule*, p. 195; M. Quinn, 'Colonial Home Rule, *Catholic Bulletin* VIII (1917), pp. 485–90.

29   F. H. O'Donnell, 'The power of the crown and the collapse of the Parliament', *New Ireland Review* XV (Mar.–Aug. 1901), p. 151. W. O'Brien, *The Downfall of Parliamentarianism: A Retrospect for the Accounting Day* (Dublin, 1918), p. 11. A. Griffith, *The Home Rule Bill Examined* (Dublin, 1912); Horgan, *Home Rule*, p. 82; S. Ó Síothcháin, *Constitutionalism and Sinn Féin*, Sinn Féin Pamphlets no. 5, NLI 1907; *Sinn Féin*, 2 May 1908.

30   See P. S. O'Hegarty, *Sinn Féin: An Illumination* (Dublin and London, 1919), p. 36.

31   *United Irishman*, 17 Feb. 1906; A. de Blácam, 'The passing of liberalism', *The Irish Commonwealth* 11 (Apr. 1919), pp. 56–7; *Catholic Bulletin* VII: 7 (July 1915), editorial.

32 See L. Barrow and I. Bullock, *Democratic Ideas and the British Labour Movement 1880–1914* (Cambridge, 1996); Biagini, *British Democracy*; Chadwick, *Augmenting Democracy*.

33 See Chadwick, *Augmenting Democracy*.

34 John Wardell, 'Certain aspects of colonial democracy', *Hermathena* XIII (1902), pp. 383–428.

35 Quoted in Barrow and Bullock, *Democratic Ideas and the British Labour Movement*, p. 163.

36 J. A. Hobson, *The Crisis of Liberalism: New Issues of Democracy* (London, 1909), p. 5.

37 A. R. Wallace, 'A new House of Lords: representatives of the best intellect and character of the nation', *Fortnightly Review*, Feb. 1907.

38 Biagini, *British Democracy*, p. 133

39 *The Leader*, 25 Oct. 1913.

40 *Irish Citizen*, 15 June 1912.

41 *United Irishman*, 1 Feb. 1913.

42 J. Connolly, 'Parliamentary democracy', 22 Sept. 1900 in A. O'Cathasaigh (ed.), *The Lost Writings of James Connolly* (London, 1997), p. 47; A. Griffith, introduction to *The Sinn Féin Policy* (Dublin 1906); A. Clery, *Dublin Essays* (Dublin and London, 1914), p. 37; G. W. Russell, *The National Being: Some Thoughts on an Irish Polity* (Dublin, 1982), p. 108; D. Figgis, *The Gaelic State in the Past and Future* (London, 1917), p. 62; A. de Blácam, *Towards the Republic: A Study of New Ireland's Social and Political Aims* (Dublin, 1919).

43 G. Baden Powell, *The Truth About Home Rule: Papers on the Irish Question* (London and Edinburgh, 1888), p. 20; On Dicey see M. Qvortrup, *A Comparative Study of Referendums: Government by the People* (Manchester, 2005); Connolly, 'Parliamentary democracy', p. 48; Rev. John Kelleher, 'Some present-day anomalies of representative government', *Irish Ecclesiastical Record* (June 1908), p. 136; *Sinn Féin*, 22 June 1907; *Sinn Féin*, 11 May 1907; *Sinn Féin*, 22 June 1907; A. O'Rahilly, The sovereignty of the people' *Studies* X (1921), pp. 39–56.

44 R. N. Tweedy, *Irish Freedom Explained: The Constitution of Saorstát Éireann* (Dublin, 1923), pp. 19–20.

45 Russell, *The National Being*, pp. 103–4; Figgis, *The Gaelic State*, pp. 65–6; De Blácam, *What Sinn Féin Stands For* (Dublin, 1921), pp. 65–6, p. 73.

46 F. W. Jowett, *What is the Use of Parliament?* (London, 1909).

47 H. Sheehy Skeffington, 'The women's movement in Ireland', *Irish Review* II (July 1912), pp. 225–7.

48 Ibid., pp. 225–7; *Irish Citizen*, 30 Nov. 1912; M. MacCurtain, 'Women, the vote, and revolution' in M. MacCurtain and D. Ó Corrain (eds), *Women in Irish Society: The Historical Dimension* (Westport, 1979), p. 50.

49 *The Leader*, 6 June 1914.

50 'Constitution of Cumann na dTeactaire', n. d., P1061 1127 Sighle Humphries Papers, UCDA.

51 MacCurtain, 'Women, the vote, and revolution', pp. 50–4.

52 'Cumann na mBan Convention', 28–29 Sept. 1918, P1061 1127, UCDA; MacCurtain, 'Women, the vote, and revolution', p. 52 p. 49; *Irish Citizen*, 11 Apr. and 2 May 1914.

53 Biagini, *British Democracy*, p. 30.

54 Chadwick, *Augmenting Democracy*, p. 169; George Gavan Duffy, *A Fair Constitution for Ireland* (2nd edn, James Duffy, 1892); Erskine Childers, *The Framework of Home Rule* (London, 1911), p. 337; J. Meredith, *Proportional Representation in Ireland* (London, 1913), pp. 33–4.

55 *The Leader*, 25 Oct. 1913. See F. C. O'Brien, *Irish Review* III (Mar. 1913–Feb. 1914), p. 439; *Irish Citizen*, 11 Jan. 1912.

56　*Sinn Féin*, 2 May 1908.

57　*Sinn Féin*, 24 Dec. 1910; *Sinn Féin*, 31 Jan. 1911; *Sinn Féin*, 4 May 1912.

58　Tom Garvin, *Nationalist Revolutionaries in Ireland 1858–1928* (Oxford, 1987), pp. 118–26.

59　R. P. Davis, *Arthur Griffith and Non Violent Sinn Féin* (Dublin, 1974), p. 153

60　A. Griffith *The Home Rule Bill Examined* (Dublin 1912); *Irish Freedom*, Oct. 1911; De Blácam, *Towards the Republic*, p. 67.

61　M. Laffan, *The Resurrection of Ireland: The Sinn Féin Party 1916–1923* (Cambridge, 1999), p. 214.

62　B. Farrell, *The Founding of Dáil Éireann: Parliament and Nation Building* (Dublin, 1971), introduction.

63　D. Shaw, *The Drama of Sinn Féin* (London, 1923), p. 116. *Sinn Féin: Local Elections*, 1920 (NLI).

64　B. Farrell, *The Creation of the Dáil* (Dublin, 1994), p. 167.

65　P. Maume, 'The ancient constitution: Arthur Griffith and his intellectual legacy to Sinn Féin', *Irish Political Studies* 10 (1995), pp. 123–38; *Sinn Féin*, 22 June 1907; S. Ó Síothcháin, *Constitutionalism and Sinn Féin*, Sinn Féin Pamphlets no. 5 (NLI); 'The unconstitutional constitution', 'The criminality of constitutionalism', *Irish Freedom*, Jan. 1912

66　'Manifesto of Cumann na mBan (Irish Women's Council)', 1914 P. 48 a/20 MacCurtain, 'Women, the vote and revolution', pp. 50–4; ibid., p. 55; 'Constitution of Cumann na mBan' P48 a/12; Cumann na mBan P48 a/21; 'Statement from the Women of Ireland to the Senate and Congress of the United States', P48 a/182

67　'Re questionnaire for proposed history of C na B', n. d. P61 4 (2) UCDA.

68　'Manifesto of Cumann na mBan (Irish Women's Council)', 1914 P. 48 a/20; MacCurtain, 'Women, the vote and revolution', pp. 50–4; ibid., p. 55; 'Constitution of Cumann na mBan' P48 a/12; Cumann na mBan P48 a/21; MacCurtain, 'Women, the vote and revolution', p. 55. Cumann na mBan P48 1/21; 'Manifesto of Cumann na mBan' (Irish Women's Council)', 1914 P48 a/20. All archival references to UCDA.

69　D. P Moran, *The Philosophy of Irish Ireland* (Dublin, 1905), p. 71.

70　Sinn Féin Pamphlet, *Democracy and Nationality*, n. d. (NLI).

71　J. Hutchinson, *The Dynamics of Cultural Nationalism: The Gaelic Revival and the Creation of the Irish Nation-State* (London, 1987), p. 311.

72　*Sinn Féin Programme Session 1913–1914* (NLI).

73　*The Republic*, Dec. 1906–Mar. 1907; 'Some constitutions of the white man', *Sinn Féin*, 2 Dec. 1911; *United Irishman*, 13 Aug. 1904; *Irish Freedom*, Aug. 1912; Figgis, *The Gaelic State*, p. 3; *Irish Freedom*, May 1913.

74　Barrow and Bullock, *Democratic Ideas and the British Labour Movement*, p. 139.

75　See Chadwick, *Augmenting Democracy*, p. 207.

76　*General Election Manifesto to the Irish People* (NLI).

77　*The Republic*, 24 Jan. 1907; *United Irishman*, 11 July 1903; D. Greaves, *Father Michael O'Flanagan: Republican Priest* (A Connolly Association Pamphlet, 1954), pp. 8–9

78　T. Garvin, *1922: The Birth of Irish Democracy* (Dublin, 1996), p. 85.

79　Sinn Féin, *1919 Árd Fheis: Clár*, Sinn Féin, *Local Elections* 1920 (NLI).

80　De Blácam, *What Sinn Féin Stands For*, p. 139. Figgis, *The Gaelic State*, pp. 65–73, Russell, *The National Being*, p. 108–13.

81　De Blácam, *What Sinn Féin Stands For*, p. 141.

82 Griffith, *The Sinn Féin Policy* (Dublin 1906); Figgis, *The Gaelic State*, pp. 65–6; Russell, *The National Being*, pp. 114–15; De Blácam, *What Sinn Féin Stands For*, Sinn Féin, *Córughadh*, 1917? (NLI).

83 R. P. Davis, *Arthur Griffith and Non Violent Sinn Féin* (Dublin, 1974), p. 87.

84 D. Shaw, *The Drama of Sinn Féin* (London, 1923), p. 133.

85 Farrell, *The Creation of the Dáil*, p. 69.

86 De Blácam, *What Sinn Féin Stands For*, chapter on 'The Sinn Féin constitution'.

87 Rev. P Gaynor, *The Faith and Morals of Sinn Féin* (Sinn Féin Pamphlets, *c.*1918).

88 Sinn Féin: *Árd Fheis*, 16 Oct. 1919 (NLI).

89 Sinn Fein *Árd Fheis* (Extraordinary 8 Apr. 1919) Reports (NLI).

90 P. Pearse, 'The sovereign people', *Collected Writings of Padraig H. Pearse: Political Writings and Speeches* (Dublin, Cork and Belfast, 1924), p. 335, p. 342, p. 336, pp. 292–3.

91 *The Republic*, 2 May 1907; *United Irishman*, 14 Nov. 1903; Pearse, 'The sovereign people'; Glandon, *Arthur Griffith and the Advanced Nationalist Press*, p. 76. ; Walter O'Brien, 'Sinn Feinism', *Catholic Bulletin* III: 9 (Sept. 1918), pp. 441–5.

92 D. Shaw, *The Drama of Sinn Féin* (London, 1923), p. 121.

93 *New York Times*, 20 Sept. 1919, 30 June 1919.

94 L. T. Hobhouse, 'Irish nationalism and liberal principle' in Morgan (ed.), *The New Irish Constitution*, pp. 361–72.

95 Hobson, *Crisis of Liberalism*, p. 260; *Sinn Féin*, 15 Apr. 1911; Pearse, 'The sovereign people', p. 343; *Sinn Féin*, 18 Jan. 1913. De Blácam, 'The passing of liberalism'; O'Brien, *The Downfall*, pp. 59–60.

96 See J. Hutchinson, *The Dynamics of Cultural Nationalism: The Gaelic Revival and the Creation of the Irish Nation State* (London, 1987), p. 123–6, pp. 132–3; De Blácam 'The passing of liberalism', pp. 54–7; *The Republic*, 2 May 1907; E. MacNeill, 'Education – the idea of the state', *Irish Review*, 25 Nov. 1922; E. MacNeill, 'The view of the state in relation to education', *Irish Review*, 28 Oct. 1922.

97 *United Irishman*, 30 Nov. 1912; J. P. O'Kane, 'The Church and liberty', *The Leader*, 27 Sept. 1913, *United Irishman*, 4 June 1904; *Catholic Bulletin* 3 (1913), pp. 249–53.

98 Rev. P. Gaynor, *The Faith and Morals of Sinn Féin*, Sinn Féin Pamphlets (Clare Series *c.*1918).

99 An exception was the journalist and nationalist politician Frank Hugh O'Donnell.

100 A. O 'Rahilly, 'Suarez and democracy', *Studies* 7 (1918), pp. 1–21; 'Democracy, Parliament and Cromwell', *Studies* 7 (1918), pp. 545–52; 'The Catholic origins of democracy', *Studies* 8 (1919), pp. 1–18; 'The sources of English and American democracy', *Studies* 8 (1919), pp. 189–209; 'The democracy of Saint Thomas', *Studies* 10 (Mar. 1921).

101 O'Rahilly, 'Democracy, Parliament and Cromwell'.

102 O'Rahilly, 'Suarez and democracy', p. 20.

103 J. Rose, *The Question of Zion* (Princeton and Oxford, 2005), p. 63.

104 Shaw, *The Drama of Sinn Féin*, p. 131.

105 Ibid., pp. 114–25.

106 O Day, *Irish Home Rule*, p. 309.

107 Kelleher, 'Some present day anomalies', pp. 129–41; *Irish Freedom*, Oct. 1911; De Blácam, *Towards the Republic*, p. 139.

TWO: EXPERIMENT

1 Figgis, *The Irish Constitution*, p. 17.

2 Ibid., p. 20.

3 *Irish Independent*, 19 June 1922.

4 *Morning Post*, 17 June 1922.

5 Committee's Report, 7 Mar. 1922, K5 3/493/5 1922 CC, NAI.

6 'Constitutional Committee Meeting', 24 Jan. 1922, P/4 299 (1), UCDA.

7 Lloyd George to Griffith, 13 Dec. 1921, DFA: 'League of Nations', L258–260, NAI.

8 Kissane, *Explaining Irish Democracy*, p. 137.

9 Duffy to Collins, 15 Mar. 1922, D152/198, NAI,

10 Committee's Report, Mar. 7 1922, 3/493/5, 1922 CC K5, NAI.

11 Kennedy in L. Kohn, *The Constitution of the Irish Free State* (London, 1932), p. xl.

12 Figgis to Collins, 7 Mar. 1922, Committee Report, 1922 Constitutional Committee L-R, NAI.

13 Cosgrave to Figgis, 11 Aug. 1922, 1922 CC S-T, NAI.

14 'Representation of the People Bill', P48a/274, UCDA.

15 'Index to Constitutions: Selected for Publication', 1922 CC H-J, NAI.

16 Figgis to Collins, 13 Apr. 1922, 1922 CC U-W, NAI.

17 'Memorandum on draft C by Messrs Murnaghan and O'Rahilly', n. d. 1922 CC U-W, NAI.

18 Figgis, *The Irish Constitution*, p. 35.

19 Kohn, *The Constitution of the Irish Free State*, p. 97.

20 N. Mansergh, *The Irish Free State: Its Government and Politics* (London, 1934), p. 46.

21 Figgis, McNeill O'Byrne, to Collins, 13 Apr. 1922, 3/493/5 1922 CC, NAI.

22 Figgis's untitled note, following correspondence with Professor Culverwell: 'Correspondence from persons not on Committee', 1922 CC, S-T NAI.

23 'Notes on Draft C of the Constitution for the members of the P. G. ', 12 Apr. 1922, K5 3/493/5 1922, CC NAI.

24 A. O'Rahilly, *Thoughts on the Constitution* (Dublin, 1937), p. 51.

25 'Memorandum on Draft C by Messr Murnaghan and O'Rahilly', 1922 CC U-W, NAI.

26 'Notes on Draft C of the Constitution for the members of the P. G.', 12 Apr. 1922, K5 3/493/5 1922 CC, NAI.

27 O'Rahilly to Figgis, 21 Feb. 1922, 4 Apr. 1922, CC C-T, NAI.

28 Figgis to O'Rahilly, 5 Apr. 1922, P178/28, UCDA.

29 O'Byrne to O'Rahilly, 15 Feb. 1922, P178/10, UCDA.

30 Harty to O'Rahilly, 3 Mar. 1922, P178/24 (1) UCDA.

31 1922 CC L-R, NAI.

32 P4/331–3, Kennedy Papers, UCDA.

33 Ibid.

34 Signatories of Draft A to Collins, 21 Apr. 22, 1922 CC, NAI. .

35 Kennedy to Figgis, 6 Mar. 1922, 3/493/5, 1922 CC, NAI.

36 Figgis, McNeill, O'Byrne to Collins, 13 Apr. 1922, 3/493/5, 1922 CC, NAI.

37 Draft A P4/331, Kennedy Papers, UCDA.

38 'Secret – Copy of Constitution', P4/333, UCDA.

39 P4/332, Kennedy Papers, UCDA.

40 N. J. Brown, 'Reason, interest, rationality, and passion in constitution drafting', *Perspectives on Politics* 6: 4 (2008), pp. 675–89.

41 H. Kennedy, 'The constitution of the Irish Free State examined', 1923/24, P4/1680, UCDA.

42 B. Kissane, *The Politics of the Irish Civil War* (Oxford, 2005), p. 71.

43 Culverwell to Collins, 5 Apr. 1922, 3/493/5 1922 CC, NAI.

44 *Poblacht*, 22 Mar. 1922.

45 Culverwell to Collins, 5 May 1922, 3/493/5, 1922 CC, NAI.

46 'Observations on the criticisms of the British government on the draft Irish Constitution, May 1922, P4/352, UCDA.

47 'Criticisms of Draft B – by George O'Brien', 24 Mar. 1922, NA1 1922 CC, NAI.

48 'Committee's response to O'Brien's criticisms', Figgis to Collins, 13 Apr. 1922, 1922 CC, NAI.

49 'Notes on the British amendment to the constitution', P4/362 (12), UCDA.

50 T. Mohr, 'British involvement in the creation of the first Irish constitution, *Dublin University Law Journal* 30 (2008), pp. 72–3.

51 'Amendments to Constitution Bill: Schedule 1', P4/341, UCDA.

52 *Morning Post*, 16 June 1922.

53 Lloyd George to Griffith 1 June 1922, P4/352, UCDA.

54 *Poblacht*, 22 Mar. 1922.

55 'Cabinet Meeting', 3 June 1922, P152/206, UCDA.

56 'Cabinet Meeting', 5 June 1922, P152/206, UCDA.

57 'Notes on the British Amendments to the Constitution', P4/362 (12), UCDA.

58 Kennedy to Collins, 11 June 1922, P4/363, UCDA.

59 'Draft reply to Lloyd George', 'Observations on the criticisms of the British Government on the draft Irish constitution', P4/352, UCDA.

60 Mohr, 'British involvement', p. 175.

61 Draft reply to Lloyd George, P4/352, UCDA.

62 Kennedy notes on Article 11, 17 Nov. 1922, P4/355 (2), UCDA.

63 'Meeting at 10 Downing St', 10 June 1922, P4/367 (3), UCDA.

64 Mohr, 'British involvement', pp. 183–4.

65 O'Rahilly, *Thoughts on the Constitution*, p. 7.

66 *Irish Independent*, 23 Sept. 1922.

67 Gavan Duffy to Collins, 26 May 1922, P152/202, UCDA.

68 Letter to Collins and Mulcahy, 24 July 1922, P152/266, UCDA.

69 *Irish Times*, 17 June 1922.

70 *The Times*, 16 June 1922.

71 *Irish Independent*, 19 June 1922.

72 Notes, n. d., P4/847 (1) UCDA.

73 Mohr, 'British Involvement', p. 186.

74 Kissane, *Politics of the Irish Civil War*, pp. 86–7.

75 Magennis to O'Rahilly, *c.*Sept 1922, P178/38, UCDA.

76 Figgis, *The Irish Constitution*, p. 19.

77 *Morning Post*, 17 June 1922.

78 See H. McBain, and L. Rogers, *The New Constitutions of Europe* (New York, 1923).

79　E. M. Stephens, 'The constitution', *Saorstat Éireann: Irish Free State Official Handbook* (Dublin, 1932), p. 74.

80　Ibid., p. 9.

81　Ibid., p. 26.

82　Douglas, France, and Kennedy, to Collins, 8 Mar. 1922, 3/493/5, 1922 CC, NAI.

83　Ibid.

84　Memorandum on Draft C by Murnaghan and O'Rahilly, n. d. NAI, 1922 CC U-W, NAI.

85　O'Rahilly note, n. d., P178/17, UCDA.

86　*Irish Independent*, 23 Sept. 1922.

87　Figgis, McNeill, O'Byrne to Collins, 13 Apr. 1922, 3/493/5, 1922 CC, NAI.

88　Ibid.

89　O'Rahilly, 'Notes on Draft C', 12 Apr. 1922, 3/493/5, 1922 CC, NAI.

90　'Acting Chairman's Draft of the Executive', 12 Oct. 1922, 3/493/5 1922 CC, NAI.

91　See Mohr, 'British involvement', p. 169.

92　B. O'Neill, 'The referendum process in Ireland', *Irish Jurist* 35 (2000), p. 307.

93　Ibid., p. 306.

94　'Document no. 43: initiative and referendum'. State of Washington 1909 , P4/321, 1922 CC, NAI.

95　Tweedy, *Irish Freedom Explained*, pp. 19–20.

96　M. Qvortrup, *A Comparative Study of the Referendums: Government by the People* (Manchester, 2005), pp. 44–62.

97　*Dail Debates*, vol. 1, 5 Oct. 1922.

98　Laffan, *The Resurrection of Sinn Féin*, p. 324.

99　*Cork Examiner*, 10 Apr. 1919.

100　Laffan, *The Resurrection of Sinn Féin*, p. 327.

101　'Memo to be submitted by Griffith as basis of proposals to Ulster Unionists at Convention', *Sinn Féin*, 18 Apr. 1912.

102　Figgis to Collins, 7 Mar. 1922, 1922 CC L-R, NAI.

103　'Notes on evidence on the working of PR election by Mr J. Humphreys', 13 Feb. 1922, 1922 CC L-R, NAI.

104　Figgis to McCarthy, Feb. 2 1922, 1922 CC S-T, NAI.

105　'The Irish Free State – Schedule and Maps of Constituencies for Senate and lower House', 1922 CC LR, NAI.

106　'Department of Local Government Memo on the General Election, 27 Aug. 1923', D/T S3766A, NAI.

107　Kennedy to Churchill, 9 Aug. 1922, D/T S 2925, NAI.

108　Churchill to Cosgrave, 2 Sept. 1922, D/T S 2925, NAI.

109　'Memo on draft constitution; P4/308 (20), UCDA.

110　'Conference on Ireland: Memorandum by Lord Midleton', 29 May 1922, P4/364 (6),UCDA.

111　'Secret Document summarising conclusion of a meeting held in the room of Secretary of State for Colonies', 13 June 1922, P4/366, UCDA.

112　'Agreement between Law Officers and Provisional Government', P4/371, UCDA.

113　*Irish Independent*, 28 Sept. 1922.

114　*Dáil Debates*, vol. 1, 20 Sept. 1922.

115 'Memo on Vocational Senate elected by P. R.',1922 CC L-R, NAI.

116 *Dáil Debates*, vol. 1, 4 Oct. 1922.

117 Figgis, *The Irish Constitution*, p. 60.

118 'Criticism of draft B – by Mr George O'Brien, 24 Mar. 1922, NA 1922 CC, NAI.

119 Figgis to Collins, 13 Apr. 1922, 1922 CC U-W, NAI.

120 Local Government to Provisional Government, 13 Oct. 1922, D/T S 1817 A, NAI.

121 Kennedy, 'The constitution of the Irish Free State examined', 1923/24, P4/1680 UCDA.

122 William Cosgrave, 'Comments on the foregoing articles', *Studies* (1933), p. 551.

123 Figgis, *Irish Constitution*, p. 37.

124 'Committee's Report', 7 Mar. 1922, 3/493/5, 1922 CC, NAI.

125 T. A. Finlay, *The Constitution: Fifty Years On* (Dublin, 1988), p. 1.

126 Figgis, *Irish Constitution*, p. 48.

127 Kohn, *The Constitution of the Irish Free State*, p. 340.

128 A. Lijphart, *Patterns of Democracy: Government Forms and Performance in Thirty-Six Counties* (New Haven and London, 1999), p. 228.

129 Kennedy to Collins, 11 June 1922, P4/363, UCDA.

130 J. J. Horgan, 'The problem of government', *Studies* (1933), p. 539.

131 Kohn, *Constitution of the Irish Free State*, p. 259.

132 *Dáil Debates*, vol. 1, 25 Oct. 1922.

133 *Dáil Debates*, vol. 1, 18 Sept. 1922.

134 Cosgrave, 'Comments on the foregoing articles'.

135 I. Jennings, *The Law and Constitution* (5th edn, London, 1968), p. 8.

136 *Dáil Debates*, vol. 1, 27 Oct. 1922.

137 'Report of the Director of Organisation', Sinn Féin Árd Fheis, 16 Oct. 1919 (NLI).

138 *Dáil Debates*, vol. 1, 18 Sept. 1922.

139 'The Catholic layman in public life', *An tOglac*, Jan. 1928

140 Ibid., pp. 73–8.

141 Shaw, *The Drama of Sinn Féin*, p. 129.

142 'Amendments to Constitution Bill', Schedule 1 P4/341, UCDA.

143 'Secretary Department of Home Affairs to Minister of External Affairs', 12 Oct. 1922, DFA Early Series 145 (2), NAI.

144 T. Mohr, 'The rights of women under the constitution of the Irish Free State', *Irish Jurist* XLI (2006), p. 33.

145 Ibid., p. 33.

146 C. O'Leary, *Irish Elections 1918–1977, Parties, Voters, and Proportional Representation* (Dublin, 1979), p. 24.

147 'Memorandum of ambulance work & efforts for peace', Civil War 1922–24, 'Peace Proposal – J. F. Homan/Clontarf, D/T S 8138, NAI.

148 R. Fanning, *Independent Ireland* (Dublin, 1983), p. 10.

149 B. Farrell, 'From first Dáil through Free State' in B. Farrell (ed.), *De Valera's Constitution and Ours* (Dublin, 1988), pp. 117–19.

150 Ibid., p. 219.

151 The members were K. O'Higgins, E. Blythe, J. J. Walsh, M. Hayes Ceann Comháirle, M. O'Byrne (Attorney General), E. M. Stephens (Secretary), and Senators Douglas and Binchy, 'Amendments to the Constitution Committee 1925–26', D/T S 4656, NAI.

152 Committee, Report, 6 May 1926, 'Amendments to the Constitution Committee 1925–26', D/T S 4650, NAI.

153 Ibid.

154 Mohr, 'Rights of women', p. 55.

155 L. Karvonen, *Political Organisation and the Interwar Crisis in Europe* (Boulder, 1993).

156 J. Coakley, 'Ireland's unique electoral experiment: the Senate election of 1925', *Irish Political Studies* 20: 3 (2005), pp. 231–69.

157 B. Farrell, 'From first Dáil through Free State' in B. Farrell (ed.), *De Valera's Constitution and Ours* (Dublin, 1988), p. 219.

158 'Amendments to the Constitution Committee, 1925–26', NAI D/T S 4650.

159 Local Government Memo to Executive Council 16 Oct. 1926, D/T S 3766A, NAI.

160 *Waterford News*, 4 Apr. 1927; *An Reult*, 10 May 1930.

161 Local Government Memo to Executive Council 16 Oct. 1926, D/T S 3766A, NAI.

162 Cosgrave to Miles, 2 Oct. 1928, NAI D/T S 3766A.

163 *Waterford News*, 1 Apr. 1927.

164 John Humphreys, *Irish Free State General Election, 1933: The Workings of Proportional Representation*, PR Pamphlet 73, 1933.

165 *Irish Times*, 22 Mar. 1968.

166 A. Beattie, 'Ministerial responsibility and the theory of the British State' in R. A. W. Rhodes and P. Dunleav (eds), *Prime Minister, Cabinet and Core Executive* (London, 1995), p. 172.

167 See D. J. Elazar, ' The principles and traditions underlying state constitutions', *Publius* 12: 1 (1982), pp. 13–14.

168 2nd reading draft, 15 June 1928, D/T S4469/10, NAI.

169 Cabinet Meeting, 19 July 1922, D/T S4469/10, NAI.

170 Clifford, *Constitutional History of Eire/Ireland*, p. 53.

171 *Seanad Debates*, vol. 10, 4 July 1928.

172 Quoted in Kissane, *Explaining Irish Democracy*, p. 208.

173 Kohn, *The Constitution of the Irish Free State*, p. 245. B. O'Neill, 'The referendum process', p. 308.

174 O'Higgins, 'On democracy', *An t Oglac*, Jan. 1928, p. 81.

175 *Seanad Éireann*, vol. 10, 4 July 1928.

176 O'Neill, 'The referendum process', pp. 319–20.

177 *Dáil Debates*, 884–5, 20 June 1928.

178 See Kohn, *Constitution of the Irish Free State*, pp. 378–81.

179 *Dáil Debates*, vol. 34 col. 313–14, 2 Apr. 1930.

180 J. Hearne, 'The constitution and the national life', D/T S 9905, NAI.

181 Hogan to O'Rahilly, *c.*May 1937, P178/64 (1), UCDA.

182 Hugh Kennedy, Foreword to Kohn, *Constitution of the Irish Free State*, p. xiii.

183 A. E. Malone, 'Party government in the Irish Free State', *Political Science Quarterly* 44: 3 (1929), p. 378.

184 Richard Mulcahy, *Dáil Debates*, vol. 59, 29 Nov. 1935.

185 Karvonen, *Political Organisation and the Interwar Crisis*, p. 164.

186 O'Rahilly, *Thoughts on the Constitution* (Dublin, 1937), p. 23.

187 Farrell, 'From first Dáil through Free State', p. 31.

188 E. M. Stephens, 'The constitution', *Irish Free State Official Handbook*, p. 74.

189 D. W. Harkness, *The Restless Dominion: The Irish Free State and the British Commonwealth of Nations* (London, 1969), p. 36.

190 Sturgis telegram to Loughnane, n. d. Nov. 1922, D/T S2989, NAI.

191 O'Rahilly to Figgis, 4 Apr. 1922, 1922 CC S-T, NAI.

192 McDunphy to O'Rahilly, 12 Aug. 1922, P178/44, UCDA, see also, P 178/38, UCDA.

193 O'Rahilly to McDunphy, 2 Sept. 1922, P/78/48), UCDA.

194 O'Rahilly, *Thoughts on the Constitution*, p. 21.

THREE: CONSOLIDATION

1 E. de Valera, 'The constitution and national life', memo originally written by John Hearne, D/T S9905, NAI.

2 *Irish Times*, 1 May 1937.

3 Tierney to O'Rahilly, 4 May 1937, P178/65, UCDA.

4 J. G. A. Pocock , *The Machiavellian Moment: Florentine Political Thought and the Atlantic Republican Tradition* (Princeton, 1975), preface.

5 D. Elazar, 'The political theory of covenant: biblical origins and modern developments', *Publius* 10: 4 (1980), p. 13.

6 'President's broadcast speech', 15 June 1937, P150/2435, UCDA.

7 Ibid.

8 '"God Given Rights": principles of the New Irish constitution', 30 Apr. 1937, P150 2431, UCDA.

9 'President's broadcast on the constitution', 30 Apr. 1937, P150/2431, UCDA.

10 'President's broadcast speech', 15 June 1937, P150/2435, NAI.

11 Typescript draft of de Valera speech to Dáil seeking approval of constitution', 25 May–June 1937, P150/2441, UCDA.

12 Kissane, *Explaining Irish Democracy*, p. 187.

13 Ibid., p. 375.

14 D. Keogh and A. J. McCarthy, *The Making of the Irish Constitution 1937: Bunreacht na hÉireann* (Dublin, 2007), p. 297.

15 J. Hearne, 'Constitutional functions of the president', *President of Éire: Powers and Functions,* June 1939, D/T S9778A, NAI.

16 De Valera, *Dáil Debates*, vol. 39, 17 July 1931.

17 'President of Ireland: Powers, functions, etc, under the constitution: classified summary', prepared by the Taoiseach's Department, D/T S 9797 A, NAI.

18 J. Kelly, *The Irish Constitution* (Dublin, 1980), preface.

19 For a view sympathetic to the anti-treaty position see 'Constitutional development: 1921–1951', D/T 2001/48/123, NAI; V. Grogan, 'Irish constitutional development' *Studies* 40: 160 (1951), pp. 385–98.

20 Royal Irish Academy, *The Origins of the Irish Constitution* (project directed by G. Hogan) (Dublin, 2011).

21 Keogh and McCarthy, *The Making of the Irish Constitution*, pp. 38–60

22 Ibid., p. 207.

23 Ibid., p. 64.

24 Ibid., p. 74.

25 Kelly, *Irish Constitution*, preface.

26 'Constitutional development: 1922–1951', 2001/48/123, NAI.

27 Kelly, *Irish Constitution*, preface.

28 S. Finer, *The History of Government* (Oxford 1999), p. 1501.

29 P. Mair, 'De Valera and democracy' in T. Garvin, M. Manning and R. Sinnott (eds), *Dissecting Irish Politics: Essays in Honour of Brian Farrell* (Dublin 2004), p. 44.

30 'Summary of draft heads of the constitution', D/TS 9715 A, NAI.

31 Keogh and McCarthy, *The Making of the Irish Constitution*, p. 326, p. 336, p. 337, p. 455.

32 'Summary of Draft Heads of the Constitution', D/TS 9715 A, NAI.

33 Ibid.

34 Keogh and McCarthy, *The Making of the Irish Constitution*, p. 454.

35 Figgis to Collins, 7 Mar. 1922, 1922 CC L-R, NAI.

36 See P178/60–63, UCDA.

37 When an American student requested permission to inspect the drafts in 1963, the decision was taken to transfer them to the archives The full records of the committee, and of their sources, have not survived. (Constitution, 1922 Settlement of Draft by Provisional Government D/T 2008/148/37).

38 Murnaghan to O'Rahilly, 5 May 1937, P178/55, UCDA.

39 Arthur Cox, Solicitors & Co. to O'Rahilly, 12 May 1937, P178/55, UCDA.

40 O'Rahilly, *Thoughts on the Constitution*, p. 22.

41 Ibid., p. 64.

42 See Mohr, 'British involvement', p. 27.

43 Keogh and McCarthy, *The Making of the Irish Constitution*, p. 112.

44 'Notes on Draft C', 12 Apr. 1922, 1922 CC A-C, NAI.

45 *Irish Independent*, 15 May 1937.

46 O'Rahilly, *Thoughts on the Constitution*, p. 7.

47 Cahill to de Valera, 4 Sept. 1936, P150/2393, UCDA.

48 De Valera to Cahill, 19 Sept. 1936, P150/2393, UCDA.

49 Keogh and McCarthy, *The Making of the Irish Constitution*, pp. 94–106.

50 Ibid., p. 69.

51 A. Hyland, 'The multi-denominational experience' in Constitution Review Group, *Report of the Constitution Review Group* (Dublin, 1996), pp. 631–2.

52 Keogh and McCartney, *The Making of the Irish Constitution*, pp. 108–10.

53 Ibid., p. 117.

54 McQuaid to de Valera, n. d., P150/2407, UCDA.

55 On Articles 38–42, P150/2407, UCDA.

56 Extracts on basis of authority from Papal Pronouncements, P150/2406; Memo in handwriting of Philip O'Donoghue, Legal Advisor, Office of the Attorney General, n. d., P150/2412, UCDA.

57 Keogh and McCarthy, *The Making of the Irish Constitution*, pp. 121–2.

58 Ibid., p. 161.

59 Ibid., pp. 167, pp. 154–5, p. 172.

60 Memo in handwriting of Philip O'Donoghue, n. d., Legal Advisor, Office of the Attorney

General, n. d., P150/2412 NAI.

61 Mair, 'De Valera and democracy', p. 45.

62 Ward, *The Irish Constitutional Tradition*, p. 219.

63 See M. MacCartaigh, *Accountability in Irish Parliamentary Politics* (Dublin, 2005), pp. 64–70.

64 J. Hearne, 'Preliminary drafts of heads of a constitution for *Saorstát Éireann*', 18 May 1935, P150/370, UCDA.

65 Roche to McDunphy, 13 Apr. 1937, D/T S10159, NAI.

66 'Observations of the Attorney General', 22 Mar. 1937, D/T S9715 B, NAI.

67 Comments of Finance, 23 Mar. 1937, D/T S 9715 B, NAI.

68 'Observations of the Department of the President', 23 Mar. 1937, D/T S 9715 B, NAI.

69 Hearne, 'The constitution and the national life', D/T S9965, NAI.

70 Draft speech to Dáil seeking approval for constitution, May–June 1937, P150/2441, UCDA.

71 Keogh and McCarthy, *The Making of the Irish Constitution*, p. 297.

72 'Summary of draft heads of the constitution', First Draft, D/T S9715 A, NAI.

73 Mair, 'De Valera and democracy', p. 44.

74 Keogh and McCarthy, *The Making of the Irish Constitution*, p. 297.

75 Ibid., p. 339.

76 Ibid., p. 83.

77 Ibid., p. 456.

78 D. Barrington, 'The presidency', *Hibernia* (Mar. 1958), p. 1.

79 Quoted in B. Kissane, 'Eamon de Valera and the survival of democracy in inter-war Ireland', *Journal of Contemporary History* 42: 2 (Apr. 2007), pp. 213–26.

80 Hearne, 'Constitutional functions of the president'.

81 Ibid.

82 See Keogh and McCarthy, *The Making of the Irish Constitution*, pp. 306 p. 327, p. 366.

83 'De Valera interview with Daniel Lord', n. d., P150/2328, UCDA.

84 Report on Joint Committee on the Constitution', 1928, 'Memo on Article 45 of the Constitution', D/T, S 4469/10, NAI.

85 *Dáil Debates*, vol. 67, 1 June 1937.

86 Mr Healy, *Dáil Debates*, vol. 233, 20 Mar. 1968.

87 *Dáil Debates*, vol. 67, 1 June 1937.

88 James Meredith, *Proportional Representation in Ireland* (London, 1913), p. 3.

89 Kissane, *Explaining Irish Democracy*, p. 212.

90 Figgis to McCarthy, 2 Feb. 1922, 1922 CC S-T, NAI.

91 The cabinet instructed the Minister of Local Government to consider electoral redistribution and to submit a report on 24 May 1937, 'Revision of constituencies 1932–41', D/T S1817 B, NAI.

92 Maguire to Secretary of the Department of the President, 13 Feb. 1934, D/T S2245, NAI.

93 'Abolition of the Senate', D/T S 2245, NAI.

94 Keogh and McCarthy, *The Making of the Irish Constitution*, pp. 86–8.

95 A. O'Rahilly, 'The constitution and the Senate', *Studies* 25: 97 (1936), pp. 2–7.

96 M. Tierney, 'The new constitution', *The Leader*, 5 June 1937.

97 Keogh and McCarthy, *The Making of the Irish Constitution*, p. 88.

98 Ibid., p. 79.

99 'Plan of fundamental constitutional law', 14 Oct. 1936 (P150/2370) UCDA. 100 McQuaid, 'Re suggested method of dealing with directive principles', Mar. 1937, P150/2407, UCDA.

101 Keogh and McCarthy, *The Making of the Irish Constitution*, p. 378.

102 Ward, *The Irish Constitutional Tradition*, p. 255.

103 Mair, 'De Valera and democracy', p. 44.

104 See B. P. Kennedy, 'Appreciation: John Hearne and the Irish constitution', *Eire/Ireland* 24: 2 (1989), pp. 121–8.

105 'President's broadcast on the constitution', 20 Apr. 1937, P150/2431, NAI.

106 Keogh and McCarthy, *The Making of the Irish Constitution*, p. 178.

107 'Interview given by the President to Mr Joseph Driscoll, *New York Herald Tribune*, 27 May 1937, P150/2351, 'Interview given to John Grade', P150/2284, 'Interview given by the President to Mr Milton Bronner', 27 Feb. 1936, P150/2328, NAI.

108 *Irish Independent*, 8 May 1937.

109 P. V. Uleri, 'Introduction' in M. Gallagher and P. V. Uleri (eds), *The Referendum Experience in Europe* (New York, 1996), p. 3.

110 Grogan, 'Irish constitutional development', p. 398.

111 *Dail Debates*, vol. 69, 21 June 1937.

112 *Dail Debates*, vol. 67, 1 June 1937.

113 Douglas to McDunphy, 21 May 1937, D/T S9856, NAI.

114 Keogh and McCarthy, *The Making of the Irish Constitution*, p. 178.

115 *Daily Telegraph*, 1 May 1937, *Manchester Guardian*, 3 May 1937, *Sunday Times*, 2 May 1937, *Irish Independent*, 11 May 1937, *Irish Independent*, 8 May 1937.

116 *The Leader*, 8 May 1937.

117 *Irish Press*, 10 May 1937.

118 Interviews with Mr Lake, P150/2436, with *New York Times*, 6 May 1937, P150/2438, and with Mr D. P. Sestner of the *International News Service*, 28 May 1937, P150/2438, NAI.

119 'Interview given by the President to Mr Milton Bonner', 27 Feb. 1936, P150/2328, UCDA.

120 Keogh and McCarthy, *The Making of the Irish Constitution*, p. 337.

121 G. Cappocia, 'Defending democracy: reactions to political extremism in inter-war Europe', *European Journal of Political Research* XXXIX (2001), p. 432.

122 'President's interview given by Mr Julian Grande', 17 Aug. 1934, P150/2284, UCDA.

123 'Constitution Committee 1934: Report on Part 1 of terms of Reference', P150/2365, UCDA.

124 D. M. Clarke, 'Emergency legislation, fundamental rights, and Article 28.3.3 of the Irish constitution', *Irish Jurist* XII (1977), p. 283.

125 Sean MacBride, *Civil Liberty Towards a New Ireland* (Dublin 1949), p. 12.

126 Moss Twomey Papers, P69/54/262, UCDA.

127 Kissane, *Explaining Irish Democracy*, p. 187.

128 R. Fanning, *Independent Ireland* (Dublin, 1983), p. 119.

129 *Irish Press*, 1 May 1937.

130 'Interview with a Representative of the *New York Times*', published 26 Jan. 1938, 2000/8/4, Jack Lynch Papers, NAI.

131 *An Phoblacht*, 29 May 1937.

132 Keogh and McCarthy, *The Making of the Irish Constitution*, pp. 353 324 334.

133 Cearbhall Ó Dálaigh, *Irish Press*, 16 Apr. 1953.

134 Hogan to O'Rahilly, Mar. 1937 1781/64 (1), UCDA.

135 *Irish Independent*, 6 May 1937.

136 New Year's Day Speech, Galway Cathedral, *Irish Press*, 3 Jan. 1938.

137 'Mr Hugh Smith's Interview with the President for the *New York Times*', 9 May 1937.

138 See D. Barrington, *The Church, the State, and the Constitution* (Dublin, 1959), p. 14.

139 Hogan to O'Rahilly, Mar. 1937, 1781/64 (1), UCDA.

140 *Irish Independent*, 15 May 1937.

141 McQuaid to de Valera Apr. 1937, P150/2395, UCDA.

142 'On occasion of official visit by de Valera to the Pontifical Palace of Castel Gandolfo, Oct. 1957', *Irish Independent*, 10 Mar. 1954.

143 *Irish Independent*, 10 Mar. 1954.

144 'Parliamentary draft of Heads of A Constitution for Saorstát Éireann', 18 May 1935, P150/2375, UCDA.

145 D. Keogh, 'The Irish constitutional revolution: an analysis of the making of the constitution' in F. Litton (ed.), 'The constitution of Ireland 1937–1987', *Administration* 35: 4 (1988), p. 18.

146 'President's broadcast speech', 15 June 1937, P150/2435, UCDA.

147 Elazar, 'The political theory of covenant: biblical origins', pp. 3–30.

148 See draft speech to Dáil seeking approval for Constitution, May–June 1937 (P150/2441), UCDA.

149 De Valera, Griffith and Plunkett to Clemenceau, 26 May 1919, Documents on Irish Foreign Policy, no. 12, DFA ES parl 1919, NAI.

150 Barrington, 'The Church, the State, and the Constitution', p. 14.

151 Elazar, 'The political theory of covenant', p. 26.

152 Ibid., p. 6.

153 E. Gellner, *Plough, Sword, and Book: The Structure of Human History* (Chicago, 1988).

154 'Interview given by Mr de Valera to Mr Henri de Kerilles', 14 July 1931, P150/2166, UCDA.

155 Quoted in P. Murray, *Oracles of God: The Roman Catholic Church and Irish Politics, 1922–37* (Dublin, 2000), p. 257.

156 'Parliamentary draftsman to president', 1 Mar. 1937, P150/2397, UCDA.

157 Keogh and McCarthy, *The Making of the Irish Constitution*, p. 490.

158 McQuaid to de Valera on Article 43, n. d., P150/2407, UCDA.

159 Keogh and McCarthy, *The Making of the Irish Constitution*, p. 490.

160 *Irish Press*, 12 May 1937.

161 MacArdle to de Valera, 1 May 1937, D/T S 9880, NAI.

162 D. Macardle, 'The Irish nation and majority rule', *Irish Press*, 18–20 Oct. 1933.

163 *Irish Independent*, 19 Nov. 1936.

164 'Women: constitutional and economic position in Saorstát Éireann', D/T S 9278 NAI.

165 See L. O'Dowd, 'Church state and women: the aftermath of partition' in C. Curtis, P. Jackson, and B. O'Connor (eds), *Gender in Irish Society* (Galway, 1987), p. 9.

166 G. Hogan, 'Foreword', to Keogh and McCarthy, *The Making of the Irish Constitution*, pp. 26–33.

167 'Women, the vote, and revolution', p. 56

168 Report of Cumann na mBan Annual Convention, 22–23 Oct. 1921, P1061 1127, UCDA.

169 This applied beyond 1925 'Cumann na mBan', P48 1/12; 'Letter from HQ', 18 May 1924, P48 a/19 (10) Mary MacSwiney Papers, UCDA.

170 M. Mazower, *After the War Was Over: Reconstructing the Family, Nation, and State in Greece, 1943–1960* (Princeton and Oxford, 2000), p. 15.

171 'Press Speech' 1936 P61 &c (4), Eithne Coyle Papers, UCDA.

172 'Resolution for discussion at Convention', 10 June 1931 P48 a/10 (1) UCDA; 'Summary of Speech at Conference, 3 Nov. 1929, P48 a/11 (1) UCDA.

173 'Interview given by Mr de Valera to representatives of the United Press', 29 Oct. 1931, P150/2168, UCDA.

174 'Broadcast Speech', 30 Apr. 1937, P150/2431, UCDA.

175 R. Slagstad, 'Liberal constitutionalism and its critics' in J. Elster and R. Slagstad (eds), *Constitutionalism and Democracy* (Cambridge, 1988), pp. 104–12.

176 Exchange with Cahill, 7 Apr. 1935, P152/39, UCDA.

177 M. Oakeshott, *The Social and Political Doctrines of Contemporary Europe* (Cambridge 1939), pp. 45–72.

178 H. Krieger, 'Comment' in G. Nolte, *European and US Constitutionalism* (Cambridge 2005), p. 194.

179 D. Grimm, 'The protective function of the state' in Nolte, *European and US Constitutionalism*, pp. 138–43.

180 Elazar, 'The political theory of covenant', p. 21.

181 See M. Mazower, *Dark Continent: Europe's Twentieth Century* (New York, 1999), p. 19.

182 Lorenz von Stein, quoted in R. Koselleck, 'Historical prognosis in Lorenz von Stein's essay on the Prussian constitution' in Koselleck, *Futures Past: On the Semantics of Historical Time* (New York, 2004), p. 66.

183 Ibid., p. 69.

FOUR: CHALLENGE

1   *Irish Press*, 7 Dec. 1971.

2   Ibid.

3   'Constitution of Ireland: 1937. 'Amendment consequential on membership of the European Community', D/T 2002/8/282, NAI.

4   'Re examination of the provisions of the constitution: Notes for discussion', Lemass to London, 25 July 1966, D/T 97/6/515, NAI.

5   *Report of the Committee on the Constitution* (Dublin 1967).

6   'Informal Committee on the Constitution: Notices and minutes of meetings, Aug. 1966', D/T 2001/48/46, NAI.

7   L. A. Walter, 'Law as literature: illuminating the debate over constitutional consistency' *Cork Online Law Review* XI (2004).

8   D. Barrington, 'Uniting Ireland', Tuarim Research Pamphlets (Dublin, 1958?): Gavan Duffy, 'Notes on constitutional reform', *Irish Jurist* (Winter 1966), pp. 271–2: 'J. Kelly, 'Revision of the constitution of Ireland', *Irish Jurist* 1 (Summer 1966), pp. 1–15. G. R. J. O'Hanlon, 'A constitution for a free people', *Administration* 15: 1 (Summer 1967), pp. 85–101.

9   B. Corish, *The New Republic* (Dublin, 1968).

10   L. P. Ua Corbaidh, *Irish Democracy: Republicanism, Nationalism and Socialism*, n. d, Sean O'Mahoney Collection, NLI.

11 Fine Gael, *Planning a Just Society* (Dublin, 1965), *Winning Through to a Just Society* (Dublin 1961), NLI.

12 Devlin, *The Price of My Soul*, p. 88.

13 Mark McNally, 'Countering the hegemony of the national canon: the modernist rhetoric of Sean O'Faoláin (1938–50)', *Nations and Nationalism* 15: 3 (2009), p. 541.

14 Corish, *The New Republic.*

15 *Irish Independent*, 6 Dec. 1971.

16 Fine Gael, *A Better Future: Fine Gael: Let the Country Win* (Dublin, 1982).

17 Garret FitzGerald, *Towards a New Ireland* (Dublin, 1973), p. 156.

18 Sinn Féin, *Women in Ireland: Sinn Fein Update*, Mar. 1999, NLI.

19 A. Connelly, 'Women and the constitution of Ireland' in Y. Galligan, E. Ward, and R. Wilford (eds), *Contesting Politics: Women in Ireland, North and South* (Boulder, 1999), p. 23.

20 R. B. Finnegan and J. L. Wiles, *Women and Public Policy in Ireland: A Documentary History* (Dublin, 2005), p. 167.

21 E. Mahon, 'Women's rights and Catholicism in Ireland' in M. Threlfell (ed.), *Mapping the Women's Movement: Feminist Politics and Social Transformation in the North* (London, New York, 1996), pp. 184–216.

22 Y. Scannell, 'The constitution and the role of women' in A. Hayes and D. Urquhart (eds), *The Irish Women's History Reader* (London and New York, 2001), pp. 71–9.

23 Mahon, 'Women's rights and Catholicism', p. 189.

24 *Irish Press*, 2 June 1972.

25 For a re-assessment see G. Hogan, 'Foreword' to Keogh and McCarthy, *The Making of the Irish Constitution.*

26 See Finnegan and Wiles, *Women and Public Policy in Ireland*, p. 210.

27 Mahon, 'Women's rights and Catholicism', p. 188.

28 F. Gardiner, 'The Impact of EU equality legislation on Irish women' in Galligan, Ward and Wilford (eds), *Contesting Politics*, p. 52.

29 N. Fennell, *Irish Marriage How Are You?* (Dublin and Cork, 1974).

30 See interview with Mr Terence Prittie of *The Guardian*, 28 May 1965.

31 'Northern Ireland – Policy Statement by Fine Gael front bench', Sept. 1969.

32 'Inter-departmental Unit on the North of Ireland, Minutes of Sixth Meeting, 12 Nov. 1970', Department of External Affairs, 2001/ 8 /14 (2), Jack Lynch Papers, NAI

33 Whitaker to Lynch, 24 Nov. 1969, 2001/8/6, Lynch Papers, NAI.

34 *Irish Times*, 8 Sept. 1969.

35 *Irish Press*, 12 Sept. 1969.

36 *Irish Times*, 8 Sept. 1969.

37 *Irish Times*, 1 Oct. 1969.

38 *Church of Ireland Gazette*, 22 Oct. 1969.

39 *Tipperary Star*, 5 Sept. 1970.

40 ' Report of party delegation to six counties and British Labour Party', 16–19 Aug. 1969', signed by C. C. O'Brien, 26 Aug. 1969, P82/219 (1), UCDA.

41 Appendix A: 'Northern Crisis. Suggested course of action: steps to be taken by Labour Party', P82 1219 (8), UCDA.

42 'Speech to the Annual General Meeting of the Irish Association in Belfast', 16 May 1972', P82/261 (1) UCDA; ' Confidential Memorandum on middle and long term prospects in relation to the situation in the Six Counties of Northern Ireland and to the eventual unity of Ireland', 1970, P82/220, UCDA; O'Brien to FitzGerald (Feb.–Apr. 1974) P215/567 UCDA.

43 Minutes of Meeting, 10 July 1974, 2005/151/307, NAI.

44 O'Brien to FitzGerald, 7 Jan. 1974, O'Brien to Cosgrave 4 Jan. 1974, P215/567 UCDA; 'A new constitution', Address by Conor Cruise O'Brien to meeting on new constitution organised by Dublin North Central Constituency Council, 26 Jan. 1977, P82/277 (1) UCDA.

45 'Inter Party Committee on the Implications of Irish Unity', D/T 2005/7/622, NAI.

46 'Memo to the All Party Committee on Irish Relations', 30 Apr. 1974, ibid.

47 'Memorandum for SDLP meeting with All Party Committee on Irish Relations', 18 Jan. 1974, D/T 2005/7/621, NAI.

48 Towards a New Ireland: Proposals by the Social Democratic and Labour Party (1975, NLI).

49 *Dáil Debates*, vol. 248, 28 July 1970. *Irish Press*, 22 Sept. 1969. 'Constitution 1937: position of religion', reply to Desmond, 22 July 1971, D/T 20003/6/64, NAI. *Irish Times*, 24 Feb. 1971.

50 Quoted in T. P. Coogan, *The Troubles: Ireland's Ordeal and the Search for Peace, 1966–1996* (New York, 2002), p. 136; *Dáil Debates*, vol. 256, 10 Nov. 1971; *Irish Press*, 2 Dec. 1971); FitzGerald, *Towards a New Ireland*, pp. 156–7. 'Transcript of interview with RTÉ's Seven Days, 30 Nov. 1971', D/T 2003/6/64, NAI.

51 'All Party Committee on Irish relations', July 1973, D/T 2005/ 151/ 307, NAI.

52 *Irish Press*, 13 Dec. 1971.

53 *Sunday Press*, 5 Dec. 1971.

54 *Irish Times*, 1 May 1967, D/T 2001/6/99 NAI.

55 Article by Taoiseach on Northern Ireland, *Foreign Affairs*, 849, 3 July 1972 P125/4 UCDA

56 Lynch to Walters, *Irish Press*, 29 June 1972.

57 *Irish Independent*, 25 Oct. 1969.

58 *Irish Times*, 21 Mar. 1971.

59 'Transcript of interview with RTÉ's Seven Days, D/T 2003/6/64, NAI.

60 *Irish Press*, 29 May 1972.

61 Attorney General's Committee on the Constitution, 'Draft Report', Aug. 1968, D/T 2005/151/307, NAI.

62 *Irish Times*, 24 Nov. 1970.

63 'Bunreacht na hÉireann: Quo Vadis', speech to a meeting of the Solicitors Apprentice Society of Ireland, 25 Feb. 1972, D/T 2005/151/307, NAI.

64 *Irish Times*, 20 Oct. 1976.

65 *Irish Times*, 6 Dec. 1971.

66 'Report of Committee on the Constitution', May 1974, Knights of Saint Colombanus D/T 2005/7/622, NAI.

67 'Oireachtas Committee to Review the Constitutional, Legislative and Institutional bases of government', 2002/8/358, NAI. *Irish Times*, 9 Nov. 1970.

68 Ibid.

69 Letter to press, D/T S 2001/6/52, NAI.

70 Letters to press, Mary Bourke, John Temple Lang, *Irish Press*, 1 Sept. 1972.

71 D. O'Sullivan, 'The Good Friday Agreement: a new constitutional agreement for Northern Ireland', *Dublin University Law Review* 22 (2000), p. 115.

72 'Notes for the Taoiseach's Information', D/T 2005/15 307, NAI.

73 All Party Committee on Irish Relations, Nov. 1975, D/T 2005/15/ 307, NAI.

74 F. O'Connor, *An Only Child and My Father's Son* (London, 2005), p. 344.

75 D. Waxman, *Hegemony Lost: The Crises of National Identity in Israel and Turkey* (Paper prepared for annual meeting of International Studies Association, Montreal Canada, 18 Mar. 2004), pp. 1–24.

76 B. Devlin, *The Price of My Soul* (London 1965), p. 380.

77 J. Dearlove, 'Bringing the constitution back in: political science and the state', *Political Studies* 37: 4 (1989), p. 534.

78 G. Hogan, review of Murphy and Twomey (eds), *Ireland's Evolving Constitution, 1937–1997*, *Bar Review* 3: 9 (2002), p. 268.

79 K. Boyle and D. S. Greer, *The Legal System North and South: A Study Prepared for the New Ireland Forum* (Dublin, 1984), pp. 20–1.

80 'Referendum Act 1942', D/T S10050 A, NAI.

81 Arthur Matheson (parliamentary draftsman) to Attorney General, 22 July 1940, ibid.

82 Department of Local Government and Public Health Memo, 19 Feb. 1942, D/T S10050 A NAI.

83 M. Suksi, *Bringing in the People: A Comparison of Constitutional Forms and Practices of The Referendum* (London, Dordrecht, 1993).

84 A. Lijphart, *Democracies: Patterns of Majoritarian and Consensus Democracy in Twenty-One Countries* (New Haven and London, 1984), p. 296.

85 J. Carey, 'Does it matter how a constitution is created?' in Z. Barany and R. G. Moser (eds), *Is Democracy Exportable?* (Cambridge, 2009), p. 160, p. 176.

86 M. Suksi, *Bringing in the People: A Comparison of Constitutional Forms and Practices of the Referendum* (Dordrecht 1993), p. 149.

87 H, Kelsen, *General Theory of Law and State* (New York, 1961), p. 259.

88 Department of Local Government and Public Health Memo, 'Referendum Bill 1941', 19 Feb. 1942, D/T S10050 A, NAI.

89 Speech to Fianna Fáil Cumann Limerick, 25 Mar. 1966, D/T 97/6/515, NAI.

90 11th Meeting, 12 Oct. 1967, 'Informal Committee on the Constitution: Notices and Minutes of Meetings', D/T 2001/45/46, NAI.

91 P. Pettit, *Republicanism: A Theory of Freedom and Government* (Oxford, 1997), p. 181.

92 M. Gallagher, 'Ireland: the referendum as a conservative device?' in M. Gallagher, and P. Vincenzo (eds), *The Referendum Experience in Europe.* (London, 1996), pp. 99–100.

93 Inter Party Committee on the implications of Irish unity: Minutes of Meeting, 2 Feb. 1972, P215/10, UCDA.

94 *Irish Press*, 6 Dec. 1971.

95 *Irish Times*, 3 Nov. 1972; *Irish Times*, 13 Nov. 1972; *Irish Times*, 3 Nov. 1972.

96 J. Newman, *Ireland Must Choose: Religion, Politics and the Law in Ireland Today* (Dublin, 1983), pp. 42–54.

97 'Speech delivered by Mr Peter Sutherland, S. C. Attorney General, to Members of Irish-American Lawyers Association, Dublin, 23 Sept. 1981'. Personal copy.

98 *Irish Times*, 28 Sept. 1981.

99 Ibid.

100 Interview with Peter Sutherland, LSE, 16 June 2009.

101 *New Ireland Forum Report*, 2 May 1984, p. 23.

102 Quoted in Ward, *The Irish Constitutional Tradition*, p. 263.

103 Meeting with New Ulster Movement delegates, 30 Apr. 1974, 2005/7/618, NAI.

104 'A new constitution', address by Dr Conor Cruise O'Brien at a meeting organised by Dublin North Central Constituency Council, 26 Jan. 1977, UCD P52/277 (1), UCDA.

105 *The Party Programme*: Labour Party Annual Conference 1980.

106 G. FitzGerald, *Irish Identity*, Richard Dimbleby lecture (London, 1982).

107 *Irish Times*, 1 Oct. 1981.

108 *Irish Times*, 24 Sept. 1981.

109 'The Constitution/Peter Sutherland Attorney General' interview by Michael Johnson, Opinion RTÉ Radio 1, 25 Sept. 1981 (copy given to me by Peter Sutherland).

110 Dennis Kennedy, 'Wholly Catholic Ireland', *Irish Times*, 11 June 1981.

111 Interview with Peter Sutherland, LSE, 16 June 2009.

112 Ibid.

113 J. Coakley, 'Moral consensus in a secularising society: the Irish divorce referendum of 1986', *West European Politics* 10: 2 (1987), p. 292.

114 T. Hesketh, *The Second Partitioning of Ireland: The Abortion Referendum of 1983* (Dublin, 1990). p. 77.

115 B. Girvin, 'Moral politics and the Irish abortion referendum 1992', *Parliamentary Affairs* 47: 2 (1994), p. 206.

116 Ibid., p. 205.

117 B. Girvin, 'Church, state and the Irish constitution: the secularisation of Irish politics' *Parliamentary Affairs* 49: 4 (1996), p. 603.

118 T. Fahey, B. C. Hayes and R. Sinnott, *Conflict and Consensus: A Study of Values and Attitudes in the Republic of Ireland and Northern Ireland* (Dublin, 2005), pp. 69–70.

119 Basil Chubb, who thought much of the constitution 'premature and clumsy' in 1978, expressed frustration with the slow pace of change; *The Constitution and Constitutional Change* (Dublin, 1978), p. 94. For an opposite position see K. Boland, *The Constitutional Scam: New Meanings for Words to Neuter the hoi polloi* (Ireland, n. d.).

120 The All-Party Oireachtas Committee on the Constitution, *Sixth Progress Report: The Referendum* (Dublin, 2001), p. 5.

121 M. Gallagher, 'The changing constitution' in J. Coakley and M. Gallagher (eds), *Politics in the Republic of Ireland* (3rd edn, London and New York, 1999), p. 93.

122 G. FitzGerald, 'The constitution in its historical context' in Murphy and Twomey (eds), *Ireland's Evolving Constitution*, p. 38. P. Sutherland, 'Twin perspectives: an Attorney General views political and European dimensions' in Farrell (ed.), *De Valera's Constitution and Ours*, p. 174.

123 'Constitutional change not a change in attitudes', *Irish Times*, 16 Sept. 2009.

124 Hogan, Foreword to Keogh and McCarthy, *The Making of the Irish Constitution*, p. 24, p. 35.

125 Interview with Peter Sutherland, LSE, 16 June 2009.

126 Z. Elkins, T. Ginsburg and J. Melton, *The Endurance of National Constitutions* (Cambridge, 2009), p. 89.

127 Ibid., p. 74.

128 Gallagher, 'The changing constitution', p. 84.

129 Ibid., p. 85.

130 Ibid., p. 91.

131 Ibid.

132 T. A. Finlay, *The Constitution: Fifty Years On* (Dublin, 1988), p. 10.

133 'Time for debate on basic rights', *Irish Times*, 24 Sept. 1981.

134 Speech Delivered by Mr Peter Sutherland, Attorney General, to members of Irish-American Lawyers Association, Dublin, 23 Sept. 1981, Government Information Services.

135 Justice Ronan Keane, quoted in B. Sullivan, 'The Irish constitution: some reflections from abroad' in Carolan and Doyle (eds), *The Irish Constitution: Governance and Values*, p. 8.

136 See G. Hogan and G. Whyte (eds), *J. M. Kelly: The Irish Constitution* (4th edn, Dublin, 2006), pp. 2090–99.

137 J. N. Earle, 'Judicial review of direct democracy', *Yale Law Journal* 99 (1989–1990), pp. 89–90.

138 G. Rahat, 'Elite motivations for initiating referendums: avoidance, addition and contradiction' in M. Setala and T. Schiller (eds), *Referendums and Representative Democracy: Responsiveness, Accountability, and Deliberation* (New York, 2009), pp. 98–117.

139 'President's broadcast on the constitution, April 30 1937' (P150/2431), UCDA.

140 Interview with Michael McInerney, *Irish Times*, 30 Aug. 1975.

141 R. Aman, 'The central meaning of Republican government: popular sovereignty, majority rule, and the denominator problem', *University of Colorado Law Review* 65 (1993–4), p. 762.

142 Kohn, *Constitution of the Irish Free State*, pp. 240–1: See R. Dahl, *A Short Preface to Democratic Theory* (New Haven, 1956). p. 38.

143 G. Sartori, *The Theory of Democracy Revisited: Part One the Contemporary Debate* (Chatham, NJ, 1987), pp. 136–7.

144 'First Draft Report of the Attorney General's Legal Committee on EEC Position – Amendments to the Constitution', 26 Oct. 1967, D/T 2002/8/282, NAI.

145 'Memorandum for the government, third amendment of the Constitution Bill, 1971', 8 Nov. 1971, D/T 2002/8/282, NAI.

146 Hogan and Whyte, *J. M. Kelly The Irish Constitution*, p. 517.

147 M. Gallagher, 'The referendum as a conservative device?', p. 94.

148 Russell Hardin, *Liberalism, Constitutionalism, and Democracy* (Oxford, 1999), p. 140.

149 P. Bew, *Ireland: The Politics of Enmity 1789–2006* (Oxford 2007), p. 575.

150 T. K. Whitaker, 'A note on North–South policy', for the Minister of External Affairs, 11 Nov. 1968, P175 (81), UCDA.

151 Boyle and Greer, *The Legal System North and South*, p. 18.

152 'The case for the retention of Articles 2 and 3', *Irish Times*, 4 Sept. 1981.

153 'Memo to the All Party Committee on Irish Relations, 30 Apr. 1974', D/T, 2005/7/620, NAI.

154 Whitaker, 'A note on North–South policy'.

155 Qvortrup, *A Comparative Study of Referendums*, p. 91.

156 On change and continuity see B. Girvin, 'Continuity, change and crisis in Ireland: An introduction and discussion', *Irish Political Studies* 23: 4 (Dec. 2008), p. 464.

157 M. Mendelsohn and A. Parkin (eds), *Referendum Democracy: Citizens, Elites and Deliberation in Referendum Campaigns* (Basingstoke, 2001), p. 2.

FIVE: CO-ORDINATION

1   B. O'Leary and J. McGarry, 'Introduction: consociational theory and Northern Ireland' in J. McGarry and B. O'Leary (eds), *The Northern Ireland Conflict: Consociational Engagements* (Oxford, 2004), p. 2

2   See K. Boyle and T. Hadden, 'Northern Ireland' in R. Blackburn and R. Plant (eds), *Constitutional Reform: The Labour Government's Constitutional Reform Agenda* (London and New York, 1999), p. 282.

3   See J. Coakley, 'Ethnic conflict and its resolution: the Northern Ireland model', *Nationalism and Ethnic Politics* 9: 3 (Sept. 2003), pp. 25–53.

4   G. Sartori, *The Theory of Democracy Revisited: Part One the Contemporary Debate* (Chatham, NJ, 1987), p. 131.

5   B. O'Leary, The nature of the agreement' in McGarry and O'Leary (eds), *The Northern Ireland Conflict*, p. 274.

6   Ibid., p. 272.

7   B. O'Duffy, *British-Irish Relations and Northern Ireland* (Dublin, 2007), p. 156.

8   McEvoy, *The Politics of Northern Ireland*, p. 118.

9   Ibid.

10   O'Sullivan, 'The Good Friday Agreement', p. 122.

11   See A. Reynolds, 'A constitutional pied piper: the Northern Ireland Good Friday Agreement', *Political Science Quarterly* 114: 4 (Winter 1999–2000), p. 622.

12   M. Rosenfeld, 'The European treaty-constitution: a view from America', *International Journal of Constitutional Law* (2005), p. 318.

13   Ibid., pp. 326–7.

14   A. Sajo, *Limiting Government: An Introduction to Constitutionalism* (Budapest, 1999), p. 2

15   See J. Ruane and J. Todd, 'The Northern Ireland conflict and the impact of globalisation' in W. Crotty and D. E. Schmitt (eds), *Ireland on the World Stage* (Harlow, 2002), p. 121

16   O'Leary, 'The nature of the agreement', pp. 280–1

17   'Interview with John Hume' in F. Millar, *Northern Ireland: A Triumph of Politics: Interviews and Analysis 1998–2008* (Dublin, 2009), p. 13.

18   Ibid., p. 3.

19   Ibid., p. 2.

20   Annex 1: Received from the SDLP (Messrs Hume and Devlin) on 17 Oct. 1973, D/T 2004/21/624, NAI.

21   'Legal committee on Northern Ireland', 29 May 1973, D/T 2004/21/624, NAI.

22   Inter-departmental unit on Northern Ireland, *Council of Ireland: Functions and Structure. Interim Report*, D/T 2004/21/624 NAI.

23   'Report by Minister of Foreign Affairs in the possible functions and structure of a Council of Ireland', 30 July 1973, D/T 2004/21/624, NAI.

24   'Summary of outcome of talks with British at official level on 28 and 29 Dec. 1973', D/T 2004/21/624, NAI.

25   See B. Kissane, 'Power sharing as a form of democracy for Northern Ireland', *Review of Politics* 68: 4 (Fall, 2006), pp. 663–75,

26   G. FitzGerald, *Reflections on the Irish State* (Dublin, 2003), p. 180.

27 For a discussion see B. O'Duffy, 'British and Irish conflict regulation from Sunningdale to Belfast: Part 2: playing for a draw, 1985–1999', *Nations and Nationalism* 6:3 (2000), pp. 399–45.

28 B. O'Leary, 'The Conservative stewardship of Northern Ireland: sound-bottomed contradictions or slow learning?' in McGarry and O'Leary (eds), *The Northern Ireland Conflict*, p. 235.

29 J. Darby, *Scorpions in a Bottle: Cultures in Conflict in Northern Ireland* (London, 1997).

30 Reynolds, 'Constitutional pied piper', p. 615.

31 M. Kerr, 'A culture of power sharing' in R. Taylor (ed.), *Consociational Theory: McGarry and O'Leary and the Northern Ireland Conflict* (Oxford, 2009), p. 210.

32 Boyle and Hadden, 'Northern Ireland', pp. 285–8.

33 See McEvoy, *The Politics of Northern Ireland* (Edinburgh, 2008), pp. 74–5.

34 Ibid., p. 85.

35 G. di Palma, *To Craft Democracies: An Essay on Democratic Transitions* (Berkeley, 1990), p. 87.

36 O'Leary, 'The nature of the agreement', p. 263.

37 Ibid., p. 265.

38 Ibid., pp. 265–6.

39 Ibid., pp. 290–1.

40 Ibid., p. 271.

41 See R. MacGinty, 'Issue hierarchies in peace processes: the decommissioning of paramilitary arms and the Northern Ireland peace process. Lessons for ending civil conflicts', *Civil Wars* 1: 3 (1998), pp. 24–45.

42 J. Ruane and J. Todd, 'The Belfast Agreement: context, content, and consequences' in J. Ruane and J. Todd (eds), *After the Good Friday Agreement: Analysing Political Change in Northern Ireland* (Dublin, 1999), p. 23.

43 Hardin, *Liberalism, Constitutionalism, and Democracy*, p. 103.

44 M. Kerr, *Imposing Power-Sharing: Conflict and Co-existence in Northern Ireland and the Lebanon* (Dublin, 2005), p. 99.

45 O'Duffy, *British–Irish Relations*, p. 190.

46 McGarry and O'Leary, 'Consociational theory and Northern Ireland', p. 10.

47 See essays in Taylor (ed.), *Consociational Theory*.

48 J. McGarry and B. O'Leary, 'Power shared after the deaths of thousands', in Taylor (ed.), *Consociational Theory*, p. 34.

49 J. McGarry, 'Democracy in Northern Ireland' in McGarry and O'Leary (eds), *The Northern Ireland Conflict*, p. 344.

50 Quoted in Kerr, 'A culture of power sharing', p. 217.

51 On such changes see R. Humphreys, *Countdown to Unity: Debating Irish Reunification* (Dublin, 2009).

52 Rosenfeld, 'The European treaty – constitution', p. 317.

53 E. Mallie and D. McKittrick, *The Fight for Peace: The Secret Story behind the Irish Peace Process* (London, 1996), p. 338

54 O'Duffy, *British–Irish Relations*, p. 160.

55 T. Nairn, *After Britain: New Labour and the Return of Scotland* (London, 2002), p. 305.

56 *Sunday Times*, 18 Apr. 1999.

57 R. Hardin, *Liberalism, Constitutionalism, and Democracy* (Oxford, 1999), p. 85

58 J. Morison, 'Ways of seeing? Consociationalism and constitutional law theory' in R. Taylor (ed.), *Consociational Theory: McGarry and O'Leary and the Northern Ireland Conflict* (London and New York, 2009), p. 287.

59 F. O'Toole, 'The peace process' in A. Higgins Wyndham (ed.), *Re-imagining Ireland* (University of Virginia Press, 2006), pp. 206–7.

60 Ibid., p. 206.

61 A. Aughey, 'Unionism' in Higgins Wyndham (ed.), *Re-imagining Ireland*, p. 210.

62 P. Shirlow, 'Northern Ireland: a reminder from the present' in C. Coulter and S Coleman (eds), *The End of Irish History? Critical Reflections on the Celtic Tiger* (Manchester, 2003), p. 198.

63 Aughey, 'Unionism', p. 215.

64 See R. Bourke, *Peace in Ireland: The War of Ideas* (London, 2003), p. 307.

65 See H. Lerner, 'Constitution writing in deeply divided societies: the incrementalist approach', *Nations and Nationalism* 16: 1 (Jan. 2010), pp. 68–89.

66 Bourke, *Peace in Ireland*, p. 308.

67 Ibid., p. 3.

68 Ibid., p. 5.

69 See Elkins, Ginsburg, and Melton (eds), *The Endurance of National Constitutions*, pp. 66–71.

70 See V. Bogdanor, 'Devolution and the British constitution' in D. Butler, V. Bogdanor and R. Summers (eds), *The Law, Politics, and the Constitution: Essays in Honour of Geoffrey Marshall* (Oxford, 1998), p. 59.

71 C. McCrudden, 'Northern Ireland and the British constitution since the Belfast Agreement' in J. Jowell and D. Oliver (eds), *The Changing Constitution* (6th edn; Oxford, 2007), p. 229.

72 Ibid., p. 269.

73 Ibid., p. 303.

74 Hardin, *Liberalism, Constitutionalism, and Democracy*, pp. 119–29.

75 J. Smith, *Making the Peace in Ireland* (Pearson, 2002), p. 243.

SIX: CONCLUSION

1 J. Habermas, *Legitimation Crisis* (London, 1976).

2 Section based on G. Hogan, 'Economic mire not caused by constitution', *Irish Times*, 14 Nov. 2009; E. F. Biagini, 'A new constitution can never be an antidote to all our ills', *Irish Times*, 29 June 2010; M. Gallagher, 'Does Ireland need a new constitution?' Politicalreform.ie, posted on 22 May 2010.

3 F. Panizza, 'Introduction', *Populism and the Mirror of Democracy* (London and New York, 2005), pp. 3–31.

4 See Sinn Féin, *Government by the People*, n. d. (NAI).

5 D. O'Brien, 'How inertia became the iron law of Irish politics', *Irish Times*, 7 Nov. 2009.

6 See M. O'Sullivan, 'Crash may offer chance of a Second Republic', *Irish Times*, 20 Aug. 2009.

7 See MacCartaigh, *Accountability in Irish Parliamentary Politics*.

8 *Irish Times*, 13 Mar. 2010.

9 Nuala O'Connor, 'Reviving the momentum of activism that made us', *Irish Times*, 17 Mar. 2010:

10 Jacobsohn, *Constitutional Identity.*

11 *Dáil Debates*, vol. 67, 1 June 1937.

12 See J. O'Dowd, 'The impact of the constitution in the deliberations of the Houses of the Oireachtas', in Carolan and Doyle (eds), *The Irish Constitution*, pp. 181–95.

13 Lynch speech, 28 Sept. 1968 D/T S 99/1/279, NAI.

14 F. D. Wormuth, *The Origins of Modern Constitutionalism* (New York, 1949), p. 3.

15 Bulsara and Kissane, 'Arend Lijphart and the transformation of Irish democracy'.

16 A. O'Halloran, 'Transformation in contemporary Ireland: society, economy and polity: an era of post-parliamentary governance', *Administration* 53: 1 (2005), p. 55.

17 See Fíach MacConghail, *Irish Times*, 17 Mar. 2010.

18 *Irish Times*, 17 Mar. 2010.

19 See Jacobsohn, *Constitutional Identity.*

20 G. Hogan, 'Constitutional interpretation' in Litton (ed.), 'The constitution of Ireland', p. 174.

21 Much of this paragraph is based on J. Kristeva, 'What of tomorrow's nation?' *Nations Without Nationalism* (New York, 1993), pp. 1–47.

22 Ibid.

23 O'Hegarty, *Sinn Féin An Illumination*, pp. 55–6.

24 FitzGerald, 'The constitution in its historical context', p. 38.

25 M. Rosenfeld, 'The identity of the constitutional subject', *Cardozo Law Review* 16 (1994–5), p. 1068.

26 MacEntee to Lynch, 6 Nov. 1969, 2001/8/5, Jack Lynch Papers, NAI.

27 'A note on north–south policy', 11 Nov. 1968, P175 (81) UCDA.

28 Whitaker to David Jones 10 Aug. 1972, P215/4, Garret FitzGerald Papers UCDA.

29 K. Hayward, *Irish Nationalism and European integration: The Official Redefinition of the Island of Ireland* (Manchester, 2009).

30 B. Farrell et al. (ed.), *De Valera's Constitution and Ours* (Dublin, 1988).

31 Quoted in T. Judt, *Ill Fares the Land* (London, 2010), p. 168.

32 See F. O'Toole, *Ship of Fools: How Stupidity and Corruption Sank the Celtic Tiger* (London, 2009), epilogue on 'The Second Republic', pp. 212–24.

33 G. FitzGerald, 'Apocalypse may yet spark the rebirth of civil morality', *Irish Times*, 16 Oct. 2010.

34 See O'Hegarty, *Sinn Féin: An Illumination*, pp. 55–6.

35 Memo on Amnesty, 5 May 1924, D/T S 581.

36 Quoted in Kissane, *Politics of the Irish Civil War*, p. 98.

37 J. de Romilly, *The Rise and Fall of States According to Greek Authors* (Ann Arbor, 1991), p. 40.

38 Judt, *Il Fares the Land*, p. 167.

39 See J. Prager, *Building Democracy in Ireland: Political Order and Cultural Integration in a Newly Independent Nation* (Cambridge, 1986).

Bibliography

—

PRIMARY SOURCES

PARLIAMENTARY DEBATES

Dáil Éireann Debates
Seanad Éireann Debates

GOVERNMENT PAPERS

NATIONAL ARCHIVES OF IRELAND
Department of An Taoiseach Files
Department of Justice Files
Department of Foreign Affairs Files
Office of the Attorney General Files

THE NATIONAL ARCHIVES (UK)
Foreign Office Files

PRIVATE PAPERS

NATIONAL LIBRARY OF IRELAND
Thomas Johnson Papers

NATIONAL ARCHIVES OF IRELAND
Liam Cosgrave Papers
George Gavan Duffy Papers
Jack Lynch Papers

UNIVERSITY COLLEGE DUBLIN ARCHIVES
Ernest Blythe Papers
Maire Comerford Papers
John A. Costello Papers
Eithne Coyle O'Donnell Papers
Conor Cruise O'Brien Papers
Eamon de Valera Papers
Desmond FitzGerald Papers

Garret FitzGerald Papers
George Gavan Duffy Papers
Sighle Humphreys
Hugh Kennedy Papers
Seán Lemass Papers
Seán MacEntee Papers
Eoin MacNeill Papers
Mary MacSwiney Papers
Patrick McGilligan Papers
Richard Mulcahy Papers
Kevin O'Higgins Papers
Alfred O'Rahilly Papers
Michael Tierney Papers
Michael Hayes Papers
T. K. Whitaker Papers

PERIODICALS/NEWSPAPERS

Catholic Bulletin
Dana
Fortnightly Review
Hermathena
Irish Citizen
The Irish Commonwealth
Irish Ecclesiastical Record
Irish Freedom
Irish Historical Studies
Irish Independent
Irish Jurist
Irish Political Studies
Irish Press
Irish Times
Irish Review
Irish Rosary
The Leader
New Ireland Review
United Irishman
The Republic
Sinn Féin
Studies

OFFICIAL PUBLICATIONS

Amendments to Constitution Committee Report, 6 May 1926.
Committee on the Constitution, *Report of the Committee on the Constitution* (Dublin: Stationery
    Office, 1967).

Commission on the Status of Women, *Progress report on the implementation of the recommendations in the report of the Commission on the Status of Women* (Dublin, 1976).

All Party Oireachtas Committee on the Constitution. *Sixth Progress Report – The Referendum* (Dublin: Stationery Office, 2001).

Second Commission on the Status of Women: Report to Government (Jan. 1993).

Women's Representative Committee. *Second Progress Report of the Implementation of the Recommendations of the Report of the Commission on the Status of Women* (Dublin, 1978).

PAMPHLETS/CONTEMPORARY PUBLICATIONS

Ashtown, F., *The Unknown Power Behind the Irish Nationalist Party: Its Present Work. . . and Criminal History* (London, 1907).

Corish, B., *The New Republic* (Oct. 1967), Irish Labour Party conference speech.

De Blácam, A., 'The passing of Liberalism', *The Irish Commonwealth* 2 (Apr. 1919), pp. 56–7.

De Blácam, A., *What Sinn Féin Stands For: The Irish Republican Movement: Its History, Aims and Ideals, Examined as to Their Significance to the World*, chapter on 'The Sinn Féin constitution (London, 1921).

De Paor, L., 'The case for the retention of Articles 2 and 3', *Irish Times*, 4 Sept. 1981.

Fianna Fáil and Labour, *Programme for a Partnership Government 1993–1999* (1993)

Fine Gael, *Winning Through to a Just Society* (1961?).

Fine Gael, *Planning a Just Society* (1965).

Fine Gael, *Ireland: Our Future Together* (1979).

Fine Gael, *A Better Future: Let the Country Win* (1982).

Fine Gael, *A Government of Renewal: A Policy Agreement between Fine Gael, The Labour Party, and Democratic Left* (1994).

Fine Gael, *21st Century Fine Gael: Report of the Standing Review Group* (2002).

FitzGerald, G., *Irish Identity*, The Richard Dimbleby Lecture (BBC, 1982).

Gaynor, P. *The Faith and Morals of Sinn Féin* (Sinn Féin Pamphlets: Clare Series no. 1 c.1918).

Greaves, D., *Father Michael O'Flanagan: Republican Priest* (A Connolly Association Pamphlet, 1954).

Griffith, A., *The Sinn Féin Policy* (Dublin 1906).

Griffith, A., *The Home Rule Bill Examined* (Dublin, 1912).

Hazleton, R. 'The Irish Senate', *United Irishman*, 9 Nov. 1912.

Hobson, B., *The Creed of the Republic* (Belfast, 1907).

Hobson, B, 'Introduction', *Irish Free State Official Handbook* (London, 1932), pp. 15–17.

Horgan, J. J., 'The problem of government', *Studies* (1933).

Hutchinson, J. H., 'Intolerant democracy', *New Ireland Review* XXV: 5 (July 1906).

Kelleher, Rev. J., 'Some present-day anomalies of representative government, *Irish Ecclesiastical Record* XXIII: 1 (June 1908), p. 139.

Kelleher, Rev. J., *Private Ownership: Its Basis and Equitable Conditions* (Dublin, 1911).

Kennedy, D., 'Wholly Catholic Ireland', *Irish Times*, 11 June 1981.

Labour Party, *The Party Programme* (Labour Party Annual Conference, 1980).

Labour Party, *Shaping Ireland's Future: Labour in Government* (1996).

Mac Donagh, M., *The Life of William O'Brien: The Irish Nationalist* (London, 1928).

MacNeill, E., 'The view of the state in relation to education', *Irish Review*, 28 Oct. 1922.

MacNeill, E., 'Education – the idea of the state', *Irish Review*, 25 Nov. 1922.

New Ireland Forum, *New Ireland Forum Report* (Dublin, 1984).

Nugent, D., *The AOH and its Critics* (Dublin, 1911).

O'Brien, W. *The Irish Cause and the Irish Convention* (Dublin, 1917).

O'Brien, W., 'Sinn Féinism', *Catholic Bulletin* III: 9 (Sept. 1918), pp. 441–5.

O'Brien, Rev. W., 'Monarchy or republic?', *Catholic Bulletin* VIII: 5 (May 1918).

O'Donnell, F. H., 'The power of the crown and the collapse of the Parliament', *New Ireland Review* XV (Mar.–Aug. 1901), pp. 146–52.

O'Higgins, K., The Catholic layman in public life', *An tOglac* (Jan. 1928), pp. 73–8.

O'Kane, J. P. 'The Church and liberty, *The Leader*, 20, 27 Sept. 1913),

O'Rahilly, A., 'Suarez and democracy', *Studies* VIII (1918), pp. 1–21;

O'Rahilly, A., 'Democracy, Parliament and Cromwell, *Studies* 7 (1918), pp. 545–52;

O'Rahilly, A., 'The sources of English and American democracy', *Studies* 8 (1918), pp. 189–209.

O'Rahilly, A., 'The Catholic origins of democracy, *Studies* 8 (1919), pp. 1–18;

O'Rahilly, A., 'The democracy of Saint Thomas, *Studies* 9: 33 (Mar. 1920).

O'Rahilly, A., 'The sovereignty of the people', *Studies* 10 (1921), pp. 39–56.

O'Rahilly, A., *The Case for the Treaty*, n.d. (NLI).

O'Rahilly, A., 'The constitution and the Senate', *Studies* XXV: 97 (1936), pp. 2–7.

Ó Síothcháin, S., *Constitutionalism and Sinn Féin*, Sinn Féin Pamphlets no. 5, NLI.

Pearse, P., 'The sovereign people', *Collected Works of Padraig Pearse: Political Writings and Speeches* (Dublin, Cork and Belfast, 1924).

Progressive Democrats, *Agreed Programme for Government 1989–1993* (Dublin, 1993).

Proportional Representation Society of Great Britain, *A Short Account of the Movement in Favour of Proportional Representation in Ireland during the Year 1911 and of the All Ireland Model Election held in December 1911* (PR Pamphlet, Jan. 1912).

Proportional Representation Society of Great Britain, *Irish General Election, 1933: The Workings of Proportional Representation* (PR Pamphlet 73, 1933).

Purcell, W. J., 'Democracy vanquished', *New Ireland Review* XXX: 1 (Sept. 1908), p. 169.

Quinn, M., 'Colonial home rule, *Catholic Bulletin* VIII (1917), pp. 485–90.

Ryan, A., 'The justice of British democracy', *New Ireland Review* XXXI (Mar.–Aug. 1909), pp. 244–5.

Ryan, F., 'Young Ireland and Liberal idea', *Dana* (Feb. 1904), pp. 62–4.

Ryan, F. 'Empire and liberty', *Dana* 4 (1904), pp. 111–17.

Ryan, F., 'Democracy as a discipline', *New Ireland Review* XXV: 6 (Aug. 1906), p. 336.

Seanacus, 'The question of Catholic organisation, *Irish Rosary* VI (1902), p. 729.

Sheehy Skeffington, H., 'The women's movement in Ireland', *Irish Review* II (July 1912), pp. 225–7.

Sinn Féin, *Women in Ireland*. Sinn Féin update policy document (March 1999).

Social Democratic and Labour Party, *Towards a New Ireland*. Proposals by the Social Democratic and Labour Party (1975).

Stephens, E. M., 'The constitution' in *Irish Free State Official Handbook* (London, 1932), pp. 72–80.

Tierney, M., 'The new constitution', *The Leader*, 5 June 1937.

Ua Corbaidh, P. *Irish Democracy, Republicanism, Nationalism and Socialism* (1982?).

Vane, L., 'Wanted: a democratic spirit', *Dana* (12 Apr. 1905), p. 355.

Wallace, A.R., 'A new House of Lords: representatives of the best intellect and character of the nation', *Fortnightly Review* (Feb. 1907).

Wardell, J., 'Certain aspects of colonial democracy', *Hermathena* XII (1902), pp. 383–428.

Williamson, C. H., 'Democracy or revolution', *Irish Ecclesiastical Record* XVII (1921), p.79.

SECONDARY SOURCES

Ackerman, B., *We the People: Foundations* (Harvard, 1991).

Ackerman, B., 'The rise of world constitutionalism', *Virginia Law Review* 83: 4 (1997), pp. 771–97.

Akenson, D. H., and J. F. Fallon, 'The Irish Civil War and the drafting of the Free State constitution', *Eire/Ireland* (Spring 1970), pp. 10–26; (Summer 1970), pp. 42–93; (Winter 1970), pp. 28–70.

Aman, R, 'The central meaning of republican government: popular sovereignty, majority rule, and the denominator problem', *University of Colorado Law Review*, 65 (1993–4), pp. 749–86.

Aughey, A., 'A new beginning? prospects for a politics of civility' in J. Ruane and J. Todd (eds), *After the Good Friday Agreement: Analysing Political Change in Northern Ireland* (Dublin, 1999), pp. 122–44.

Aughey, A., 'Reimagining Ireland: Unionism' in A. Higgins Wyndham (ed.), *Reimagining Ireland* (Virginia, 2006), pp. 208–12.

Azkin, B., 'On the stability and reality of constitutions' in R. Bachi (ed.), *Studies in Economic and Social Science* (Jerusalem, 1956), pp. 314–15.

Bacik, I. and S. Livingstone, *Toward a Culture of Human Rights in Ireland* (Dublin, 2002).

Baden Powell, G., *The Truth About Home Rule: Papers on the Irish Question* (London and Edinburgh, 1888).

Barrington, D., 'The presidency', *Hibernia* (Mar. 1958), 1–2, 11.

Barrington, D., 'Uniting Ireland', Tuarim Research Pamphlets (Dublin, 1958?).

Barrington, D. 'The Church, the state and the constitution', Catholic Truth Society of Ireland (Dublin, 1959).

Barrow, L., and I. Bullock *Democratic Ideas and the British Labour Movement 1880–1914* (Cambridge, 1996).

Beattie, A., 'Ministerial responsibility and the theory of the British state' in P. Dunleavy and R. A. W. Rhodes (eds), *Prime Minister, Cabinet and Core Executive* (London 1995), pp. 158–81.

Beer. S., *To Make a Nation: The Rediscovery of American Federalism* (Cambridge MA, 1993).

Bellamy, R., *Political Constitutionalism: A Republican Defence of the Constitutionality of Democracy* (Cambridge, 2007).

Bellamy, R. and D. Castiglione, 'Review article: Constitutionalism and democracy – political theory and the American constitution', *British Journal of Political Science* 27 (1997), pp. 595–618.

Bew, P., *Ireland: The Politics of Enmity: 1789–2006* (Oxford, 2007).

Beytagh, F., *Constitutionalism in Contemporary Ireland: An American Perspective* (Dublin, 1997).

Biagini, E. F., *British Democracy and Irish Nationalism 1876–1906* (Cambridge, 2007).

Bogdanor, V., 'Western Europe' in D. Butler and A. Ranney (eds), *Referendums Around the World: The Growing use of Direct Democracy?* (Basingstoke, 1994), pp. 24–98.

Bogdanor, V., 'Devolution and the British constitution' in D. Butler, V. Bogdanor and R. Summers (eds), *The Law, Politics, and the Constitution: Essays in Honour of Geoffrey Marshall* (Oxford, 1998), pp. 54–77.

Bogdanor, V., 'Geoffrey Marshall' in D. Butler, V. Bogdanor and R. Summers (eds), *The Law, Politics, and the Constitution: Essays in Honour of Geoffrey Marshall* (Oxford, 1998), pp. 1–19.

Bogdanor, V., *The New British Constitution* (Oxford and Portland Oregon, 2009).

Boland, K., *The Constitutional Scam: New Meanings for Words to Neuter the hoi polloi* (Ireland, n.d.).

Boyle, K. and D. S. Greer, *The Legal System North and South: A Study Prepared for the New Ireland Forum* (Dublin, 1983).

Boyle, K. and T. Hadden, 'Northern Ireland' in R. Blackburn and R. Plant (eds), *Constitutional Reform: The Labour Government's Constitutional Reform Agenda* (London and New York, 1999), pp. 282–307.

Bradley Lewis, V., 'Constitutional natural law', *Review of Politics* 60: 2 (1998), pp. 366–8.

Brown, N. J., 'Reason, interest, rationality, and passion in constitution drafting', *Perspectives on Politics* 6: 4 (2008), pp. 675–89.

Butler, A. and R. O'Connell, 'A critical analysis of Ireland's Constitutional Review Group Report', *Irish Jurist* 33 (1998), pp. 327–65.

Cappocia, G., 'Defending democracy: reactions to political extremism in inter-war Europe', *European Journal of Political Research* 39: 4 (2001), pp. 431–60.

Carey, J.M., 'Does it matter how a constitution is created?' in Z. Barany and R. G. Moser (eds), *Is Democracy Exportable?* (Cambridge, 2009), pp. 155–78.

Carolan, E. and O. Doyle (eds), *The Irish Constitution: Governance and Values* (Dublin, 2008).

Chadwick, A., *Augmenting Democracy: Political Movements and Constitutional Reform During the Rise of Labour 1900–1924* (Farnham, 1999).

Childers, E., *The Framework of Home Rule* (London, 1911).

Chubb, B., *The Government and Politics of Ireland* (Oxford, 1970).

Chubb, B., *The Constitution and Constitutional Change in Ireland* (Dublin, 1978).

Chubb, B., 'Government and Dáil: constitutional myth and political practice' in B. Farrell et al. (eds), *De Valera's Constitution and Ours* (Dublin, 1988), pp. 93–102.

Chubb, B., *The Politics of the Irish Constitution* (Dublin, 1991).

Clarke, D. M., 'Emergency legislation, fundamental rights, and Article 28.3.3. of the Irish constitution', *Irish Jurist* 12 (1977), pp. 217–82.

Clery, A., *Dublin Essays* (Dublin and London, 1914).

Clifford, A., *The Constitutional History of Eire/Ireland* (Belfast, 1987).

Clune, M. J., 'Horace Plunkett's resignation from the Irish Department of Agriculture and Technical Instruction, 1906–07', *Eire-Ireland* 17: 1 (1982), pp. 57–74.

Coakley, J. 'Moral Consensus in a secularising society: the Irish Divorce Referendum of 1986', *West European Politics* 10: 2 (1987), pp. 291–6.

Coakley, J., 'The election that made the first Dáil' in B. Farrell (ed.), *The Creation of the Dáil: A Volume of Essays from the Thomas Davis Lectures* (Dublin, 1994), pp. 31–46.

Coakley, J., 'Ethnic conflict and its resolution: the Northern Ireland model', *Nationalism and Ethnic Politics* 9: 3 (Sept. 2003), pp. 25–53.

Coakley, J., 'Ireland's unique electoral experiment: the Senate election of 1925', *Irish Political Studies* 20: 3 (2005), pp. 231–69.

Collins, N., 'Parliamentary democracy in Ireland', *Parliamentary Affairs* 57: 3 (2004), pp. 601–12.

Collins, S., *Breaking the Mould: How the PDs changed Irish Politics* (Dublin, 2005).

Connelly, A., 'Women and the constitution of Ireland' in Y. Galligan, E. Ward and R. Wilford (eds), *Contesting Politics: Women in Ireland, North and South* (Boulder, 1999), pp. 18–38.

Connolly, J., 'Parliamentary democracy' in A. O'Cathasaigh (ed.), *The Lost Writings of James Connolly* (London and Chicago, 1997).

Coogan, T. P., *The Troubles: Ireland's Ordeal and the Search for Peace, 1966–1996* (New York, 2002).

Cox, M., A. Guelke and F. Stephens, *A Farewell to Arms? Beyond the Good Friday Agreement* (2nd edn, Manchester, 2006).

Curran, J. M., *The Birth of the Irish Free State, 1921–1923* (Mobile Alabama, 1980).

Dahl, R., *A Preface to Democratic Theory* (Chicago, 1956).

Dahl, R., *Polyarchy* (New Haven, 1971).

Dahl, R., *Democracy and its Critics* (New Haven, 1989).

Darby, J., *Scorpions in a Bottle: Conflict of Cultures in Northern Ireland* (London, 1997).

Davis, R. P., *Arthur Griffith and Non Violent Sinn Féin* (Dublin, 1974).

De Blácam, A., *Towards the Republic: A Study of New Ireland's Social and Political Aims* (Dublin, 1919).

De Paor, L., *Unfinished Business: Ireland Today and Tomorrow* (London,1990).

De Romilly, J., *The Rise and Fall of States According to Greek Orders* (Ann Arbor, 1991).

Dearlove, J., 'Bringing the constitution back in: political science and the state', *Political Studies* 37: 4 (1989), pp. 521–39.

Devlin, B., *The Price of My Soul* (London, 1965).

Dyson, K., *The State Tradition in Western Europe* (Oxford, 1985).

Elazar, D., 'The political theory of covenant: biblical origins and modern developments', *Publius* 10: 4 (1980), pp. 3–30.

Elazar, D., 'The principles and traditions underlying state constitutions', *Publius* 12:1 (1982), pp. 11–25.

Elkins Z., T. Ginsburg and J. Melton, *The Endurance of National Constitutions* (Cambridge, 2009).

Elster J. and R. Slagstad (eds), *Constitutionalism and Democracy* (Cambridge, 1988),

Eule, J. N., 'Judicial review of direct democracy', *Yale Law Journal* 99 (1989–90), pp. 1503–86.

Fahey, T., B. C. Hayes and R. Sinnott, *Conflict and Consensus: A Study of Values and Attitudes in the Republic of Ireland and Northern Ireland* (Dublin, 2004).

Fair, J. D., 'The king, the constitution and Ulster: Interparty negotiations of 1913 and 1914',*Eire/Ireland* (Spring 1971), pp. 35–52.

Farrell, B., 'The drafting of the Irish Free State Constitution', *Irish Jurist* 5 (1970), pp. 115–343, and *Irish Jurist* 6 (1971), pp. 111–345.

Farrell, B., *The Founding of Dáil Éireann: Parliament and Nation-Building* (Dublin, 1971).

Farrell, B., 'The paradox of Irish politics' in B. Farrell (ed.), *The Irish Parliamentary Tradition* (Dublin, 1973).

Farrell, B., 'From First Dáil through Irish Free State' in B. Farrell (ed.), *De Valera's Constitution and Ours* (Dublin, 1988), pp. 18–32.

Farrell, B., 'The constitutions and the institutions of government: constitutional theory and political practice' in F. Litton (ed.), *The Constitution of Ireland, 1937–1987* (Dublin, 1988), pp. 162–72.

Farrell, B. (ed.), *The Creation of the Dáil* (Dublin, 1994).

Fay, P., 'Amendments to the Constitution Committee 1926', *Administration* 26 (1978), pp. 331–52.

Fennell, N., *Irish Marriage How Are You?* (Dublin and Cork, 1974).

Figgis, D. *The Gaelic State in the Past and Future* (London, 1917).

Figgis, D., *The Irish Constitution: Explained by Darrell Figgis* (Dublin, 1922).

Finer, S., *The History of Government* (Oxford, 1999).

Finlay, T. A., *The Constitution: Fifty Years On* (Dublin, 1988).

Finn J. E., 'Transformation or transmogrification? Ackerman, Hobbes (as in Calvin and Hobbes), and the puzzle of changing constitutional identity', *Constitutional Political Economy* 10 (1999), pp. 355–65.

Finnegan, R.B., *Women and Public Policy in Ireland: A Documentary History* (Dublin, 2005).

FitzGerald, G., *Towards a New Ireland* (London, 1972).

FitzGerald, G., *All in a Life: Garret FitzGerald: An Autobiography* (London, 1991).

FitzGerald, G., 'The constitution in its historical context' in T. Murphy, and P. Twomey (eds), *Ireland's Evolving Constitution 1937–1997: Collected Essays* (Oxford, 1998), pp. 29–41.

FitzGerald, G., *Reflections on the Irish State* (Dublin, 2003).

Gallagher, M., 'Ireland: the referendum as a conservative device?' in M. Gallagher, and Vincenzo, P. (eds), *The Referendum Experience in Europe.* (London, 1996), pp. 86–106.

Gallagher, M., 'The constitution and the judiciary' in J. Coakley and M. Gallagher (eds), *Politics in the Republic of Ireland* (4th edn, Oxford and New York, 2005), pp. 72–193

Galligan, Y., E. Ward and R. Wilford (eds), *Contesting Politics: Women in Ireland, North and South* (Boulder, 1999).

Gardiner, F., 'The impact of EU equality legislation on Irish women' in Y. Galligan, E. Ward and R. Wilford (eds), *Contesting Politics* (Boulder: 1998), pp. 38–55.

Garvin, T., *Nationalist Revolutionaries in Ireland 1858–1928* (Oxford, 1987).

Garvin, T., 'An Irish republican tradition?' *Working Papers in British-Irish Studies*, 39 (2004).

Gavan Duffy, C., 'Notes on constitutional reform', *Irish Jurist* (Winter 1966), pp. 271–2.

Gavan Duffy, G., *A Fair Constitution for Ireland: with an appendix containing the opinions of Unionist, Liberal, and Nationalist journals on the proposal* (2nd edn, Dublin, 1892).

Gellner, E., *Plough, Sword, and Book: The Structure of Human History* (Chicago, 1988).

Girvin, B., 'Moral politics and the Irish Abortion Referendum 1992', *Parliamentary Affairs* 47: 2 (1994), pp. 204–21.

Girvin, B., 'Church, state and the Irish constitution: the secularisation of Irish politics', *Parliamentary Affairs* 49: 4 (1996), pp. 599–615.

Glandon, V. E., *Arthur Griffith and the Advanced Nationalist Press, Ireland 1900–1922* (New York, 1985).

Grogan, V., 'Irish constitutional development', *Studies* 40: 160 (1951), pp. 385–98.

Guelke, A., 'Northern Ireland and the international system'. in W. Crotty and D. E. Schmitt (eds), *Ireland on the World Stage* (Harlow, 2002), pp. 127–39.

Gwynn, D., *The Irish Free State 1922–1927* (London, 1928).

Habermas, J., *Legitimation Crisis* (London, 1976).

Hardin, R., *Liberalism, Constitutionalism, and Democracy* (Oxford, 1999).

Harkness, D., *The Restless Dominion: The Irish Free State and the British Commonwealth of Nations, 1921–31* (London, 1969).

Hayes, A. and D. Urquhart (eds), *Irish Women's History Reader* (London, 2001).

Hayward, J. and R. N. Berki, *State and Society in Contemporary Europe* (Oxford, 1979).

Hayward, K., *Irish Nationalism and European Integration: The Official Redefinition of the Island of Ireland* (Manchester, 2009).

Hayward, K. and M. MacCartaigh (eds), *Recycling the State: The Politics of Adaptation in Ireland* (Dublin, 2008).

Hazleton, W., 'Devolution and the diffusion of power: the internal and transnational dimensions of the Belfast Agreement', *Irish Political Studies* 15 (2000), pp. 25–38.

Hesketh, T., *The Second Partitioning of Ireland: The Abortion Referendum of 1983* (Dun Laoghaire, 1990).

Higgins Wyndham, A. (ed.), *Reimagining Ireland* (Virginia 2006).

Hobhouse, L.T., 'Irish Nationalism and Liberal Principle' in J. H. Morgan (ed.), *The New Irish Constitution: An Exposition and Some Arguments* (London and New York, 1912), pp. 361–72.

Hobson, J., *The Crisis of Liberalism: New Issues of Democracy* (London, 1909).

Hogan, G., 'Irish nationalism as a legal ideology', *Studies* 75: 300 (1986), pp. 528–39.

Hogan, G., 'Constitutional interpretation' in F. Litton (ed.), *The Constitution of Ireland 1937–1987* (Dublin, 1988), pp. 173–92.

Hogan, G., 'The Constitution Review Committee of 1934' in F. O'Muircheartaigh (ed.), *Ireland in the Coming Times* (Dublin, 1997), pp. 342–70.

Hogan, G., review of T. Murphy and P. Twomey (eds), *Ireland's Evolving Constitution, 1937–1997*, *Bar Review* 3: 9 (1998), pp. 267–70.

Hogan, G. 'De Valera, the constitution, and the historians', *Irish Jurist* XL (2005), pp. 293–320.

Hogan, G., 'Foreword' to D. Keogh and A. McCarthy (eds), *The Making of the Irish Constitution 1937: Bunreacht na hÉireann* (Dublin, 2007), pp. 13–38.

Hogan, G. and G. Whyte (eds), *J. M. Kelly: The Irish Constitution* (4th edn, Dublin 2006).

Hogan, J., *Election and Representation* (Oxford, 1945).

Horgan, J. J., *Home Rule: A Critical Consideration* (Dublin, 1911).

Humphreys, R., Review article, 'Our bilingual constitution', *Irish Jurist* 35 (2000), pp. 375–87.

Humphreys, R., 'Constitutional contradictions: accommodating multiple identities after the Good Friday Agreement' in E. Carolan and O. Doyle (eds), *The Irish Constitution: Governance and Values* (Dublin, 2008), pp. 114–21.

Humphreys, R., *Countdown to Unity: Debating Irish Reunification* (Dublin, 2009).

Hunt, A., 'Evaluating constitutions – the Irish constitution and the limits of constitutionalism' in T. Murphy and P. Twomey (eds), *Ireland's Evolving Constitution* (Oxford, 1998), pp. 317–35.

Hutchinson, J., *The Dynamics of Cultural Nationalism: The Gaelic Revival and the Creation of the Irish Nation State* (London, 1987).

Hyland, A., 'The multi-denominational experience' in Constitution Review Group, *Report of the Constitution Review Group* (Dublin, 1996), pp. 631–2.

Jackson, A., *The Two Irelands 1798–1998: Politics and War* (Oxford, 1999).

Jacobsohn, G., 'An unconstitutional constitution? A comparative perspective', *International Journal of Constitutional Law* 4: 3 (2006), pp. 460–87.

Jacobsohn, G., 'Constitutional identity', *Review of Politics* 68 (2006), pp. 361–97.

Jacobsohn, G., *Constitutional Identity* (Cambridge, MA, 2010).

Jennings, I., *The Law and Constitution* (5th edn, London, 1968).

Jowell, J. and D. Oliver (eds), *The Changing Constitution* (6th edn, Oxford, 2007).

Jowett, F. W., *What is the Use of Parliament?* (London, 1909).

Judt, T., *Ill Fares the Land* (London, 2010).

Karvonen, L., *Political Organisation and the Interwar Crisis in Europe* (Boulder, 1993).

Kelly, J., 'Revision of the constitution of Ireland', *Irish Jurist* 1 (Summer 1966), pp. 1–15.

Kelly, J., 'Fundamental rights and the Irish constitution' in B. Farrell (ed.), *De Valera's Constitution and Ours* (Dublin, 1988), pp. 163–74.

Kelly, J., 'The constitution: law and manifesto' in F. Litton (ed.), *The Constitution of Ireland 1937–1987* (Dublin, 1988), pp. 208–17.

Kelly, J. M., *The Irish Constitution* (Dublin, 1980).

Kelsen, H., *General Theory of Law and State* (New York, 1961).

Kennedy, B. P., 'Appreciation: John Hearne and the Irish constitution', *Eire/Ireland* 24: 2 (1989), pp. 121–8.

Kennedy, H., 'Character and sources of the constitution of the Irish Free State', *American Bar Association Journal* 14 (1928), pp. 437–45.

Keogh, D., 'The Irish constitutional revolution: an analysis of the making of the constitution' in F. Litton (ed.), 'The constitution of Ireland 1937–1987', *Administration* 35: 4 (1988), pp. 4–84.

Keogh, D. and J. McCarthy, *The Making of the Irish Constitution 1937: Bunreacht na hÉireann* (Cork, 2007).

Kerr, M., *Imposing Power Sharing: Conflict and Coexistence in Northern Ireland and Lebanon* (Dublin, 2006).

Kerr, M., 'A culture of power sharing' in R. Taylor (ed.), *Consociational Theory: McGarry and O'Leary and the Northern Ireland Conflict* (Oxford, 2009), pp. 206–21.

King, A., *Does the United Kingdom Still Have a Constitution?* (London, 2001).

Kissane, B., 'Government changeover and democratic consolidation in the Irish Free State', *Journal of Commonwealth and Comparative Politics* 39: 1 (2001), pp. 1–23.

Kissane, B., *Explaining Irish Democracy* (Dublin, 2002).

Kissane, B., 'The illusion of state neutrality in a secularising Ireland', *West European Politics* 26: 1 (2003), pp. 73–94.

Kissane, B., 'Defending democracy? The legislative response to political extremism in the Irish Free State, 1922–1939', *Irish Historical Studies* 34: 134 (2004), pp. 156–74.

Kissane, B., *The Politics of the Irish Civil War* (Oxford, 2005).

Kissane, B., 'Power-sharing as a form of democracy for Northern Ireland', *Review of Politics* 68: 4 (Fall, 2006), pp. 663–75.

Kissane, B., 'Éamon de Valera and the survival of democracy in inter-war Ireland', *Journal of Contemporary History* 42: 2 (2007), pp. 213–27.

Kissane, B., 'De Valera, the 1937 constitution, and proportional representation' in E. Carolan and O. Doyle (eds), *The Irish Constitution: Governance and Values* (London, 2008), pp. 35–53.

Kissane, B., 'From people's veto to instrument of elite consensus' in M. Setala and T. Schiller (eds), *Referendums and Representative Democracy: Responsiveness, Accountability, and Deliberation* (London and New York, 2009), pp. 17–34

Kissane, B., 'The Constitutional revolution that never was: democratic radicalism and the Sinn Féin movement', *Radical History Review* (Spring 2009), pp. 77–103.

Kissane, B. and H. Bulsara, 'Arend Lijphart and the transformation of Irish democracy', *West European Politics* 32: 1 (2009), pp. 172–96.

Kissane, B. and N Sitter, 'National identity and constitutionalism in Europe: introduction', *Nations and Nationalism* 16: 1 (Jan. 2010), pp. 1–6.

Kissane, B. and N. Sitter, 'The marriage of state and nation in European constitutions', *Nations and Nationalism* (Jan. 2010) 16:1, pp. 49–68.

Kohn, L., *The Constitution of the Irish Free State* (London, 1932).

Koselleck, R., 'Historical prognosis in Lorenz von Stein's Essay on the Prussian Constitution' in *Futures Past: On the Semantics of Historical Time* (New York, 2004), pp. 58–75.

Kristeva, J., *Nations without Nationalism* (New York, 1993).

Laffan, M., *The Resurrection of Ireland: The Sinn Féin Party 1916–22* (Cambridge, 1999).

Lee, J., *The Modernization of Irish Society 1948–1918* (Dublin, 1973).

Lee, J., *Ireland 1912–1985* (Cambridge, 1989).

Lee, J., 'Peace and Northern Ireland' in A. Higgins Wyndham (ed.), *Reimagining Ireland* (Virginia, 2006), pp. 219–23.

Lerner, H. 'Constitution-writing in deeply-divided societies: the incrementalist approach', *Nations and Nationalism* 16: 1 (Jan. 2010), pp. 68–89.

Lijphart, A., *Democracy in Plural Societies: A Comparative Exploration* (New Haven and London, 1977).

Lijphart, A., *Democracies: Patterns of Majoritarian and Consensus Government in Twenty-One Countries* (New Haven CT and London, 1984).

Lijphart, A., 'Democratic political systems: types, causes and consequences', *Journal of Theoretical Politics* 1: 1 (1989), pp. 33–48.

Lijphart, A., 'Democratization and constitutional choices in Czechoslovakia, Hungary, and Poland 1989–91', *Journal of Theoretical Politics* 4: 2 (1992), pp. 207–23.

Lijphart, A., *Patterns of Democracy: Government Forms and Performance in Thirty-Six Countries* (New Haven, CT and London, 1999).

Litton, F. (ed.), *The Constitution of Ireland 1937–1987* (Dublin, 1988).

Loughlin, M., *The Idea of Public Law* (Oxford, 2003).

MacCartaigh, M., *Accountability in Irish Parliamentary Politics* (Dublin, 2005).

MacCartaigh, M., 'The recycling of political accountability' in K. Hayward and M. MacCartaigh (eds), *Recycling the State: The Politics of Adaptation in Ireland* (Dublin, 2008), pp. 201–23.

McCartney, D., *Democracy and its Nineteenth Century Critics* (Dublin, 1979).

MacCurtain, M., 'Women, the vote, and revolution' in M. MacCurtain and D. Ó Corrain (eds), *Women in Irish Society: The Historical Dimension* (Westport, 1979).

MacDonagh, M., *The Life of William O'Brien, the Irish Nationalist: A Biographical Study of Irish Nationalism, Constitutional and Revolutionary* (London, 1928).

MacDonnell, J., 'The constitutional limitations upon the powers of the Irish legislation' in H. Morgan (ed.), *The New Irish Constitution: An Exposition and Some Arguments* (London and New York, 1912), pp. 90–112.

MacGinty, R., 'Issue hierarchies in peace processes: the decommissioning of paramilitary arms and the Northern Ireland peace process. Lessons for ending civil conflicts', *Civil Wars* 1: 3 (1998), pp. 24–45.

MacMillan, G., 'The referendum, the courts and representative democracy in Ireland', *Political Studies* 15 (1992), pp. 67–79.

MacPherson, C. B., *The Life and Times of Liberal Democracy* (Oxford, 1977).

Mahlmann, M. 'Constitutional identity and the politics of homogeneity', *German Law Journal* (2005), pp. 307–17.

Mahon, E., 'Women's rights and Catholicism in Ireland' in M. Threlfell (ed.), *Mapping the Women's Movement: Feminist Politics and Social Transformation in the North* (London, New York, 1996), pp. 184–216.

Mair, P., *The Changing Irish Party System: Organisation, Ideology and Electoral Competition* (London, 1987).

Mair, P., 'De Valera and democracy' in T. Garvin, M. Manning and R. Sinnott (eds), *Dissecting Irish Politics: Essays in Honour of Brian Farrell* (Dublin, 2004), pp.31–45.

Mallie, E. and D. McKittrick, *The Fight for Peace: The Secret Story behind the Irish Peace Process* (London, 1996).

Malone, A.E., 'Party government in the Irish Free State', *Political Science Quarterly* 44: 3 (1929), pp. 363–78.

Mansergh, N., *The Irish Free State: Its Government and Politics* (London, 1934).

Mansergh, N., *The Unresolved Question: The Anglo-Irish Settlement and its Undoing 1912–72* (New Haven and London, 1982).

Martin, F. F., *The Constitution as Treaty: The International Legal Constructionist Approach to the U.S. Constitution* (Cambridge, 2007).

Maume, P., 'The ancient constitution: Arthur Griffith and his intellectual legacy to Sinn Féin', *Irish Political Studies* 10 (1995), pp. 123–38.

Mazower, M., *Dark Continent: Europe's Twentieth Century* (New York, 1999).

Mazower, M. (ed.), *After the War Was Over: Reconstructing the Family, Nation, and State in Greece, 1943–1960* (Princeton and Oxford, 2000).

McBride. L., *The Greening of Dublin Castle: The Transformation of Bureaucratic and Judicial Personnel In Ireland 1892–1992* (Washington DC, 1992).

McCrudden, C., 'Northern Ireland and the British constitution since the Belfast Agreement' in J. Jowell and D. Oliver (eds), *The Changing Constitution* (6th edn, Oxford, 2007), pp. 227–70.

McEvoy, J., *The Politics of Northern Ireland* (Edinburgh, 2008).

McGarry, J., 'Political settlements in Northern Ireland and South Africa' in J. McGarry and B. O'Leary (eds), *The Northern Ireland Conflict: Consociational Engagements* (Oxford, 2004), pp. 236–60.

McGarry, J., and B. O'Leary (eds), *The Northern Ireland Conflict: Consociational Engagements* (Oxford, 2004).

McGarry, J. and B. O'Leary, 'Power shared after the deaths of thousands', in R. Taylor (ed.), *Consociational Theory: McGarry and O'Leary and the Northern Ireland Conflict* (Oxford, 2009), pp.

McIlwain, C., *Constitutionalism: Ancient and Modern* (New York, 1947).

McNally, M., 'Countering the hegemony of the national canon: the modernist rhetoric of Sean O'Faolain (1938–50)', *Nations and Nationalism* 15: 3 (2009), pp. 524–4.

Mendelsohn, M. and A. Parkin (eds), *Referendum Democracy: Citizens, Elites and Deliberation in Referendum Campaigns* (Basingstoke, 2001).

Menendez, A. J., 'Three conceptions of the European constitution', Working Paper, Arena, pp. 1–40.

Meredith, J., *Proportional Representation in Ireland* (London, 1913).

Millar, F., *Northern Ireland: A Triumph of Politics: Interviews and Analysis* (Dublin, 2009).

Mohr, T., 'The rights of women under the constitution of the Irish Free State', *Irish Jurist*, 41 (2006), pp. 20–59.

Mohr, T., 'British involvement in the creation of the first Irish constitution', *Dublin University Law Journal* 30 (2008), pp. 166–87.

Moran, D. P., *The Philosophy of Irish Ireland* (Dublin, 1905).

Morgan, D. G., *The Separation of Powers in the Irish Constitution* (London, 1997).

Morgan, J. H. (ed.), *The New Irish Constitution: An Exposition and Some Arguments: edited on behalf of the Eighty Club* (London, 1912).

Morrison, J., 'Constitutionalism, civil society and democratic renewal in Northern Ireland' in Michael Cox, Adrian Guelke and Fiona Stephen (eds), *A Farewell to Arms? Beyond the Good Friday Agreement* (2nd edn, Manchester, 2006), pp. 226–36.

Moss, W., *Political Parties in the Irish Free State* (New York, 1933).

Munro, C., *Studies in Constitutional Law* (2nd edn, Butterworth 2002).

Murphy, J. A., 'The achievement of Eamon de Valera' in J. P. O'Carroll and J. A. Murphy (eds), *The Life and Times of Eamon de Valera* (Cork, 1983), pp. 1–7.

Murphy, T. and P. Twomey, *Ireland's Evolving Constitution, 1937–* (Oxford, 1998).

Murray, P., *Oracles of God: The Roman Catholic Church and Irish Politics, 1922–37* (Dublin, 2000).

Nairn, T., *After Britain: New Labour and the Return of Scotland* (London, 2000).

Newman, J., *'Ireland Must Choose': Religion, Politics and Law in Ireland Today* (Dublin, 1983).

Newman, J., *Puppets of Utopia: Can Irish Democracy be Taken for Granted?* (Dublin, 1987).

Norman, H. F., *George Russell* (Frome, 1935).

Nwabueze, R., *Constitutionalism in the Emergent States* (London, 1977).

Oakeshott, M., *The Social and Political Doctrines of Contemporary Europe* (Cambridge, 1939).

O'Brien, W., *The Downfall of Parliamentarianism: A Retrospect for the Accounting Day* (Dublin and London, 1918).

O'Connell, M. R., 'Irish constitutionalism: a rescue operation', *Studies* 75: 299 (1986), pp. 317–28.

O'Connor, F., *An Only Child and My Father's Son* (London, 2005).

O'Corrain, D., 'Articles 41 and 44: minority religious opinion 1937–1986' in E. Carolan and O. Doyle (eds), *The Irish Constitution: Governance and Values* (Dublin, 2008), pp. 35–53.

O'Day, A., *Irish Home Rule 1867–1921* (Manchester, 1998).

O'Dowd, J., 'The impact of the constitution in the deliberations of the houses of the Oireachtas' in E. Carolan and O. Doyle (eds), *The Irish Constitution: Governance and Values* (Dublin, 2008), pp. 181–95.

O'Dowd, L., 'Church, state, and women: the aftermath of partition' in C. Curtis, P. Jackson and B. O'Connor (eds), *Gender in Irish Society* (Galway, 1987), pp. 3–36.

O'Duffy, B., 'British and Irish conflict regulation from Sunningdale to Belfast. Part 1: Tracing the status of contesting sovereigns, 1968–1974, *Nations and Nationalism* 5: 4 (1999), pp. 523–42.

O'Duffy, B., 'British and Irish conflict regulation from Sunningdale to Belfast. Part 2: playing for a draw 1985–1999', *Nations and Nationalism* 6: 3 (2000), pp. 384–99.

O'Duffy, B., *British Irish Relations and Northern Ireland: From Violent Conflict to Conflict Regulation* (Dublin, 2007).

O'Halloran, A., 'Transformation in contemporary Ireland: society, economy, and polity: an era of post-parliamentary governance', *Administration* 53: 1 (2005), pp. 54–79.

O'Halpin, E., 'Parliamentary party discipline and tactics: the Fianna Fáil archives 1926–32', *Irish Historical Studies* XXX: 120 (1997), pp. 581–91.

O'Halpin, E., 'Politics and the state, 1922–32' in J. R. Hill (ed.), *A New History of Ireland:* vol. 7, *Ireland, 1921–84* (Oxford, 2003), pp. 86–125.

O'Hanlon, R. J., 'A constitution for a free people', *Administration* 15: 1 (Spring 1967), pp. 85–101.

O'Hegarty, P. S. *Sinn Féin: An Ilumination* (Dublin and London, 1919).

O'Leary, B., 'The Conservative stewardship of Northern Ireland, 1979–97: sound-bottomed contradictions or slow learning?', *Political Studies* 45: 4 (1997), pp. 663–76.

O'Leary, B. 'Afterword: what is framed in the framework documents?' *Ethnic and Racial Studies* 18: 4 (1999), pp. 862–72.

O'Leary, B., 'The nature of the Agreement' in J. McGarry and B. O'Leary (eds), *The Northern Ireland Conflict: Consociational Engagements* (Oxford, 2005), pp. 260–94.

O'Leary, B. and B. O'Duffy, 'Tales from elsewhere and a Hibernian sermon' in H. Margetts and G. Smith (eds), *Turning Japanese: Britain with a Dominant Party of Government* (London, 1995), pp. 193–210.

O'Leary, C., *Irish Elections 1918–1977: Parties, Voters and Proportional Representation* (Dublin, 1979).

O'Neill, B., 'The referendum process in Ireland', *Irish Jurist* 35 (2000), pp. 305–44.

O'Rahilly, A., *Thoughts on the Constitution* (Dublin, 1937).

O'Sullivan, D., *The Irish Free State and its Senate: A study in Contemporary Politics* (London, 1940).

O'Sullivan, D., 'The Good Friday Agreement: a new constitutional agreement for Northern Ireland, *Dublin University Law Journal* 22 (2000).

O'Toole, F., 'The peace process' in A. Higgins Wyndham (ed.), *Reimagining Ireland* (Virginia, 2006), pp. 206–8.

O'Toole, F., *Ship of Fools: How Stupidity and Corruption Sank the Celtic Tiger* (London, 2009).

Ó Tuathaigh, G., 'De Valera and sovereignty: a note on the pedigree of a political idea' in J. P. O'Connell and J. A. Murphy (eds), *De Valera and His Times* (Cork, 1983).

Pakenham, F., *Peace By Ordeal: The Negotiation of the Anglo-Irish Treaty, 1921* (London, 1992).

Panizza, F., 'Introduction', *Populism and the Mirror of Democracy* (London and New York, 2005).

Pettit, P., *Republicanism: A Theory of Freedom and Government* (Oxford, 1997).

Pocock, J. G. A., *The Machiavellian Moment: Florentine Political Thought and the Atlantic Republican Tradition* (Princeton, 1975).

Prager, J., *Building Democracy in Ireland* (Cambridge, 1986).

Qvortrup, M., *A Comparative Study of Referendums: Government by the People* (Manchester, 2005).

Rahat, G., 'Elite motivations for initiating referendums: avoidance, addition and contradiction' in M. Setala and T. Schiller (eds), *Referendums and Representative Democracy: Responsiveness, Accountability, and Deliberation* (New York, 2009), pp. 98–117.

Regan, J. M., 'The politics of reaction: the dynamics of treatyite government and policy, 1922–33', *Irish Historical Studies* XXX: 120 (1997), pp. 542–64.

Regan, J. M., *The Irish Counter-Revolution 1921–36: Treatyite Politics and Settlement in Independent Ireland* (Dublin, 1999).

Reynolds, A., 'A constitutional Pied Piper: The Northern Irish Good Friday Agreement', *Political Science Quarterly* 114: 4 (Winter 1999–2000), pp. 613–37.

Rokkan, S., *Citizens, Elections, Parties: Approaches to the Comparative Study of the Processes of Development* (New York, Oslo, 1970).

Rosenfeld, M., 'The identity of the constitutional subject', *Cardozo Law Review* 16 (1994), pp. 1049–1994.

Rosenfeld, M., 'The European treaty – constitution and constitutional identity: a view from America', *International Journal of Constitutional Law* (2005), pp. 316–31.

Royal Irish Academy, *The Origins of the Irish Constitution* (project directed by G. Hogan) (Dublin, 2011).

Ruane, J. and J. Todd (eds), *After the Good Friday Agreement: Analysing Political Change in Northern Ireland* (Dublin, 1999).

Ruane, J. and J. Todd, 'The Belfast Agreement: Context, content, consequences' in J. Ruane and J. Todd (eds), *After the Good Friday Agreement: Analysing Political Change in Northern Ireland* (Dublin, 1999), pp. 1–30.

Ruane, J., and J. Todd, 'The Northern Ireland conflict and the impact of globalisation' in W. Crotty and D. E. Schmitt (eds), *Ireland on the World Stage* (Harlow, 2002), pp. 111–27

Russell, G. W., *The National Being: Some Thoughts on an Irish Polity* (Dublin, 1982).

Sajo, A., *Limiting Government: An Introduction to Constitutionalism* (Budapest, 1999).

Sartori, G., *The Theory of Democracy Revisited: Part One the Contemporary Debate* (Chatham, NJ, 1987).

Scannell, Y., 'The constitution and the role of women' in A. Hayes and D. Urquart (eds), *The Irish Women's History Reader* (London and New York, 2001), pp. 71–9.

Schapiro, R.A., 'Identity and interpretation in state constitutional law', *Virginia Law Review*, 84: 3 (Apr. 1998), pp. 389–457.

Shaw, D., *The Drama of Sinn Féin* (London, 1923).

Shirlow, P., 'Northern Ireland: a reminder from the present' in C. Coulter and S. Coleman (eds), *The End of Irish History? Critical Reflections on the Celtic Tiger* (Manchester, 2003), pp. 192–208.

Slagstad, R., 'Liberal constitutionalism and its critics' in J. Elster and R. Slagstad (eds), *Constitutionalism and Democracy* (Cambridge, 1988), pp. 104–12.

Smith, G., 'The functional properties of the referendum', *European Journal of Political Research* 4: 1 (1976), pp. 1–23.

Smith, J., *Making the Peace in Ireland* (Harlow, 2002).

Smith, M., 'The title An Taoiseach in the 1937 constitution, *Irish Political Studies* 10 (1995), pp. 179–85.

Smith, R., *Garret: The Enigma* (Dublin, 1985).

Suksi, M., *Bringing in the People: A Comparison of Constitutional Forms and Practices of the Referendum* (London, Dordrecht, 1993).

Sunstein, C., 'On the expressive function of law', *University of Pennsylvania Law Review* 144 (1996), pp. 2021–53.

Sutherland, P., 'Twin perspectives: an attorney general views political and European dimensions' in B. Farrell (ed.), *De Valera's Constitution and Ours* (Dublin, 1988), pp. 174–88.

Swift MacNeill, J.G., *Studies in the Constitution of the Irish Free State* (Dublin Cork, 1925).

Taylor, R. (ed.), *Consociational Theory: McGarry and O'Leary and the Northern Ireland Conflict* (Oxford, 2009).

Tonge, J. *Northern Ireland: Conflict and Change* (2nd edn, Harlow, 2002).

Tonge, J., *The New Northern Irish Politics* (Basingstoke, 2005).

Towey, T., 'The reaction of the British government to the 1922 Collins–de Valera pact', *Irish Historical Studies* 22: 85 (1980), pp. 65–77.

Townshend, C., 'The meaning of Irish freedom: constitutionalism in the Free State', *Transactions of the Royal Historical Society* 6th series, 8 (1998), pp. 45–70.

Tushnet, M., *The New Constitutional Order* (Princeton, 2003).

Tushnet, M., 'Potentially misleading metaphors in comparative constitutionalism: moments and enthusiasm' in J. H. Weiler and C. L. Eisgruber (eds), *Altneuland: The EU Constitution in a Contextual Perspective* (Jean Monnet Working Paper 5/04, 2004).

Tweedy, R. N., *Irish Freedom Explained: The Constitution of Saorstát Éireann* (Dublin, 1923), pp. 19–20.

Uleri, P. V., 'Introduction' in M. Gallagher and P. Vincenzo (eds), *The Referendum Experience in Europe* (London, 1996), pp. 1–20.

Walker, N., *After the Constitutional Moment*, The Federal Trust for education and research (Online Paper 32/03, Nov. 2003), pp. 1–15.

Walter, L.A., 'Law as literature: illuminating the debate over constitutional consistency', *Cork Online Law Review* 10 (2004).

Ward, A., *The Irish Constitutional Tradition: Responsible Government in Modern Ireland* (Dublin, 1994).

Ward, A. 'The Constitution Review Group and the "Executive State" in Ireland, *Administration* 44: 4 (1997), pp. 42–63.

Weiler, J. 'A constitution for Europe? Some hard choices' in G. A. Berman and K. Pastor (eds), *Law and Governance in an Enlarged European Union: Essays in European Law* (Oxford, 2004), pp. 39–61.

Wheeler, H., 'Constitutionalism' in Y. I. Greenstein and N. W. Polsby (eds), *Handbook of Political Science* (Reading, Mass., 1975), pp. 1–93.

Wilson, G., 'The Westminster model in comparative perspective' in I. Budge and D. McKay (eds), *Developing Democracy: Comparative Research in honour of J. F. P. Blondel* (London, 1994), pp. 190–3.

Wormuth, F. D., *The Origins of Modern Constitutionalism* (New York, 1949).

Index

—